The Playful Self

Rebecca Abrams is a social researcher and award-winning journalist. Her articles and reviews have appeared in many national newspapers and magazines. She is a regular contributor to the *Guardian* and the author of two previous books, *When Parents Die*, shortlisted for the 1996 Mind Award, and *Woman In A Man's World*. She is currently researching women's friendship at Nuffield College, Oxford.

The Playful Self

Why Women Need Play in Their Lives

Rebecca Abrams

FOURTH ESTATE • *London*

First published in Great Britain in 1997 by
Fourth Estate Limited
6 Salem Road
London W2 4BU

1 3 5 7 9 10 8 6 4 2

A catalogue record for this book is available from the British Library.

ISBN 1-85702-550-4

Typeset by MATS, Southend-on-Sea, Essex
Printed in Great Britain by Clays Ltd., St. Ives plc, Bungay, Suffolk

For Jessica

'There can be no effective and satisfactory work without play; there can be no sound and wholesome thought without play.'

Charles Dickens, *Hard Times*

Contents

Acknowledgements

An inherent irony of writing a book about the importance of play has been that doing so has at times drastically reduced the degree of play possible in my own life. My first acknowledgement of debt therefore must be to all the good friends who, in the face of my frequent refusals, persisted in phoning, issuing invitations, suggesting meetings and generally not allowing me to cease altogether practising what I preached.

Writing this book has by no means been all hardship, however, for it has also brought the profound pleasure of sharing my ideas about play and playfulness with many other people, of listening to their thoughts and learning from their professional expertise and their personal experiences. I am indebted to every one of them for the confidence and encouragement they have given me, knowingly or otherwise, to start, continue and finish this book.

Above all I wish to thank David Bodanis, my erstwhile café companion, who was the first person to believe that there was a book here, who urged me to develop my fledgling ideas into a coherent proposal and to submit it without delay to my agent. It was David who left on my doorstep a copy of Johan Huizinga's classic work, *Homo Ludens* (then unknown to me), thus providing crucial early inspiration as well as a key secondary source.

Catherine Clarke, Richard Cockett, Ellen Jackson, Rachel Polonsky and Katherine Rake most kindly read through the manuscript in various draft forms, and all made pertinent comments, contributions and criticisms. I am also most grateful to Christina Hardyment, Stephen Harrison, Susan Sellers and John Walsh, who gave valued advice on draft chapters. In addition I should like to take the opportunity to thank Dominic Abrams, Michael Argyle, Kate Bailey, Ilana Ben-Amos, Penny Boreham, Madeleine Bunting, Wendy Buonaventura, Paul David, Robert French, Duncan Gallie, Diego Gambetta, David Goldie, Elizabeth Grice, Janie Hampton, Leo Hendry, Elaine Herman, Michael Holyoke, Anne Horner, Sonia

Jackson, Chris Kiddy, Richard Layte, Cathy Lloyd, Simon Mason, Jon Mee, Susie Moreira, Robert Needham, Avner Offer, Gilda O'Neill, Marc Polonsky, Beattie Rubens, Helen Russell, Katie Sampson, Keith Skeats, Cathy Troupp, Megan Vaughan, Veronica Wadley, Helen Watson, Charles Webster, Julie Wheelwright, Araminta Whitley, John Whitwell and Jane Wood. I also wish to acknowledge the financial support of a timely award from the Authors' Foundation and the K. Blundell Trust.

Special thanks to Elinor Goldschmied, at whose instigation the Play Day workshop took place in London in 1990. To Elinor and to all the women who attended the workshop, and who agreed to be interviewed afterwards, I can only say that the book would have been immeasurably the poorer without the valued contribution of your thoughts and feelings. I am likewise immensely grateful to *all* the women and men who have granted me permission to quote their words in the pages that follow.

On a more personal note, I owe particular thanks to John Slim, private cuttings service supreme, for keeping me up-to-date with newspaper coverage of 'women's things'. I am grateful to Robert and Sarah Whyte, who kindly provided this writer's dream location for a crucial few weeks while a first draft of the manuscript was finished. Many thanks are also due to Marc and Rachel Polonsky again, for allowing me to commandeer their study while I edited the final draft.

My husband Hugo has had to live with this book for as long as he has known me, and will be even gladder than I to see it in published form. His many invaluable suggestions, ideas and comments, still more his support and love are more appreciated that he will ever know. Finally, I should like to thank my daughter Jessica, to whom this book is dedicated. Her own irrepressible playfulness has been – and is – the best possible inspiration.

Ltd, 1985, 1993, reproduced by kind permission of Macmillan Press Ltd; 'Men Talk' from *True Confessions and New Cliches* by Liz Lochhead, Polygon, 1985; *A Night Out With the Girls: Women Having a Good Time* by Gilda O'Neill, first published in Great Britain by The Women's Press Ltd, 1993, 34 Great Sutton Street, London EC1V 0DX, used by permission of The Women's Press Ltd; *Man Made Language* by Dale Spender, reproduced by kind permission of HarperCollins Ltd; *Women's Talk: A Social History of Gossip in Working-Class Neighbourhoods 1880-1960* by Melanie Tebbutt, reproduced with kind permission of Scolar Press; *Country Hoard* by Alison Uttley, published by Faber and Faber, 1943, reproduced by kind permission of Faber and Faber Ltd; *From the Beast to the Blonde* by Marina Warner, reproduced by kind permission of Chatto and Windus, © Marina Warner 1994; 'Whale Nation' by Heathcote Williams, reproduced by kind permission of Jonathan Cape.

Introduction

'Life must be lived as play'
(Plato, *The Republic*)

Walking through town at lunchtime the other day, I saw a group of men kicking a ball back and forth. They were laughing and joking and generally having a good time. They were playing. Looking around me, I could see plenty of women, but all of them looked too busy to play. They were hurrying somewhere with bags of shopping and young children in tow. This small episode stuck in my mind because it reminded me of how this book began, over ten years ago, when I was in my early twenties and for a couple of years shared a house with a group of friends. It was a fairly typical student household: there were intermittent wrangles about cleaning the bath and hogging the telephone; bicycles blocked the entrance, unwashed plates blocked the sink. On the whole, though, we got on well enough and, despite the fact that there were two women to four men, gender was seldom the cause of conflict when it did arise: Clare and I were no more vigilant about washing up than Craig, Paul, Richard or Tod, nor were they any more innocent of hogging the phone. When it came to sport, however, a marked difference emerged between the male and the female occupants. Every day, significant amounts of Craig's, Paul's, Richard's and Tod's time would be taken up with sport, whether playing it, reading about it, listening to it or watching it. I got up in the morning to the sound of the sports bulletins on the radio and I went to bed at night to the sound of the soccer highlights on the TV; the newspapers which littered the kitchen table lay open at pages devoted to an assortment of men chasing, kicking and hitting balls of various shapes and sizes. Something was going on here. Why were so much time and so much space dedicated to these activities, especially when they were primarily of interest to just one half of the population? After all, it was not as if the papers gave five pages a day to aerobics or cookery or cross-stitch, or any other activity that might pull a similarly disproportionate number of female readers. The more I thought about it, the more I puzzled about it. Men and male activities predominated across the board in media coverage, not just in sport, but in all spheres. However, to me this matter of the sports coverage seemed significantly different. It was not that I objected to sport itself. I objected to what it symbolised: the aggrandisement of a form of male play, the permission it gave men to value their play and their playfulness, in the absence of equivalent permission being given to women.

In the years that followed, I became increasingly intrigued, and troubled, by this apparent devaluation of women's play, increasingly aware of the paucity of play in many women's lives. I started looking around at the women I knew and puzzling over their, *our*, frequent lack of playfulness. I began to pay closer attention to other women, too: women in the street, women in the news, women in history, women in novels; I began listening more carefully to the women I was interviewing in the course of my work as a journalist and sociologist; reading between the lines of books I was studying on women's work and leisure, on women's experience of sexuality, identity, maternity. It became increasingly clear to me that an issue of major importance was being consistently neglected.

Both today and in the past, women have been overlooked, and have overlooked themselves, when it comes to play. The ability and the need to play are both there, yet the opportunities for play in many women's lives are under threat, the value of women's play is undermined, and – most worrying of all – the sense of entitlement to play has been eroded. A considerable body of literature exists on the subject of play, but I have yet to find a reference to women's play in any index of any book. Even books written in recent years dedicating themselves to exploring female experience, whether professional, personal, sexual or familial, omit to mention either the role of play in women's lives or its relation to well-being. No systematic work has ever been carried out on what play means for women. This omission is itself a clear indicator of how absent play is, and long has been from the lives of women.

A woman's capacity for play is very often at odds with the other aspects of her life; the pressures of work, the expectations of parents, partners and children, and, not least, her own expectations of herself. In general, women continue to be seen as the facilitators of other people's play. They appear as adjuncts to children's play in the socially acceptable role of mother, childminder, play-school worker and teacher. They appear as props for men's social and sexual play in adverts, soap operas, videos, films and magazines. Being fun and giving fun are regarded as two more items on a woman's list of that day's Things To Do, aspects of her role as mother, wife, girlfriend, lover. As such, she is very often the provider of pleasure rather than the recipient.

Of course there is a genuine pleasure in making others happy, especially where children are concerned: last summer, our two-year-old encountered the seaside for the first time; she splashed in the breakers, gathered pebbles and seaweed to put in her bucket, shouted at the kites flying high overhead, inscribed mysterious signs and symbols on the sand with a razor-shell. For five days, she was in a delirium of happiness. In the face of such pleasure, how could I regret the day-long cliff-top walks that were my idea of fun? Instead I splashed in the breakers too, gathered seaweed for her bucket, helped her make her first sandcastles, and, catching her happiness, was happy too. Vicarious pleasure is not to be sneered at; some would say that vicarious pleasure is the best kind of pleasure there is. But to be *always* content with making others happy? Such selflessness makes me uneasy. I am reminded of the mother of a friend of mine who offered round the after-dinner chocolates, urging everyone to have another one, until it was pointed out that she had not even had her first. 'Oh, that's all right. I'll have mine when you've all had enough.' She was enjoying watching us enjoying them, she explained.

In life's intermittent joy rides, is it right that we should so readily assume the passenger seat? Should we not, at least some of the time, be sitting at the wheel? Of course, we *are* bound to others' needs. Someone *does* have to ensure there is food for supper, shoes that fit, money for the milkman. However much we may want to, we *cannot* always meet our own needs whenever we please. None the less, we can come many steps closer to living a life in which there is space, not only for our responsible, caring, other-focused selves, but also for our carefree, self-focused, playful selves.

In addressing these issues, this book proposes a shift in the direction of feminist thinking. Until now much of the emphasis within feminism has been focused on changes in the world of work as the way forward in the quest for sexual equality. The quest to improve working conditions for women is by no means over, but we can no longer afford to ignore other dimensions of our lives. Work alone has not proved a successful route to improving the quality of women's lives today. This is a fundamental and extremely unpopular problem in feminist camps, yet the facts cannot be ignored: women still work longer hours in total than men of equivalent employment status, still have less time off, and are still doing most of the housework and childcare.

As Camille Paglia puts it, 'Professional functioning in the Apollonian capitalist machine . . . must not be confused with full human identity.'[1] Work, however important, is never going to turn us into happy, fulfilled individuals, and it is foolish to think it can or will. It has solved certain problems and introduced a number of new ones: on the plus side, there is evidence that paid work for women is linked to self-esteem, good mental health, a sense of self-efficacy; on the minus side, there is evidence of role strain, stress, chronic fatigue. Work is not the sole solution to sexual inequality and personal unhappiness, and never will be. In seeking to share the advantages that work offers men, we find ourselves sharing also its disadvantages. In failing to see that quality of life is about more than the sum of our occupation – for men as well as for women – we have missed a crucial point, which is in increasingly urgent need of recognition. Women are workers *par excellence*, but what of our playful selves?

What seems to me incontestable, though so long ignored, is the fact that women's play has been and still is deprioritised in our culture. On an individual day-to-day level this down-grading of women's play can be extremely hard to combat. The man in Prestoprint, who faxed the original synopsis of this book through to my agent, neatly summed up the situation when he said, 'I hope my wife doesn't read this – it'd interfere with my rugby.'

Like those of a great many women, my days are dominated by the sense of there being too much to do and not enough time to do it in; there is certainly not enough time to play with the purity of intention and absorption that my young daughter does. I observe her absorption with delight and wonder. I marvel at her intent participation in these games of her own making, her single-minded dedication to the task in hand. As she plays, she breathes deeply and unselfconsciously; her feet twirl round and round; she leans this way and that; she pauses, she starts again; her whole body is concentrating. Watching her at play, it is impossible not to be charmed. But it is equally impossible not to be reminded of the scarcity of this kind of play in my own life these days. Sometimes, I confess, my heart sinks when she wants to play ball: I was just about to wash up/write a thank-you letter/empty the dishwasher – even, heaven forbid, read the newspaper. Other times, her play gives me the excuse to play: we chase and hide and tickle and giggle, we sing songs, we dance, we pull silly faces, we make funny noises. And, when I can forget the washing up, the thank-you letter and the dishwasher, it is wonderful. And I wonder why it is not a more valued aspect of life, this playing, when it makes me feel so good, when, just for a moment, it puts everything else into perspective. I wonder why I need the uninhibited enthusiasm of a little girl to legitimate this instinct for playfulness, why it is not easier to be playful just for myself, why, for so many women like me, the playfulness that formed an integral part of our lives and of our very identity as children gradually gets written out of how we view the world and how we see ourselves.

The Playful Self is not intended to be the definitive word on the matter; my aim in writing this book has been to put the issue on the agenda, to start people talking and thinking about the role of play in women's lives, the importance of playfulness. This is not a paean for hedonism, so much as a plea for balance, a call to all those who find themselves stressed out by their daily lives, who cannot seem to find a moment for themselves, who do not recall when they last lost track of time. This book will speak to some women more than others, for not all women are out of touch with their playful self. Some are strikingly playful, a few are effortlessly so; others work hard at their play, and some seem to have no need of it. Nevertheless, most women, I believe, do feel the lack of play in their lives and would have it otherwise, but are unsure how to change the situation. To them, this book is addressed. In all probability, some of what it has to say will speak as much to men as to women, for men too can have a hard time when it comes to play. My hope is that someone out there at this very moment is writing a book about *men's* need to recapture the playful self. If someone is, however, I suspect that person will not be saying quite the same things, because the reasons why women find it so hard to play are essentially bound up with being female, and with the social conventions, expectations and restrictions that accompany femaleness. While the problem of valuing the playful self in a work-obsessed culture is one that we all face, the relationship of women to play is a very particular one, borne out of the experience of being female in our culture.

An important moment in the writing of *The Playful Self* came in 1990 when I was lucky enough to meet a remarkable woman called Elinor Goldschmied. Elinor has a worldwide reputation in the field of social work for her documentary training films, and within Europe is an acknowledged expert on the management of day care services. I had contacted Elinor to request an interview for the oral history project I was working on at the time, *Lives of Distinguished Women*, a series of interviews for the National Life Story Collection in London. Elinor was then in her late seventies, and still working as a childcare expert. She had worked extensively in the UK and abroad with children and adults, developing her theory of heuristic play: the discovery of the world through playing. I quickly found out that Elinor's insatiable curiosity meant that she was as interested in finding out about my life as telling me about hers. When she heard that I was preparing a book on the subject of women and play, she responded with interest and enthusiasm, and suggested that we run a one-day workshop together, aimed at giving women the opportunity to explore and, in some cases, rediscover their instinct and ability for play. Elinor had run workshops of this kind previously, in Spain and Italy, with a view to helping women understand how children play, but she was interested now in seeing what happened when women's own play was made the focus of the workshop. The Play Day took place in London in November 1990. Twenty women attended, some were friends, some were colleagues, some had responded to advertisements posted in shop windows. They ranged in age from 25 to 60; some were single, some lived with a partner, some were married; some had young children, some had grown-up children; some had high-powered careers, some had routine jobs, some were full-time housewives. All shared a desire to make play a central part of their lives; only one felt she did so already; most felt their lives suffered from a lack of play; several felt it had been squeezed out entirely. The day was structured around a few key exercises, with opportunities for discussion after each one. These exercises were all designed to reawaken, release and stimulate playfulness. The responses to these exercises were fascinating in their variety. In some cases, the response was intense and even shocking. One woman in her fifties discovered that her playful self was not as sweet and agreeable as she'd assumed, but an angry, disobedient self, who wanted to play by destroying. Another woman had come to the Play Day because she saw herself as a playful person, but in fact discovered in the course of the day how very difficult she found it to play. The exercises, and the women's responses to them, are described in detail in Chapter 9. Ten of the women agreed to be interviewed a fortnight after the Play Day about the day itself and about the role of play in their lives generally. Their thoughts and feelings are threaded through the book, and, along with those of the many women that I have interviewed over the years, have added muscle and bone to my ideas, fleshed out the theory, and rooted it in real life.

The book is divided into three parts. The first part of the book analyses what play is and what play does. Chapter 1 looks at the current state of play in society today and shows how a culture of work flourishes at the expense of play, how the conditions of work, and the state of the labour market in Britain today, militate against playfulness by creating an atmosphere of instability, uncertainty and anxiety. Chapter 2 defines what is meant here by 'play' and 'playful'. It distinguishes 'play' from 'leisure', and sets out to explain how we may know when we are playing. This chapter also shows how the word and the concept 'play' have changed over time, to suit the needs of different eras, and how play has gradually become disassociated with adulthood. Chapter 3 asks, so what? Do we actually need to play? Does it really matter if we don't? Drawing evidence from a range of social and scientific research, the chapter argues that play is good for us in a number of important ways, and that we suffer when we cannot or do not play. The first three chapters having established that we do not play, that we need to play, and that we know what play is, Chapter 4 locates play in its historical context and considers the role of play at different times in the past, tracing the story back to a time when play held a respected and accepted place in culture, and showing how the playful self gradually became identified with indolence, childishness and, ultimately, immorality. This chapter argues that as our nation industrialised so did the individuals within it.

Part Two of the book focuses more specifically on women, and the reasons why it is that women seem to lose out when it comes to play, why we find it so hard to nurture the playful self within us. Chapter 5 looks at the practical, external obstacles to play, the sheer lack of time in our lives, the sheer bulk of work, paid and unpaid. This chapter shows how leisure is often a myth in women's lives, merely work in another guise. The next two chapters look at the key internal obstacles to play, the psychological and emotional factors that inhibit playfulness in women. Chapter 6 argues that, from childhood, women are socialised into ways of thinking geared to serving others, caring for others, and feeling responsible for others, and that this 'imperative of service' wages war on the playful self within us, undermining both our capacity for play and our inclination for play. Chapter 7 exposes the second major opponent of play: self-consciousness. In this chapter, we see how self-consciousness becomes like an internal mirror we carry around with us, and how this habit of self-consciousness makes genuine playfulness impossible. Chapter 8 concludes this part of the book by looking at the role of semantics in play, arguing that through the very language we use we have been cut off from our playful selves, but that through that same language we can also reclaim our playfulness in immediate and powerful ways.

Part Three of the book looks at solutions; drawing from interviews with the women who attended the London Play Day, this section sets out the means for revitalising the playful self and reincorporating it into the centre of our lives. Chapter 9 looks at how the play of children can often show adults the way, helping us to get in touch with our ability to play, helping us to rediscover habits of playfulness. Chapter 10 tackles the problem which so many women identify as the chief cause for their lack of play: lack of time. This chapter argues that it is only by playing that we will find the time to play, that only when we allow ourselves to be playful do we discover that playfulness is possible. Chapter 11 focuses specifically on certain aspects of our lives which can be anything but playful, such as our relationship with our bodies, food and sex, and shows how, by approaching them with our playful self to the fore, we can let them become boundlessly rich sources for play. Chapter 12 puts the personal in the context of the political and argues that play is not just a matter for the individual, but is a concern for society as a whole. In a just, humane society, the playful self is regarded with respect, and play is considered not an indulgence, but a right. Only the society that upholds, rather than negates, the right to play – for women and men, for young and old – can truly be said to value the individuals who comprise that society.

Thus we start with the self and come back to the self. The playful self.

Twenty years ago, Susie Orbach and other feminists began to decode women's language to reveal for the first time the anguish and suffering related to food, buried in casually dropped phrases, such as 'I'm trying to lose weight' and 'I'm not eating today'. This book seeks to decode the wider, deeper meanings held in phrases commonly used by women today, such as 'I'm so tired' and 'I never get a moment to myself'. These words are the key to a hidden yet shared world of self-denial, frustrated creativity, dissatisfaction, unfulfilled potential, oppressive responsibility, over-work and self-doubt. It is not an exaggeration to amend Orbach's phrase and say that, like fat, play is a feminist issue, one that until now has been overlooked. Like fat, play cuts across boundaries of age and class. The paucity of play in so many women's lives today is an indication that, and a crucial reason why, the crusade for genuine equality in contemporary society is not yet over.

I am convinced, both from my heart and from my research, that the issue of lack of play, this urgent need to rediscover our playful selves, is one that cuts across the board and has relevance for all women today. Any activity that releases a person, however temporarily, from the troubles and concerns of daily life can be called 'play', and as such deserves respect for the simple reason that women need to be carefree – literally, free from cares – from time to time. Without play as a central, thriving aspect of our lives, we are emotionally, physically, spiritually and socially disadvantaged. The poet-philosopher Friedrich Schiller wrote 'Man only plays when he is in the fullest sense of the word a human being, and he is only fully a human being when he plays.'[2] Our quest for a balanced life, for genuine quality of life, as opposed to quasi-equality, can only truly begin once we recognise and reclaim this fundamental right: the right to our playful selves.

PART ONE

1

The State of Play

'There are two ways of doing injury to mankind: one, the introduction of pains; the other, exclusion of pleasures. Both are acts of tyranny, for in what does tyranny consist, if not in this?'
(Jeremy Bentham, *Theory of Legislation*)

Play is many things: a concept, an activity, an experience, an attitude. It is also a fundamental human need, one of the first skills we master, one of the last skills we relinquish. It is one of the most essential sources of human joy, one of the most effective forms of education, one of the most successful routes to scientific and artistic discovery. Play fuses our earliest years and has the potential to redeem our final ones. Long before we can walk or talk or feed ourselves, we are capable of play and playfulness. After sucking and crying, comes smiling and laughing. A baby of just three or four months old has already developed a sense of fun. It will gurgle and giggle at the mere suggestion of a game, is not only capable of playing, but enthusiastic to do so. From the very beginning, the world is a storehouse for play. We assert ourselves through play and we bind ourselves to one another through play. Nature and evolution would not have wasted their combined resources on play were it not truly an essential for human survival from the outset.

Adults, too, need play in their lives. Specialists from a wide range of disciplines are united on this issue, and, as we shall see in Chapter 3, contemporary research provides abundant evidence for the primacy of play for social and psychological well-being at *all* ages. Throughout history, play has been considered a topic of philosophical and practical significance, so much so that many of the great philosophers from Plato on have written about the importance of play in human society. In the twentieth century, the Dutch historian Johan Huizinga, in his classic work on the subject, *Homo Ludens*, argued that 'Genuine, pure play is one of the main bases of civilisation'.

It is therefore deeply troubling, and cause for genuine concern, that a great many people today are not playing. In spite of all the evidence testifying to the importance of play, most of us have less and less time for play in our lives, and even when we do have the time to play, we are no longer sure how to play. Far from being a basis of civilisation, play in contemporary culture has become a relic of bygone days, a curiosity; the very word 'play' has a quaint ring to it, and comes with dubious connotations of self-indulgence, frivolity and immaturity. Instead, we live in a society that attaches great and growing importance to the world of work.

Working Our Lives Away

In the back windscreen of a Mini somewhere in south London there is a sign that reads: 'WORK – RETIRE – DIE'. This dour little adage sums up the way most of us feel about our lives from time to time, and for many of us it encapsulates an on-going and unpleasant reality. We don't just *feel* as if we're working our lives away, we *are* working our lives away. Whether our work is running a household or running a company, whether it is stacking supermarket shelves or drafting legal enactments, whether it is managing a hospital ward or driving minicabs, the chances are that work, of one kind or another, will be taking up a great and increasing amount of time, leaving us less and less time for the other things in life: family, friends, fun – the things that make life more than an uninspiring journey from pay slip to handshake to grave. We know the balance is wrong, but we do not know what to do about it. We think to ourselves, maybe, if we work hard enough now, we will reach a stage in the future where we can stop working altogether. We'll emigrate, we'll retire early, we'll live in the sun, we'll play tennis all day, we will never attend another meeting, never cook another meal, never wash another sock. But, in the meantime, there are bills to pay and food to buy and kids to feed.

We live in a culture obsessed with work. This is not just a women's problem; it is a problem for everyone. Increasingly, we define ourselves and others not by what we are but by what we do. 'What do you do?' we ask someone on first meeting. 'How's work?' we enquire of friends and relations, as if that were the most significant part of them. And certainly, for those in work, it takes up the significant part of their time. Employees are working longer hours than ten years ago. Many of us are less contented with our work than ten years ago. More than half of us are suffering from stress.[1] In a survey of eleven countries, Britain came eighth on employees' job satisfaction, with only four out of ten British employees saying they were happy in their work. They were more likely than workers in other countries to find work stressful, to feel underpaid, and to feel exhausted by their work.[2] Work-related ill-health is an increasing problem for employers, and increases the risk of marital difficulties and breakdown.[3] It is known that the risk of divorce goes up for women who are also economically active.[4] This is usually explained as a result of the woman's increased chances of being financially independent and therefore having the option of divorce, but could just as well be a result of the greater stress that comes from trying to hold down a job, a family and a marriage.[5] Low-level persistent fatigue has become a recognised medical condition, affecting up to 48 per cent of the adult population at some time in their lives.[6] Claims in the seventies that the world of work was changing, that we were moving towards a 'leisure society', that the three-day week was only a step away, have come to nothing. On the other hand, 'jobs for life' are becoming rarer; the 1990s have witnessed a growth in the numbers of people employed in temporary jobs, and, amongst professionals, there has been an increase in short-term contracts. Technological advance is releasing many of us from full-time, life-long employment, whether we like it or not. But while the work-place may be changing, work of one kind or another still determines how most of us spend our time, and how most of us feel about our lives.

In Britain, the average employee currently works almost 40 hours a week, with men clocking up nearly 45 hours a week on average.[7] One in four male employees in the UK now works more than 48 hours a week, while one in eight British managers works more than 60 hours a week.[8] Amongst white-collar workers, two-thirds now work 40 hours or more a week, while a quarter work 50 hours or more.[9] What does that mean for the quality of life in those households? It is no longer just men who are subject to the demands of the work-place. The biggest growth area in the work force is amongst female employees. Women now comprise half of the work force, up from a third in 1950. In some parts of the country there are now more women in paid employment than men. In the late 1970s, 60 per cent of women aged 24–55 had a job; in 1991, that figure had risen to 75 per cent.[10] While the majority of employed women are in part-time jobs, they are nevertheless working more than 30 hours a week on average.[11] In addition, the number of women classed as part-time workers, but actually holding down two jobs, has almost doubled in the last ten years – and that is the official statistic. The true figure is without doubt much higher.[12] Almost half of all couples of working age are now *both* in paid employment of some kind, and in

28 per cent of households with dependent children, both parents are working full-time, on top of their domestic responsibilities.[13]

This trend is by no means restricted to Britain. Although average hours have fallen by half an hour a week in European Union countries, in many sectors of the European work force, employees are working longer than before.[14] In the USA, it has been estimated that the average worker does the equivalent of one month more work each year than in the 1970s. Two-thirds of American households now have two adults in work.[15]

Contemporary society attaches great importance to the work that people do, yet the conditions of work are deteriorating. A climate of insecurity and anxiety hovers over the world of employment. Predictions and evidence that job security will not be a feature of employment in the future are causing considerable anxiety for both employed and unemployed – those with jobs feel anxious about keeping them, those without can't see how they'll ever get them. The future of work, we are told by economists, journalists, labour market forecasters and trends analysts, will be characterised by part-time employment, short-term contracts, high staff turnover and increasing mechanisation. These developments might be considered good news, were it not for the fact that so many people today derive their core sense of identity and self-worth from the work that they do.[16] Faced with the prospect of enforced leisure time, most of us feel panicked, not relieved. Confronted with increasing insecurity in the work-place, we accept unacceptable work-loads and working conditions. We stay late at the office, to demonstrate our commitment as much as to clear some of the backlog. We put up with short-term contracts, even though that may mean we cannot get a mortgage or personal insurance or pension plan. We put up with inadequate support and insufficient training, rather than risk what job security we have, despite the costs to our psychological and physical health. We make do with low wages and pathetic pay rises, rather than be labelled as a troublemaker, regardless of the costs to our loved ones.

The prevailing economic situation tells us we are right to be anxious. Fluctuating house prices, rising taxation, high unemployment, rising crime and the clampdown on credit all contribute to the pressure to keep our heads down, to keep working, whatever the price paid by ourselves, our families, our communities.

While those of us with work are worried, over-stretched and exhausted, the unemployed and retired face stigmatisation for their lack of employment. Their low status in the eyes of society is often accompanied by low self-esteem, depression and poor physical health.[17] As one commentator succinctly put it: 'The one thing that has been worse in popular experience than work has been the lack of it.'[18] Yet one in six households currently has no paid employment at all. We have created an 'economic apartheid', in which 29 per cent of households in the UK have two earners, but 34 per cent have no earners.[19] The new-look work-place may have introduced flexibility, but it has also created insecurity and inequality. Some of us have more work than we can cope with, others have no work and desperately need it.

Over-work has been dubbed 'the nineties' disease', and we are all suffering from its effects.[20] According to a survey of around one million British employees, more than three-quarters of white-collar employees say that over-work is affecting their health, over half agreed that their personal lives were suffering as a result of long working hours.[21] For the vast majority of men, a sense of identity and self-worth is inextricably linked to paid employment, reflected in the fact that men are particularly vulnerable to the negative consequences of unemployment, redundancy and retirement. Out-of-work delinquents describe their illegal activities as 'jobs', without apparent trace of irony.[22] A significant proportion of men suffer from depression after stopping work, and their likelihood of dying of a heart attack also rises steeply around retirement age.[23]

Working Women

Women are especially prey to the culture of over-work. If anything, women are *more* at risk than men, for the simple reason that women's work tends not to stop and men's does. However long the hours he has worked, a man tends to leave his work at the door of the office, shop or factory; most women, on the other hand, get home from work only to start on the housework, the cooking, the childcare, even, increasingly, the DIY. The stock cartoon of the woman hoovering under the feet of the man in the armchair reading his newspaper is rooted in mundane reality. A survey in 1993 by the British market research group Mintel found that only one man in a hundred does an equal share of the housework, while 85 per cent of working women almost always do all the laundry and ironing.[24]

In addition, there are important differences between men's and women's experiences of work. Men's work often incorporates and encourages opportunities for leisure in a way that women's does not. Business is conducted over a game of golf or a pint of beer; meetings are held in a club or restaurant. Initiatives such as works football, rugby or cricket teams all enhance men's enjoyment of their job by fostering positive experiences and friendships, as well as providing legitimate contexts for non-work within the working day. While these practices make work more enjoyable for men, they frequently disadvantage women who are unable or unwilling to participate in such activities. A banker friend in her thirties is quite certain that her reluctance to go from the office to one of the numerous City wine-bars is a check on her career, but finds the overwhelmingly male atmosphere intimidating and unpleasant. 'It's bad enough having to work in that environment all day, without having to spend my evenings in it too,' she says. For a great many women, there will be children to collect from a childminder, nursery or school, which make it impossible either to 'waste time' socialising during the day or to stay on after work.

The culture of work is placing women under incredible pressure, as they find themselves caught in a pincer movement of paid and unpaid work. More women are now in paid employment than ever before: an estimated 74 per cent of women will be economically active by 2001, compared to 47 per cent in 1961.[25] Most of those women work from necessity as often as from inclination, and tend to be in low-paid, low-status jobs, with little security and few prospects. Time out from paid work to have children or care for elderly relatives is rewarded by reduced chances of promotion, diminished earning prospects and a shrinking pension fund.[26] Professional women on a recognised career path suffer less in these respects[27] but they will often have to contend with intense pressure to put in the same hours as their male colleagues and show the same commitment to their careers. Here again, few concessions are made to other demands there may be on a woman's time, such as young children or elderly parents, despite the fact that society still regards their care as her responsibility. Many young middle-class women are attempting to get ahead with their careers while they can, working ferociously hard in their twenties, putting off having children until they are in their thirties. Even then, the trend is to rush back to work within weeks of giving birth, partly in response to external pressures, partly driven by internal ones. Terrified of losing professional status, unable to find self-worth other than in the furtherance of their careers, many young women today have become 'hooked' on work. A direct product of society's fixation with work, the female workaholic is a very long way from the feminist ideal of women being as free as men to find fulfilment through paid work. She is more akin to the compulsive gambler or the bulimic: hers is a dependence detrimental to both health and happiness, a dependence fuelled by economic necessity and by the values of the society she lives in. At the other end of the economic spectrum, a growing number of women are having to take on two, sometimes three, part-time jobs in an attempt to make ends meet. Fiona, a mother and grandmother in her fifties, is a typical example: she gets up at six every morning, fixes her husband's breakfast and packed lunch, then goes off to her job as an office cleaner. She finishes work at midday, then cleans people's houses every afternoon for three hours. From four to six-thirty, she looks after her four small grandchildren while her daughter goes out to work. After that, it is time to make supper for her husband, tidy the house, watch some television and go to bed. Officially, Fiona works 20 hours a week; the real total is much closer to 60 hours a week, although she is paid for just 35 of them.

While a substantial body of research shows that women's employment prospects suffer as a result of trying to combine work and parenthood, the extent to which women themselves suffer from the toll of unremitting hard work has not been studied. The few studies that have looked at women's situation from this angle do not make cheerful reading: sociologists Gregson and Lowe point to a 'crisis in day-to-day social reproduction' for women trying to combine paid work, housework and responsibility for childcare.[28]

The strain of over-work is greatest for women in their thirties and forties with young children. The largest proportion of women going out to work fall into this age group, yet these women are also the ones coping with the heaviest burden of unpaid work in the home.[29] In 45 per cent of households with dependent children, both adults are also going out to work.[30] For many women the effort of trying to combine these two demanding jobs is not just exhausting, it is also profoundly undermining. Catherine, in her late thirties with three young children, says with despair in her voice, 'I'm not being a very good mother, and I'm not doing my job very well either. It's just too much. I constantly have the sense that I'm failing at both. Sometimes it makes me quite despairing, but I can't see a way out. I'm giving everything I've got, I've nothing left over for myself, but it's still not enough.'

For most women today, work, paid or unpaid, consumes vast amounts of time and energy. Women's total work time is going up, meanwhile, according to trends analysts Demos, women's free time is going down: with a fall of 10 per cent since the mid-1980s, women's free time currently stands at 15 hours a week less than men's.[31] Clearly, the quality of women's lives has not been improved. Journalist Ginny Dougary, describing in *The Times* her daily scramble to combine career and family, articulates the feelings of many women today when she writes; 'I have the fears, the doubts, the intermittent sense that it cannot be healthy for working parents – those of us who attach some importance to the second word – to be leading such driven, exhausted and, quite often, joyless lives.'[32]

Overworked And Underplayed

We know something is not right with the way we live our lives today, but we are unsure what to do about it. 'All work and no play makes Jack a dull boy' goes the childhood rhyme – and the same applies to Jill too. Yet this is exactly the state of affairs in which we find ourselves. The heart of the problem is that we have allowed our preoccupation with work to blind us to an equally significant dimension of human activity.

Play, once scrutinised with the same fervent attention currently devoted to the realm of employment, has been made redundant in the course of this century. Play, once a meaningful and popular concept, has gradually fallen into disuse. While work has been regularly analysed and periodically redefined to take account of, for example, industrialisation, Marxism, the decline of the servant class, technological advance and the growth of the service industry, play, by contrast, has been increasingly ignored.[33] Both as a concept and in practice, play has been edged out of our line of vision by the all too dominant face of work. Consequently, many of us are no longer clear what play is: we are uncomfortable with the abstract notion of play, and have difficulty in pinpointing examples from our own lives. We are not even sure whether we *should* be playing: children and animals may play, but we are profoundly uncertain what part, if any, play should have in adulthood.

On the Women's Play Day which Elinor Goldschmied and I ran in November 1990, the extent of this uncertainty quickly became apparent. Of the twenty participants, all twenty agreed that play was important (although they weren't quite sure what it was) but only two were confident that they enjoyed play in their life on a regular basis. More typical were the responses of 34-year-old Rachel, a journalist: 'I ring up a friend once in a while and say, "Let's go on the rampage." Does that count as play?' or 42-year-old Deborah, a solicitor and mother of two: 'Play? What's that? With two small children and a full-time job I don't have time for it, whatever it is,' or 25-year-old Cathy, who works full-time at her local job-centre, and also has a part-time evening job at the ice-rink: 'I don't know if I play exactly, but I go riding every Saturday. I'd go mad if I didn't.'

Western culture has exalted the role of work and, as a consequence, lost sight of play as an equally essential aspect of human life. Robert Louis Stevenson pointed this out as long ago as 1876, complaining that 'Perpetual devotion to what a man calls his business, is only to be sustained by perpetual neglect of many other things, and it is not by any means certain that a man's business is the most important thing he can do.'[34] The time and energy we devote to work is still causing, or forcing, us to neglect many other things in our lives, most notably the time and energy to play.

Many traditional communities have succeeded better than we in this respect. In Ladakh, an ancient culture on the Tibetan Plateau, work and play have a very different place in people's lives than here in the west. Anthropologist Helena Norberg-Hodge has spent many years living alongside the Ladakhi people and describes in her book *Ancient Futures* the way they live:

> People work hard, but at their own rate, accompanied by laughter and song. The distinction between work and play is not rigidly defined. Remarkably, Ladakhis only work, really work, for four months of the year. In the eight winter months, they must cook, feed the animals, and carry water, but work is minimal. Most of the winter is spent at festivals and parties. Even during summer, hardly a week passes without a major festival or celebration of one sort or another, while in winter the celebration is almost nonstop.[35]

Norberg-Hodge was impressed by the balance that the Ladakhi people achieved in the different aspects of their lives. In particular, she was struck by the way that they succeeded in fusing both work and leisure with a spirit of playfulness, with clearly visible benefits: 'The Ladakhi people exude a sense of well-being, vitality, and high spirits. In terms of physique, almost everyone is trim and fit – only rarely overweight and even more rarely obese . . . The old are active until the day they die.'[36]

Sadly, this is a tale with a depressing ending. As western influences have encroached on the insulated world of the Ladakhis, the delicate equilibrium of their lives has been disrupted. In search of higher wages in the city, the young men now spend many hours away from the village, see little of their families, and are no longer involved with domestic and agricultural work, which is left to the women and old people. The gradual segregation of Ladakhi society has eroded the inter-generational harmony that previously existed, and a hitherto unknown degree of domestic conflict has become commonplace.

During her most recent visit to Ladakh, Norberg-Hodge observed increasing levels of dissatisfaction, particularly amongst the young, while the older people were prey for the first time to feelings of isolation and loneliness.

In Ladakh, as has happened so often elsewhere, the west has imported not only its achievements, but also its failures. Instead of seeing that here was a society where work had a place but stayed in its place, and learning from the people of Ladakh, western developers have imposed their own values, chief amongst which is an obsession with paid employment and crude market values.

Of course we need work in our lives. It serves an important role beyond the money it brings in. At its best, work is a source of dignity and self-respect. Paid work may no longer be an option for every individual, but it is nevertheless a valid goal, a worthy aspiration, arguably a universal right. What is quite wrong is the situation that we now find ourselves in, where the very idea of work has become so dominant that it has crowded out other, vital, states of mind. We need to recover play as a central, defining part of our lives. Rather than segregating play to a few small corners, we need to find ways of infusing play, and still more importantly, a spirit of playfulness into every aspect of our lives.

Women And Play

While both sexes experience considerable pressure on their play in what is an overwhelmingly work-focused culture, and while we could all benefit from increased access to play, nevertheless, the play deficit is especially acute in women's lives. In this age of so-called equality, play, in its very broadest sense of informal, unstructured time-off for oneself, is still easier for men than it is for women. A man can go to the pub, go to the club, go for a walk, potter about in the garden, tinker about in the shed. Women, however, seldom have the place or the space to play. It is hard for a woman to sit alone in a pub or restaurant, or even on a park bench, without feeling conspicuous and vulnerable. It is hard for a woman to potter about in the garden or sit and read a book when there are clothes to wash, children to bath, supper to cook. The division of domestic labour is changing, but only very slowly, and in the meantime women continue to bear the main responsibility for running the home, a significant burden of work on which it is hard to turn one's back. Opportunities for formalised play, such as physical sports, are also harder for women to take advantage of. In purely practical terms, fewer such opportunities exist and, even when they do, the other pressures on a woman's time and energy often make it difficult to make the most of them.

Even if these obstacles are overcome, the very act of taking time for play can meet with strenuous resistance. I got into conversation recently with a man in his mid-forties whose marriage was breaking up. He placed the blame squarely at the feminists' door. 'It's that Further Education course she went on last year,' he explained. 'If she hadn't done that course, she'd never have met the people she met, and she'd never have got all those ideas in her head. It's talking to them that's caused all this trouble.' 'Those ideas' turned out to be nothing more earth-shattering than his wife attempting to renegotiate aspects of their marriage that over the last twenty-two years had ceased to make her happy. She no longer saw any reason to cook supper every night, nor to spend so much of her time on housework. She wanted to do something different, something just for herself. She wanted to get out of the house a few evenings a week, learn something new, meet some different people. The children had left home; she had done her duty by them. Now she felt it was time to look to her own needs. But, as far as her husband was concerned, her needs did not come into it, and that included her play needs. He did not want his wife developing a life of her own, not surprisingly given the service she had provided all those years. Who would be there to make supper when he got home? Who would do the shopping? Who would answer the phone (and take his business calls) when he was out? The smooth running of his life was based on the assumption that she would be there to do these and many other things besides.

The assumption that men are more entitled to play than women is widespread and deep-rooted. It is held by women and men of every age, race and class, and mirrored in the inequality of opportunity for play in men and women's lives. Manners mock reality in this respect. The requirement that a gentleman should stand when a lady enters the room, and remain standing until she has either sat down or gone away, is an inversion of what usually happens: many women sit only when everyone else is seated, eat only when everyone else is fed, sleep only when everyone else is sleeping, rest only when everyone else is tended to. A woman's needs for genuine time off must often wait until the needs of all those around her have been met. 'Play', as one working mother put it, 'is something I get the children to do so that I can get on with clearing up tea, putting on a wash and running their bath.' Lack of money obviously limits both women's and men's opportunities for play, but her play is first to go by the board when money is short. This principle cuts across class: her night out with the girls goes before his evening in the pub; her piano lessons go before his literary lunches; her health club membership goes before his golf. Financial considerations reflect some unappealing but widely held attitudes towards women's play – in short, that it is of less value than men's. A woman's role, after all, is to meet everyone else's needs, not indulge her own. In a culture that is uneasy with the possibility of a woman finding fulfilment other than through her loved ones, the idea of a woman out and about while her partner sits at home alone rouses considerable anxiety. Conversely, and illogically, where the man is busy with his work, out with his friends, or away on business, our culture praises this same woman's ability to amuse herself as an admirable display of resourcefulness and self-sufficiency. The message is unambiguous: when the cat's away, the mouse can play, but otherwise, she must stay home and behave. Given the many constraints on women's play – practical, emotional and cultural – claiming some real time off can be nothing short of hard work. It may mean finding and paying someone to babysit, or putting up with the resentment and hostility of a partner. It may mean ignoring implicit and explicit accusations of selfishness and, last but not least, it may mean combating one's own feelings of uncertainty about one's entitlement to play.

Twenty-seven-year-old Margaret is happily married, with a well-paid job as an industrial psychologist, yet she made this comment on her life: 'At weekends, me and my girlfriends sit around feeling so tired, and asking each other why it all feels such hard work. "Is this what it's all about?" we say.' Margaret's words give voice to a fatigue and a sneaking sense of futility that many thousands of women will recognise from their own lives. But what is this 'it' that she describes as being so exhausting? Margaret's words are shocking because they are honest. We are not supposed to be ground down and exhausted anymore; we are supposed to be empowered and fulfilled.

Work is one aspect of a fulfilled life, but it will never be the panacea for all ills. For many women, paid employment has brought new troubles to replace the old ones, or rather, it has not so much replaced the old problems as obscured them. Scores of books are now being published with titles like *Juggling It All, Executive Mothers, The Juggling Act*, and *The Mother Puzzle.* One leading women's magazine uses the slogan 'The Magazine For Women Who Juggle Their Lives'. While this slogan acknowledges the demanding reality of many women's lives today, it comes perilously close to celebrating a state of affairs it should deplore. At the same time, the number of books and articles about coping with stress and stress-related illness is on the increase. One publisher alone offers *The Book of Stress Survival,*

Coping with Stress at Work, Stress Busters, The Stress Protection Plan and *Banish Anxiety*.[37] Newspapers too are full of gloomy predictions: 'Overwork: The Nineties' Disease', claimed a feature in the *Independent on Sunday*, 'Alarm Bells Sound In Vain As More People Feel Tired All The Time', tolled the *Observer*.[38] Occupational stress – as well as its counterpart, the stress of not having an occupation – seems set to be the illness of the new millennium.

Never have women had more need of play than right now, when the juggling act that so many of us perform in our daily lives leaves us ever less time for ourselves, when the hours we spend working, whether paid or unpaid, grow ever longer. The end of the day comes not when we leave the office, but the moment when our heads finally hit the pillow. Posy Symmonds depicts this brilliantly in one of her cartoons, showing a woman arriving home from work to be greeted at the door by her toddler wanting to show off his painting, her teenage step-daughter wanting help with her homework, and her husband wanting to talk over his day. When, finally, they have been played with, listened to, talked with, fed, bathed and put to bed, the cat appears demanding to be stroked. For many women, the end of one kind of working day often simply signals the start of another. No wonder Margaret and her friends, and millions of other women like them, are exhausted much of the time. In interviews I have conducted up and down the country with women from all walks of life, ranging in age from 20 to 90, I've encountered the same story over and over again: lives of unrelenting hard work. Paid and unpaid work comprise a great and growing component of women's existence, yet the pay-offs are not as obvious as they should be.

Dismounting The Work Horse

In late-twentieth-century western culture, work has become something of a god, and women have increasingly joined men in worshipping at the altar of employment. Many of us travel longer distances to work than ever before, and when we get there we work longer hours than before. Technological advance has added to the bulk of work, not diminished it. Anxiety about job security has increased, as has the pressure on people's time. So-called labour-saving devices, both in the office and the home, simply prove the amazing elastic properties of work, which will expand in proportion to the space available for it.

The material quality of life may have improved for many women over the last hundred years: gone are the days when a woman could not rent a television, let alone buy a house, without a man's signature.

Today, more women than ever before have some money of their own, and with it some control of their daily lives and of their future. But the emotional and psychological quality of their lives has not so obviously improved. The sources of stress in women's lives today may look different, but at root they are pretty much the same: the stress of not genuinely being the author of one's own life, the stress of having little say over how one's time is spent, the stress of having to work so hard for such short moments of freedom. 'I never have any time,' says Gillian, 30, a producer in local radio. 'I feel as if I've sold my life. I want to buy some of it back, but I don't know how.'

Where we have gone wrong has been in searching for the key to fulfilment in the realm of work alone. By eradicating the inequalities that exist in the work-place, we thought we would be able to grow and fulfil our potential at last. Instead, we find we are working harder than ever, feel as hidebound as ever, and in many respects have simply taken on the limitations of men's social roles in addition to our own. As Camille Paglia says, 'Getting women out of the kitchen and into the office, we have simply put them into another bourgeois prison.'[39]

Life is hard work, but it need not be *all* hard work. We are the ones who can change things, if we want them changed, because improving the quality of life does not lie solely in terms of access to the work-place and more money in the pocket. Women need to recognise that they are entitled to a reasonable *quality* of life. Working for 90 per cent of your waking hours is not reasonable for anyone.

Feminism in the twentieth century has concentrated much of its efforts on improving the lot of the working woman, whether or not she is paid for her labour. Tremendous advances have undoubtedly been achieved in this respect, although there is still much room for improvement. Women are still concentrated in low-status, poorly paid sectors of the labour market; their wages and their promotion prospects still suffer greatly from breaks for child-bearing and child-rearing; their pension receipts at retirement are consistently lower than men's, and poverty in old age is a considerable problem of women, and for the state. The way in which the world of paid employment is structured continues to disadvantage women in work and out of it. The work-place itself remains in need of radical overhaul if it is to accommodate the needs of its increasing numbers of female employees.

But seeing the problem only in terms of work is like only ever looking out of the windows of a house on one side, forgetting that the view from the other side might look rather different. For too long now we have been looking out of one side of the house. By placing so much emphasis on our working selves, we have obscured an equally firmly entrenched area of inequality that, once unearthed, is perhaps more deeply shocking: the fact that women, past and present, have very rarely had regular, extended opportunities to play.

It is in the realm of our playful selves that persistent and invidious inequality remains, unacknowledged and unchallenged. Work alone cannot improve the quality of women's lives, because it can too easily become yet another form of enthralment. If women genuinely wish to improve the quality of their lives, they must do so through other, more resilient, means than the market-place. Women work for many reasons: financial necessity, personal choice, mental stimulation, company and friendship, moral and social pressure. Many women feel guilty if they do not work and guilty if they do. What was intended to bring freedom, through social autonomy, economic power and professional status, has in many cases only forged a new lock on the prison door. What we need now is to quest not only for equality of work, but equality of play.

Just over two hundred years ago, Jeremy Bentham argued that to remove the pleasure from people's lives was as much a form of tyranny as to introduce pain. A life of work without adequate play does just that: creates a life of pains without the pleasures. Instinctively we know this, which makes it all the more puzzling and troubling that we have allowed play to become so marginalised in our lives. Play gives colour to the monochrome of daily existence. It is the salt to the meat of our everyday lives. A world of work without play is a recipe for tense, stressed, bored people, who are not only not working to the best of their ability, but not *living* to the best of their ability. The point now is that women must recognise and claim not only the right and need to work, but also – crucially – their right and need to play.

2

What is Play?

'Play is not a behaviour per se, or one particular type of activity among others. It is determined by a certain orientation of the behaviour.'
(Jean Piaget, *Plays, Dreams and Imitation in Childhood*)

Relatively few people today can confidently define play, or easily describe what relevance it has in their life. Their hesitation is interesting. Does it expose a basic lack of familiarity with the experience of play or merely a reluctance to frame their experience as play? In all likelihood, it derives from a combination of the two: as play is increasingly marginalised in our lives, we become less acquainted with it and, as it becomes less familiar, we find it increasingly difficult to recognise. As the word 'play' falls into disuse, we apply other words to describe the experience of playing, words like 'leisure' and 'recreation', which do not perhaps apply so well, but which we get used to using all the same, until we are no longer clear what the difference is.[1]

While I was researching and writing this book, people frequently asked me, 'What *is* play exactly?' To begin with, I took the question at face value, treating it as a straightforward request for more information. Gradually, however, I began to understand that it was something more than that: it was an expression of a widely shared cultural ignorance, highlighting the degree to which the fundamental concept of play – and, more specifically, adult play, and, more specifically still, adult *female* play – has been devalued in our society. Women I spoke to seemed particularly uneasy about the notion of play. 'Women and play? What do you mean?' they asked. Or they would say, 'Play? Isn't that just for children?' Or, sometimes, 'What about *men* and play?' It is as if many of us no longer have a mental image of ourselves as players. Instead, our mental self-portraits are of being busy, coping, juggling, organising, managing. We know we are entitled to many things that our great-grandmothers were not: university education, a mortgage, free contraception, abortion, equal pay. We know that we are entitled to sexual desire, to physical appetite, to intellectual stimulation. But we seem profoundly unsure whether or not we are entitled to play. Interestingly, the men I spoke to about the book did not seem to have a problem with the notion. They sometimes said, 'And what about men?' and they too sometimes wanted to know what I meant by the word 'play', but not one of them directly challenged the basic premise that women would benefit from more play in their lives. This sense of unentitlement was exclusively female.

Defining Play

Both as an abstract entity and as a practical reality, play has become increasingly alien to us. Part of the difficulty of defining play lies in the fact that play is a paradoxical phenomenon and definitions of play are as various as play itself. Many people have tried to define play in terms of what it is not: not bound by formal rules and regulations; not bound by necessity; not pre-planned; not done for an end-result. But most of these conditions of play collapse under scrutiny. Much of children's play is highly ritualised and structured, with very specific rules and regulations. Similarly, in many cases play *will* be linked to a specific goal or end-product, such as wanting to win a game, or paint a picture. Nor need play be entirely spontaneous: it can just as easily be motivated by seriousness and undertaken with immense deliberation. Think of dress-making, acting, mountaineering.

Since the nineteenth century, our conception of play has tended to focus on what play *does*, rather than what play *is* (rather as our conception of people has). The psychologist Stanley Hall, writing at the end of the nineteenth century, described play as an evolutionary throwback, an expression of primitive urges left over from an earlier phase of our evolution. This explanation of play identified it as fundamentally undesirable, and *not* playing became a way of distinguishing oneself from the childish, the uncivilised and the primitive. It was also argued by an eminent philosopher of the day, Herbert Spencer, that play had a physiological basis, being a way of releasing tension and resting fatigued nerve centres. Both these explanations of play adopt a resolutely functional approach to the subject. In so doing, they reflect the spirit of an age concerned with order and control, in which Man stands proudly at the helm of the good ship *Progress*, as it sails away from the limitations of the past, out into the twentieth century.

This functional view of play has coloured our understanding ever since. Mirroring the scientific age we inhabit, preoccupied by notions of cause and effect, twentieth-century definitions have tended to recreate play in ways which we can quantify and test, allowing us in turn to pinpoint its various applications and effects. Karl Groos, for example, in his two major works, *Play of Animals* and *Play of Man*, propounded the view that play enables the young of a species to learn and practise in a non-essential context the various skills essential for survival, an idea taken up with enthusiasm by biologists since, who have found in animal play abundant 'proof' of this theory. To be fair to Groos, he was also one of the first people to challenge the accepted view of the time that play was fundamentally trivial. He argued instead that play was of central importance to animal and human well-being, asserting that 'The more earnest is a man's life, the more he will enjoy the refuge afforded by play . . . There he is released from the bondage of his work and from all the anxieties of life.'[2] Despite these brave words, Groos's account of the more existential aspects of play have received far less attention than his theory of 'play as practice'.

Freud, and much of the psychoanalytic thought that came after him, has emphasised the cathartic function of play, seeing it as the means by which we work out repressed consciousness of unpleasant experiences. In *Beyond the Pleasure Principle*, Freud describes how a small boy turned his mother's upsetting absences into a game in which he would make his toys disappear and then appear again. In this way, play allowed the child to take control of distressing emotions caused by circumstances that in reality were beyond his control.[3] Thus, Freud maintained, we use play to master disturbing experiences. This is, arguably, what children are doing when they play blind-man's-buff or hide-and-seek; it is what adults are doing when they go to see a Shakespearian tragedy or a Stephen King movie. Through play, fear becomes a source of enjoyment rather than distress.[4] Freud concluded from this that 'play and art are evasions of reality'.[5] He maintained that we are avoiding life as it really is when we play, or, rather, attempting to recreate it in ways which seem to us safe.

While such explanations go a long way towards a definition of play, they do not go far enough. Each leaves something crucial out. In trying to pin down play, these theories tend instead to end up curiously wide of the mark. Part of the tantalising nature of play is that it glitters enticingly on the edges of one's view, but shimmies away on closer inspection. Play cannot satisfactorily be limited to one particular purpose or to one particular activity. Functionalist explanations may explain why the impulse to play exists in humans, and what the various functions of play are, but they do not begin to approach the experience of playing. For an analysis of what that experience consists of, we need to turn to the work of two more psychologists: Jean Piaget and Mihaly Csikszentmihalyi.

Jean Piaget was a Swiss psychologist whose interest in play came out of his studies of how children develop the necessary skills of speech and numeracy, how they negotiate the social skills they require to live alongside one another and to mature from children into socially effective adults. Piaget became particularly interested in the play phenomenon in the 1940s, and set out to define play according to the player's experience of it, as distinct from the observer's. In doing so, Piaget identified that it is not what we are doing, but the way we feel and think while we are doing something, that determines whether or not we are playing. In Piaget's words, 'Play is not a behaviour per se, or one particular type of activity among others. It is determined by a certain orientation of the behaviour.'[6] The key words here are 'orientation of the behaviour', by which Piaget means behaviour oriented towards assimilation rather than accommodation, or, in other words, behaviour which is geared towards absorbing the external world into oneself, rather than adapting oneself to fit in with the external world. 'Play', he argues, 'is essentially assimilation, or the primacy of assimilation over accommodation . . . [it] proceeds by relaxation of the effort at adaptation and by maintenance or exercise of activities for the mere pleasure of mastering them.'[7] Piaget's definition points, correctly in my view, not to a specific activity or intention, but to a specific state of mind, and it is this state of mind that inclines us to play. Piaget specifies what this state of mind consists of: the 'relaxation of the effort at adaptation'.[8] With Piaget's definition in hand, it begins to make sense to talk about a playful self, a self oriented towards the possibilities for play, rather than turned away from such possibilities, a self that can allow room for assimilation as well as accommodation, a self, to return to an earlier metaphor, that can take the driver's seat as well as the passenger's, a self that is not always oriented towards others, but retains the ability to serve the needs of self. This is the self that is willing to become engrossed, to lose track of time, to do something for the sheer enjoyment of doing it.

While Piaget identifies the state of mind that *precedes* and *enables* play, he falls short in distinguishing it from the state of mind that *accompanies* play. The American psychologist Csikszentmihalyi takes us the crucial step further by identifying the features of this second state of mind. The focus of Csikszentmihalyi's research is why certain activities and behaviour lead to the psychological phenomenon he calls 'flow', a state which appears to be beneficial to physical and mental well-being. 'Flow' is summarised as 'the experience of intense involvement . . . where there is total concentration, little or no self-consciousness and a sense of self-transcendence resulting from a merging of consciousness with action.'[9] Although Csikszentmihalyi's concern is not with play explicitly, his definition of 'flow' is nevertheless indistinguishable in all its key features from the state of mind that characterises play. It is reasonable, then, to assume that when we experience 'flow', we are in fact at play, and, conversely, that when we are playing, we will experience the state Csikszentmihalyi terms 'flow'.

Piaget and Csikszentmihalyi are not the only people who have sought to encapsulate this special state of mind. The psychologist Graham Privette writes about 'peak experiences', rather than 'flow', summarising the key ingredients as: absorption, focused attention, awareness of power, intense joy, value and meaning, spontaneity, effortlessness, integration and identity.[10] Once again, the similarities between 'peak' experiences and the state of mind of a person at play are striking. Historian Johan Huizinga, coming at the matter from a different angle, talks of 'the play-mood', which he describes as 'one of rapture and enthusiasm . . . sacred or festive in accordance with the occasion. A feeling of exaltation and tension accompanies the action, mirth and relaxation follows.'[11] Call it 'flow', call it 'peak', call it the 'play-mood', this special state of mind defines whether or not we are playing, and can now be identified with some precision. Its chief components are:

- deep concentration
- involvement
- heightened awareness
- focused attention
- absorption of self in action
- diminished self-consciousness
- sense of self-transcendence
- feeling of spontaneity
- sense of purpose and mastery
- excitement, rapture, delight

There are, then, two distinct states of mind associated with play and, in the playful self, these two states are both present: on the one hand, the playful self is open to the possibility of play, rather than closed off to such a possibility; on the other hand, the individual must be capable of playing once given the opportunity. For women, giving rein to the playful self has a particular pertinence, for it means giving oneself permission to put oneself first, to put oneself at the very centre of one's concerns, and to stop, if only briefly, worrying about accommodating others. It means valuing the impulse and the ability to play, and being able to benefit from the actual experience of playing.

In Search Of The Playful Self

Equipped with this definition of play, we can now begin to search for the play in our own lives, to sort out what constitutes genuine play for us and what is just a pale imitation of it.

A crucial first step is to distinguish 'play' from 'work' and 'leisure'. This is not always easy. Because of the emphasis we place on work, or the lack of work, it is work that tends to dominate our mental and emotional viewfinder. Because work fills up so much of our time and takes up so much of our energy, we tend to take work as the focal point around which other aspects of our lives must be arranged. As a result, play is often wrongly assumed to be the opposite of work. The effect of this is two-fold: first, it means that the ways in which work can be a source of play are often overlooked, and secondly, it means that play is often confounded with work's true opposite, leisure.

Play is neither the same as leisure, nor the opposite of work. While we can define leisure as a range of activities that take place outside of time designated for work, play will not be squeezed into this definition, for play can and does occur in the course of doing one's job; work can be playful. Artists, musicians, writers, scientists, even a City broker I know, will describe their work as play. It could be argued that what makes some kinds of employment highly rewarding, and others profoundly tedious, is the degree of play in those various kinds of work. But it is not the work *per se* that leads to play: the coat must be cut to fit the wearer. Carpentry would drive me mad, writing books might well exasperate a carpenter. Shaping words is, for me, a source of pleasure as well as income, in the same way that shaping wood presumably is for a carpenter, but our respective sources of pleasure are not interchangeable. In Tolstoy's novel *Anna Karenina*, the eponymous heroine reflects that, 'If there are as many minds as there are heads, then there are as many kinds of love as there are hearts.' The same can be said of play. To involve an element of play, an activity must first suit the skills and the personality of the individual doing it, whether that activity come under the category of leisure or work.

Victoria and Sue run a small flower shop in Oxford. It has just one room, with plain white walls and black and white lino on the floor. There is no heating, and in winter they have to huddle round a small heater in the back room. Twice a week they get up at 4 a.m. to drive to New Covent Garden Market, returning in time to unload the van and open the shop at ten. By Thursday evening, they are exhausted. But the sheer sense of fun that emanates from that one little room is utterly infectious: it is impossible to look in the window without smiling. This is not just a flower shop, it is a playground. There are miniature pineapples, enormous poppies, tropical plants that resemble exotic birds, willow branches, palm fronds, roses of impossible hue, even, in one corner, small prickly green balls, aptly named 'testiculi'. There is nothing ordinary or mundane or serious here; everything is outrageous, eye-catching, startling – whether in colour, shape or mere suggestiveness. People go to the shop just to see what new marvel has arrived that week, and then cannot resist buying some for themselves. Victoria and Susan work long, hard hours, but what comes across is their creativity and exuberance. One day before Christmas I dropped by and found the shop adorned with miniature fir trees, all decorated with heart-shaped sequins and smiling plastic cherubs. Instead of the conventional garlands of holly and red berries, the walls were covered with hoops of ivy and scarlet chilli peppers. 'You two are just playing!' I declared teasingly. And, with five grown-up children between them, Victoria and Sue did not deny it for an instant. 'Yes!' they agreed, happily. 'We are!'

Confounding leisure and play is a curiously modern tendency, in part caused, in part mirrored, by the gradual substitution in the last hundred years or so of the word 'leisure' for the word 'play', without due attention being paid to the ways in which these two entities differ from one another. Social scientists interested in the causes of well-being in adulthood have made life unnecessarily difficult for themselves by ignoring the distinctions between leisure and play, and focusing instead on the distinctions between leisure and work. For when looked at without reference to the concept of play, the boundaries between leisure and work begin to appear blurred. In his study of happiness, social psychologist Michael Argyle acknowledges this blurring: 'For some people work spreads into their leisure: social workers, managers, academics, writers and artists not only take their work home, and mix their work and leisure, but for them, there is no clear distinction between the two. For many of these people, work is very satisfying because it has some of the characteristics of leisure.'[12] Argyle here makes the common mistake of trying to explain work satisfaction in terms of its similarity to leisure. This is like explaining the thirst-quenching properties of a melon in terms of its similarity to an orange. What in fact explains the connection between melons and oranges in this instance is that both are fruits with a high water content. Correspondingly, the connection between work and leisure in the context of well-being is not that one is like the other, but that they are both activities with a high play content.

As play has been subsumed into the category of leisure, it has been set up as the opposite of work. But if, as we have just seen, work can be play, leisure can be anything but. A game of netball will not be much fun if you are much worse than everyone else on the team; singing in a band will not be a playful experience if after the first song the audience bombard the stage with rotten tomatoes. It is not the activity itself, but the way you feel about it, and the way it makes you feel, which determines whether or not it can be called play. Eating, drinking, making love, resting, spending time with close friends or family, taking physical exercise, reading, listening to or making music – all these leisure activities *may* be experienced as play, but it depends who is doing them, when, where and how. The key is whether or not an activity provides a context for play.

Sociologist Ralph Glasser has argued that the commodification of leisure activities in recent years has dramatically reduced their worth:

> Instead of participation [in recreation] being an individually constructed experience, it becomes so standard that it is rather like buying a ticket for a ride on a known tram-route. The experience becomes institutionalised, and the participant feeds himself into it, helps to process himself through it, and emerges at the other end having had a completely standard, predictable experience . . . The activity, once processed in marketing and design terms, becomes *a different product*; it becomes a standard product instead of an activity that from start to finish bore the stamp of one particular person and thereby assisted the individual to realise himself uniquely.[13]

Glasser does not use the word 'play' but he is describing the process by which the play element is frequently processed out of leisure.

One reason why play and leisure tend to be conflated is that leisure activities are more likely than non-leisure activities to make us feel good, and feeling good is one of the sure signs that we've been playing in some way. A research project led by Leo Hendry and his colleagues, involving over 5000 young people aged 14-20, found a clear correlation between regular participation in some kind of leisure activity and good mental health. However, this same research failed to identify any *single* leisure activity that could be guaranteed to make people feel good: young men seemed to feel better for an evening in the pub, but it had a negative effect on some of the young women; sport, similarly, made many adolescents feel good, but not all.[14] In itself, then, leisure is not a guarantee of well-being.

Another reason why play and leisure are often confused is that, like play, leisure activities tend to be freely chosen, rather than imposed. Imposed activities are rarely playful, a point forcibly brought home to me at a party a few years ago. Half way through what had been an enjoyable afternoon, the host announced we were all going to play pass-the-parcel. My heart sank. The forfeits consisted of tasks such as kissing everyone's feet, changing clothes with the person opposite, impersonating Elvis Presley. My heart sank further. As far as I could see, this was nothing but a hideous exercise in humiliation, but, looking round the circle of faces, there could be no mistaking the mysterious fact that many of the other people were thoroughly enjoying themselves.

Similarly, activities that may *appear* alike can affect the same individual very differently, depending on the circumstances in which they take place: a child who likes colouring-in at home may detest drawing maps in geography lessons; an adult who enjoys concocting gourmet extravaganzas for dinner parties may derive no pleasure from cooking supper all the other days of the week. American psychologists have found that when teenagers perceived an activity as productive, such as school-work or a job, their perception immediately reduced the activity's positive effect on mood.[15] A woman on the Play Day described how she so hated the feeling of being coerced that she had given up a leisure activity which she'd initially enjoyed, simply because it took place at a set time each week and as a result came to seem more of a duty than a pleasure.

When it comes to play, the activity itself is only as significant as your attitude towards it. It is not what you do, but the way that you do it: choosing to do something increases the chances that it will lead to play, being forced into doing something diminishes the chances.

Play is not necessarily light-hearted or trivial. For many people, play takes a form that involves a high degree of commitment, skill and even risk. This is true of the musician, the rock-climber, the chess player. Michael Argyle calls these kinds of activities 'serious leisure'. In his study of the connection between leisure and well-being, it was this 'serious leisure' that had the most beneficial outcomes. Argyle found that, while people often described their serious leisure activities as 'stressful, challenging and absorbing', they were also more satisfied by their pursuits than people with non-serious leisure.[16] Ralph Glasser explores the concept of serious and non-serious leisure further by talking, darkly, of 'empty leisure', leisure that may fill time but nevertheless fails to fulfil; it is in itself empty and it leaves us empty. These forms of fulfilling, 'serious leisure' are precisely the ones that are also likely to lead to the experience of 'flow', described by Csikszentmihalyi, and they can thus be said to represent one particular route to play.

No single leisure activity can be called play, however. What fulfilling leisure activities do provide in many cases is a *context* for play. Importantly, it is only when a form of leisure, or work, leads to play that we begin to benefit. It is the experience of playing that transforms an activity into something special, something that makes us feel better, about ourselves, about other people, about the world we live in. It can emerge in activities as diverse as writing a memo, eating mashed potato or clearing out the cupboard under the stairs, and this diversity explains why it is that some leisure activities leave you feeling restless and dissatisfied, while others make you feel wonderful. This is why watching television, a leisure activity currently favoured by 98 per cent of the British population, is not, properly speaking, play. Watching television, unlike many other leisure activities, and despite its popularity, has little benefit in terms of feelings of well-being.

Beyond Work And Leisure

Both work and leisure can provide a context for play, and they can involve elements of play. Play, on the other hand, is distinct from both work and leisure; it has the capacity to appear in both, or in neither. The relationship between these three entities can be represented in terms of a plain sponge cake sandwiched together by a mouthwatering filling. The cake as a whole represents a person's life, the top layer of sponge represents leisure, the bottom layer of sponge represents work, the filling is play. One can prise the cake apart and eat the filling with the top layer, or with the bottom layer. Alternatively, one can scoop out the filling and just enjoy it by itself. Ideally, one can let the filling hold the two layers together and take a bite out of the whole thing so that the filling turns the dry slabs of sponge into a delicious mouthful of cake.

In a post-industrial society, leisure and work will always exist in inextricable and paradoxical relation to one another, even though they may be quite separate aspects of a person's life.[17] While leisure serves to demarcate and contain work time, work serves the same function for leisure: you know you are doing one because you are not doing the other. Leisure and work give each other their value: leisure without work is as pointless as work without leisure is unendurable. Even as children, we realise that the summer holidays are magical precisely because they are flanked by two school terms. According to Engels, leisure is a compensation for work, and it is true for many people that work does not provide much opportunity for enjoyment, and thus creates the need for it outside of work. Without formal opportunities for work, many people feel unentitled to leisure, and compensate by turning their leisure time into unpaid work. They sit on committees, they become magistrates and councillors. A fair-sized army of people take on charity work the moment they retire.

Work and leisure, then, exist in the same continuum, but play is a different concept altogether. Work and leisure are distinguishable from one another according to various conventions of time, place, money and outcome; play is governed by what might be called meta-rules, concerning attitude and state of mind. Play moves in a different sphere from work and leisure, though their flight paths may overlap. In permitting ourselves the right to play, in making space for play in our lives, we move beyond the familiar realms of work and leisure. When any activity involves play, it is instantly transformed into the source of a profound and unmistakable sense of well-being.

Femina Ludens

Play is a state of mind, a state of being, which should form a natural and central part of life from the moment we are born to the moment we die. If many of the existing theories and definitions of play have failed to recognise its importance at every stage of the life cycle, they have failed still more grievously to recognise the particular significance of play for women. None of them address the specific purpose that the playful self can serve in a woman's life. Yet with its fundamental characteristic of serving the self, and its profound affinity with freedom, play has a very special meaning for women.

From infancy we are socialised to identify ourselves in relation to other people, to gauge others' responses, to be ever-mindful of others' thoughts, feelings and needs, to be the facilitators of other people's play. What play offers women in particular is the chance to be without reference to an Other; it enables us to enjoy 'the greatest fullness of existence', not in relation to another person, as is our usual experience, but 'with the highest autonomy and freedom'. Through play, we can experience ourselves as everyday life does not commonly allow us to. Reintroducing play into our lives is thus of prime importance.

Play gives women the chance to transcend not only the vagaries of the human state, but also the cultural limitations imposed by gender. Uninhibited sexual play, for example, is a chance to be free from the everyday rules governing how a woman must dress, how she must look, how much noise she should make. A female musician, lost in the play of her creative talents, is free to savour a degree of self-absorption and unselfconsciousness normally discouraged in women. Playing with children, too, can provide a welcome opportunity for 'unfeminine' behaviour, such as rolling on the floor, talking nonsense, pulling silly faces. Play can also provide temporary release from the cultural taboos on female thought, contemplation, imagination and fantasy.

The women who attended the Play Day may have started the workshop uncertain about the meaning and role of play in their lives but, by the end of the day, all had pinpointed what it meant for them.

'Play is time off from the daily grind,' said 56-year-old Elizabeth.

'Play is like a shadow of everyday life. It's not reality, but it's the boundaries of reality,' said 30-year-old Ella.

'You can be things in play that you might not be able to be in real life,' said 32-year-old Caitlin.

'Play is a way of recharging my batteries. It helps me cope with the pressures of my job,' said 45-year-old Jane.

'Play is a state of mind, an activity, an emotional feeling – all these things and more,' said 33-year-old Beth.

'Play is a pleasurable, light activity, in which I am oblivious of time passing,' said 29-year-old Penny.

'Play puts me in touch with different aspects of myself,' said 38-year-old Alison.

'Play is enjoying life and giving everything your full attention,' said 27-year-old Maddie.

'Play is feeling alive,' said 32-year-old Emma.

Play is not a specific activity, done in a specific way, at a specific time. It can be, but it does not have to be. Play may be done with others or alone. There are no 'oughts' about play. For women, whose lives are full of 'oughts', that is one of the best things about it. Play is what you want it to be. Rather like love, play brings to the player a state of absorbed concentration that both shuts out the rest of the world and simultaneously brings it into sharper focus. For one person, play will be doing the monthy accounts, for another, it will be making ginger biscuits, for a third, play is samba dancing on a

Saturday night, for a fourth, it is staying at home with a good book. Ultimately, the opportunity to play resides in any activity that, however briefly, places you firmly at the centre of your universe, allowing you for a moment to celebrate your existence wholeheartedly and unashamedly.

Any activity has the potential to provide a context for play, whether it be knitting or mountaineering, but it is not until we are *at* play that the potentially beneficial effects of that activity can be realised. Conversely, without the core of play, an activity is no more than its utilitarian function: to procreate, to avoid dehydration, to stave off hunger, to make a garment, to produce a painting. The transformative properties of play can only be experienced through playful action. We all have the capacity to be players in life, not the archetype of the fool, but the archetype of majesty, the regal figure who is simultaneously in, of, and above the world. In *The History of the Decline and Fall of the Roman Empire*, Edward Gibbon wrote, 'There are two very natural propensities which we may distinguish in the most virtuous and liberal dispositions, the love of pleasure and the love of action . . . the character in which both the one and the other should be united and harmonised would seem to contribute the most perfect idea of human nature.'[18]

The individual – woman, child or man – who, through playful involvement with the world, combines both pleasure and action, is one of life's players in the very best sense of the word. We have seen earlier in this chapter that there are in fact two distinct states of mind associated with play, one precedes play and makes play possible, the other accompanies the act of playing. In the playful self, *both* these states are combined; we are both receptive to the possibility of play and capable of playing when the opportunity arises. The playful self is one that feels inclined to play, able to play, and, above all, *entitled* to play. By valuing the player in herself, every woman has the chance to transform herself from the object of other people's needs to the active subject of her own.

3

Why Play?

'Play is the continuous evidence of creativity, which means aliveness.'
(Donald Winnicott, *Playing and Reality*)

In the hilltop town of Monreale in northern Sicily, there is a magnificent cathedral. It sits in the middle of the market square, soaking up the Mediterranean sun, its carved stone the colour of warm butter. Inside, the walls and ceiling are covered in gold mosaics, illustrating the stories of the Old and New Testaments. The images are amazingly vivid: you can almost see the figures moving, almost hear what they are saying. None is more striking than the mosaic, high overhead in the central nave, of God, sitting comfortably on a planet, engrossed in the act of creating the heavens. His expression is solemn, conveying deep concentration, as he daubs some golden stars here, an ice-blue moon there. There is something strangely familiar about this God – and then you realise: he looks like a small child let loose with a large sheet of paper and a pot of coloured paints.

The God in Monreale cathedral is the Great Creator in the act of busily creating. He is, above all, a playful God, reminding us that play is at the heart of creation, divine and human. When we play we too are creators, in the act of creating, or more precisely, recreating. The word 'recreation' points directly towards the divine aspects of human play. We need and benefit from play because through play we are able to approach aspects of our lives creatively. When we play we are at our most creative, most able to overcome problems and meet challenges. 'The creative act does not create something out of nothing, like the God of the Old Testament,' writes Arthur Koestler. 'It combines, reshuffles and relates already existing but hitherto separate ideas, facts, frames of perception, associative contexts.'[1] It is this capacity of play to bring together disparate elements, to reconcile the irreconcilable aspects of ourselves, to make something whole and new and good out of the old, weary and troublesome, that underlies its profound importance in our daily lives.

For many of us, placing a proper value on play is achievable, but finding the time and space for play, however much we may want to, can seem impossible. This raises the question, why bother playing if it is such an effort? Do we really need to play? What happens to us when we do not? In short, does play matter? The answer is, yes, it does. In fact, play matters very much. As the psychologist Donald Winnicott has said, 'It is in playing and only in playing that the individual child or adult is able to be creative . . . and it is only in being creative that the individual discovers the self.'[2] If we wish to live lives in which we are creatively engaged with ourselves, with others and with the world around us, we need to locate play firmly at the centre of our lives.

Shakespeare's comedies and romances are full of women who save the day through their ability to think and act playfully. Portia in *The Merchant of Venice* pretends to be a lawyer (Balthazar – a man) in order to save the life of Antonio, conducting a trial that skilfully averts catastrophe. Viola in *Twelfth Night* disguises herself as a boy to save her own life, and in doing so secures a love-match for herself and her twin brother. Rosalind, the heroine of *As You Like It*, also disguises herself as a boy, but uses her disguise to test the love of her suitor, Orlando, who has failed to recognise her. She 'plays the knave' with him, persuading him to call her Rosalind, and to woo her as if she were Rosalind – which of course she is. These are all playful characters, dramatic personifications of playfulness, whose ingenuity is manifested in the words they use and the things they do.

In Elizabethan productions of these plays, an additional twist would have been added by the audience's knowledge that the female parts were played by males, and that the 'women' disguising themselves as men in reality were men. For contemporary audiences, the irony lies in noticing that the playful disguises assumed by the female characters are all male, since this both emphasises the fact that power lies with men, while at the same time undercutting that power base. In addition, the plots of these comedies often highlight their playfulness through devices such as the dreams in *The Taming of the Shrew* and *The Tempest*; the plays within plays in *A Midsummer Night's Dream*; the teasing songs and riddling epilogues in *As You Like It, The Tempest, All's Well that Ends Well* and *Twelth Night*. Structurally, each of these plays moves from threatened or actual disorder, to playful disorder, to creative resolution, to restored order. In so doing, they enact and celebrate the restorative power of playfulness, its ability to tame destructive forces, to transform chaos into order. Conversely, many of the tragedies offer a glimpse of playful capacity stifled by jealousy, greed, ambition or foolishness, with tragic consequences. In *King Lear*, Cordelia's verbal playfulness is fatally misunderstood by her father. In *Othello*, Desdemona's playful affection for Cassio is disastrously misconstrued by her husband. In *Troilus and Cressida*, Cressida's wordly playfulness helps her to survive the separation from her beloved Troilus, but is ultimately annulled by the moral and physical devastation of war. Cleopatra's sexual playfulness wins her Mark Antony, but cannot endure the political intrigues of Rome, nor the ravages of time. Ophelia, on the receiving end of Hamlet's vicious and disturbed word games, goes mad and kills herself. Where the value of play is upheld, events are resolved happily; where play is condemned, destroyed or oppressed, events culminate in catastrophe.[3] Shakespeare, as so often, identifies a profound truth about human existence. Play, though it may have the appearance of frivolity, is anything but, a frivolity. It is a priority in our lives, a profoundly serious business.

The Benefits Of Play

We are born with an instinct for playfulness, but it is an instinct that needs nurturing if we are to benefit from it. Right from the very beginning of our lives, play matters. If we want proof of its importance, we can do no better than to look at what happens when people are deprived of play. No one who saw the harrowing photographs and television footage of the Romanian orphans, blank-eyed and motionless in their rows of identical cots, depleted of the energy and curiosity we normally associate with small children, could fail to be moved by them. As experts were quick to point out, these children were not only deprived of love, they were also deprived of play. They lay in their cots with nothing to look at or respond to or engage with. There were no loving faces, no mobiles or teddies or pictures, no one to sing or coo to them. This is an extreme example, perhaps, but without opportunities to play any child will become depressed, withdrawn, aggressive and anti-social. Children brought up in institutions, where opportunities for play are often restricted, tend to be more passive, listless, apathetic and depressed, as well as less creative and spontaneous than other children. Lack of play is clearly not the only, or even the major, problem for children brought up in care, but it is a significant factor. One study found that babies living with their own families were played with *seven times as often* as those in institutions.[4]

Leaving aside for now the gender differences in childhood play, a crucial issue which I will return to in some detail in Chapters 6, 7 and 8, the main point to emerge from the above and other studies is that all children who are deprived of play suffer, while all children who have ample opportunities to play thrive. Besides the immediate pleasure it brings, play offers children a safe way of learning and mastering practical and social skills. It teaches good communication. It provides an acceptable means of expressing and exploring feelings of aggression or hatred. It helps the individual to manage uncomfortable or frightening emotions, and it is central to healthy psychological development, bridging the gap between 'inner personal reality' and 'external or shared reality'.[5] Children who spend time in imaginative thinking, pretend play and fantasising, are more likely to be creative in their handling of both materials and situations.[6] They are likely to be less aggressive, have better concentration and are more likely to enjoy what they do than children who tend not to have fantasy-play. Play also seems to be linked to intelligence, with children who score high on IQ tests playing longer than those with lower scores.[7]

A further reason for taking play seriously is that our childhood experiences of play may well influence the kind of adults we become, affecting how we relate to other people, how we handle our own emotions, how we respond to new challenges, and how we cope with stressful experiences. Experiments by Suomi and Harlow with monkeys have shown that the opportunity to play in young animals directly influences how effective they will be as adults.[8] Monkeys raised only with their mother, but without contact with their peers, become 'socially withdrawn and unusually aggressive' in adulthood, while monkeys reared in total social isolation rapidly deteriorate, become disturbed, and display clear symptoms of distress, such as intense self-clasping, compulsive rocking, thumb and finger sucking, and self-mutilation, tearing at their own skin and muscle. When reintroduced to other monkeys, they are withdrawn, antisocial, and violently hostile towards baby monkeys. They are sexually incompetent, unable to nurture infants in turn and are sometimes violent towards their own babies. Only their intellectual ability remains relatively unaffected. The researchers concluded from their observations, 'It becomes clear that play is of utmost importance for the subsequent social well-being of the individual and those around him. Play, which appears to be so spontaneous, carefree and frivolous, is actually one of the most important aspects of social development.'[9]

The same seems to be true of humans. Like the monkeys studied by Suomi and Harlow, people who have had few good experiences of play as children often have difficulties in adulthood. They are more likely to suffer from depression, often find it hard to show affection and establish trusting relationships, and have problems playing with their own children. At the Cornmarket Family Centre in Bath, depressed mothers are helped to play with their children using a system called 'relationship play'.[10] The idea is very simple: mother and child are shown how to have affectionate, physical, non-verbal play together. The mother might make a bridge with her body for the child to go under, or become a tower for the child to climb; she can sit the child on her legs, so that they can 'row' back and forth, or she can make her arms into a pretend 'prison' from which the child has to wriggle free. Relationship play can be tremendously liberating for women who have found little or no enjoyment in their children. It not only provides play for the child; it gives the mother a chance to play too. It creates a way for mother and child to communicate with their bodies, and in so doing helps them build up a sense of trust and confidence and intimacy. By creating opportunities for shared enjoyment between mother and child, relationship play also makes the adult feel better about her parenting abilities, and more inclined to play with her child. It thus sets up a positive cycle that is profoundly beneficial to all concerned.

Mothers who are not depressed need opportunities to play too. The woman who told me that play was something she got her children to do so that she could make tea may represent the majority of us but, if so, we have gone wrong somewhere along the line. As adults we too need to express our playful side, and children can be the excuse to do so. The child's lack of inhibition when it comes to playing can set the pace and show us the way, as another mother acknowledged when she explained to me, 'I learnt to play again when I had my son. He taught me everything I'd forgotten about playing.'

Far from being a frivolous activity with no discernible benefit beyond immediate enjoyment, play bears fruit in a wide range of 'serious' situations. Studies have shown that time spent playing benefits both children and adults when they later encounter 'serious' situations. In a study by Sylva, Bruner and Genova, a group of children aged 3–5 were set the task of retrieving a piece of chalk from a perspex box placed beyond their immediate reach. Some of the children in the study had been allowed to play with the chalk and the box for a while beforehand. The researchers found that the children who had played first were more efficient and imaginative in retrieving the piece of chalk than those who approached the problem cold. Playing, the researchers concluded, made the children more, not less, able to cope with 'serious', goal-directed, situations.[11]

The same principle applies to adults, hence the efficacy of 'brainstorming' sessions and 'executive stress weekends'. This latter example is interesting because of the way it so closely mimics children's play. A team-building technique which came into vogue in the 1980s, the executive stress weekend consists of a group of employees getting together in a non-work environment, usually for a weekend, but sometimes for longer. A course leader will then set up various games, such as fording a river, or beating another group to a pre-arranged goal. These are often adult versions of traditional children's games such as grandmother's-footsteps or kick-the-can (in which you try to reach a pre-agreed goal without being seen), or stick-in-the mud (in which you try to rescue trapped team mates, without getting caught yourself). The opportunity to play games in this way enables managerial staff to explore their capacity for certain skills, such as leadership, co-operation, flexibility and inventiveness. By learning to manage situations which are physically and emotionally demanding, but at the same time framed as play, participants are then able to be more creative and efficient in the way they approach problems at work.

Recently I spent an evening in the company of two men who were discussing the value of these weekends. One was the director of a multi-national organisation, the other a senior manager for the same employer. The latter was keen to try an executive stress weekend. He thought it would be helpful to have the chance to learn and develop management skills outside the context of work and the restraints of the office. The director, however, said that he had quite enough executive stress already and could think of nothing less appealing. His jokey put-down effectively dismissed the subject. Listening to the conversation, I could not help thinking that it also revealed this man's unease about play as a valid form of learning, let alone as an activity that could have any real bearing on the 'serious' world of work. Later the same evening, his wife complained jokingly about how hard her husband worked, how seldom they had proper holidays, and how little time he managed to spend with his young children. Work and play for this man were entirely separate realms of existence, and the former left him little opportunity for the latter. The discussion was good natured, but for his wife, like many women, it was no joke: she was as hampered by his lack of playfulness as he was.

The Healing Power Of Play

In cases where trauma or deprivation have suppressed or distorted the capacity for play, play itself can be an extremely effective method of healing, for play, like dreams, 'serves the function of self-revelation, and of communication at a deep level'.[12] This is the central premise behind Play Therapy. Using play as both the vehicle for coming to terms with psychological distress and the cure for that distress, play therapists aim to break the destructive circularity of that distress. At the Cotswold Community, a therapeutic centre for severely disturbed boys, play is highly valued. The community was created from the site of a former approved centre, but the barren dormitories and barred windows have long since disappeared, and it now consists of a cluster of houses in which the boys experience, often for the first time, something like close-knit family life. One of the central tenets of the Cotswold Community is that play is a vital ingredient in well-being. Playing is an essential part of the emotional 'work' that the boys must do, and this is reflected in the daily time-table, which gives as much time to play as to school-work.

However, many of the boys are unable to play, or rather their play is as disturbed as they are. Mock-fighting often escalates into real fighting; competitive games can quickly become unbearably stressful; even relatively gentle fantasy-play with toys can feel quite threatening to these children whose own lives have provided so little of the safety and stability that are the necessary pre-conditions for play. They invariably come from broken homes; many will have been in several children's homes and foster families, and the majority will have a history of delinquency. The Cotswold Community is often a last-ditch attempt to stop them sliding into juvenile crime.

In the centre's highly supportive environment, the boys are given the opportunity to discover a way of playing that is not destructive to either themselves or others. This process of self-discovery through play is extremely powerful. The boys are able to regress to the age at which they 'lost themselves' and, as it were, start again. A thirteen-year-old may retreat to the age of a three- or four-year-old, in which he clings to his teddy bear and uses it to communicate to the world. There is nothing unusual in asking a toddler 'what teddy would like for tea', but addressing a thirteen-year-old in this way is a poignant reminder of the necessity of childhood play, as necessary to our future well-being as learning to walk or talk.

'Peter' came to the community when he was ten. He seldom spoke and seemed locked away inside his head, from where he viewed the world with unconcealed mistrust and fear. The only clue he gave as to his inner state were the pictures that he drew constantly. There were several striking features about these pictures. They were always of a town encircled by high, thick walls, drawn in heavy grey or black crayon; inside the town there were a few buildings dotted about, but there were no streets or paths to connect them. On the outside of the wall, a few wiggly roads led to the perimeter of the town but no further, for there were never any gates in Peter's drawings, either into or out of the town.

For a long time, Peter's pictures, or 'maps' as he called them, remained unchanged. But very gradually they began to acquire new features. More streets and pathways appeared inside the town, connecting the different buildings; more roads appeared outside the town too, so that there were now several approach routes; a small gateway appeared on the south side of the town, although no roads as yet led directly to or from it.

The therapist working with Peter let him discuss the design and detail of his maps without making any attempt to 'connect' them to his psychological state. The turning point came one evening when the therapist came across a bundle of papers tied up in a plastic bag and dumped in the outside dustbin. The bundle turned out to be Peter's latest maps, hurriedly rejected for what they might reveal. And indeed they were revealing. He had drawn a town that resembled the maps of medieval London, bustling and teeming with life and laced with a rich network of roads. And, most startling of all, at the four compass points, there were now four gateways, permitting access to and from the town. Peter himself recognised this as a turning point, hence his frightened reaction to this brave new world he'd discovered. Nevertheless, it signalled the start of his recovery from his psychological wounds and his gradual return to the world.[13]

Many relief agencies now prioritise children's play programmes as important strategies to counter the effects of growing up with everyday conflict and violence in countries such as Northern Ireland and the Occupied Territories.[14] Play programmes and play therapy are also used to help children to recover from specific trauma. In Mozambique and Eritrea, where children as young as seven or eight were kidnapped and forcibly recruited into the army, they endured and took part in terrible atrocities. In Bosnia and Rwanda, children witnessed the slaughter of their entire families. The play of these children, if they are still capable of playing at all, often reflects the horrors they have experienced: they draw tanks and guns obsessively, their pictures are blood-splattered and scattered with corpses. Images of war, pain, death and fear stalk their play as surely as their lives.[15]

Increasingly, professionals working with child refugees are using play both to express and to heal the dreadful experiences they have survived. David Tolfree, consultant on children and war to Save The Children in Britain and Sweden, has collected case studies of different approaches to children traumatised by war in his recent book, *Restoring Playfulness.* He documents how a group of unaccompanied refugee children from south Sudan were able to work through their appalling experiences by recounting dreams, telling stories and drawing pictures. 'It would have been inappropriate to expect these children to express their feelings directly through talking,' Tolfree explains, 'but play is one of the universal means by which children work through difficult experiences, and by playing, in its very broadest sense, these children were able to do so indirectly.' Tolfree's book also provides an example of how the strength of children's ability to play can help adults. Like the depressed mothers at the Cornmarket Centre in Bath, adult refugees from former Yugoslavia were helped to overcome their traumatic experiences by seeing, and gradually connecting with, the spontaneity of their children's play.[16]

At our most desperate moments we still retain the instinct for play. It is a need as fundamental as water, food and medicine. We can, it is true, still live without play but, as e e cummings said, 'unbeing dead isn't being alive'. Even under severe pressure, play is one of the last impulses to be subdued and one of the first to reassert itself, for it is an instinct that runs close to survival. In *An Evil Cradling*, his account of the years he spent as a hostage in Beirut, Brian Keenan poignantly describes the games that he and his fellow hostage, John McCarthy, devised to pass the hours and perserve their sanity. During the Kurdish refugee crisis in April 1991, thousands of Kurds fled from Iraq to the Turkish mountains, where they lived for weeks without proper food or housing or sanitation, conditions described by one relief worker as the worst he had seen in ten years of fieldwork. Television cameras filming Inshikveren camp on the Turkish–Iraq border brought into our warm, comfortable homes the impotence, rage and fear of a whole people: the dehydrated, dying children, the grieving mothers, the bewildered old people. But as the cameras panned over these distressing scenes, they settled for a brief moment on a group of small boys, six or seven years old, scrawny from lack of food, but still smiling and laughing amidst the mud and snow and chaos. They had got hold of some empty water-bottles, trampled them flat with their bare feet, and were using them as makeshift toboggans. The camera moved on – these were not the images it was looking for – yet the laughter and smiling faces of those boys were proof that play is not the privilege of the rich and contented, but the property and pleasure of the destitute and dying too.

The instinct for play is profound and resilient. As the Kurdish children demonstrated, it will resurface even in the most desperate circumstances. In the squalor of the Rwandan refugee camps around Goma children had got hold of empty grain-sacks and turned them into makeshift kites. During the terrible 1985 famine in Sudan, sardine tins were transformed into go-carts. As one relief worker put it, 'When the children start playing, you know that the worst is over. It is the beginning of hope.'[17]

Play For Today

The capacity for play has an important role in the most extraordinary situations, but also in the most ordinary ones. In our daily lives, an ability and a readiness for play are a vital part of our relationships with other people. A trouble shared is a trouble halved, but a pleasure shared is a pleasure doubled. Experiences that make us happy are good for us, and being in a good mood has a positive knock-on effect in other areas of our lives. Experiments have shown that 'Positive moods produce positive thoughts, improved recall of happy events, better creativity and problem-solving, more helping behaviour and greater liking for other people.'[18] The exhilaration and sense of well-being after a few hours spent laughing and joking with others is tremendous. Our own pleasure is mirrored and heightened by the pleasure of our playmates, so that we not only derive enjoyment from the shared activity, but also from the shared enjoyment in that activity. When school children develop in-jokes about certain teachers, or mess around at the back of the class, they are using play, albeit of a disruptive kind, to foster a sense of community which in turn mitigates the less pleasant aspects of being at school. Amongst factory workers, joking and playing games on one another has a similar effect: it creates a strong sense of community and a context in which members of that community can enjoy themselves, thus making the monotony and boredom of work more bearable. Shared pleasure is thus a profoundly positive experience. It confirms our individual sense of self and also our sense of ourselves as successful social beings. It makes us feel happy in ourselves and with others.[19]

Play can benefit one-to-one relationships in a number of ways. As we have seen, play enhances mood, and people in a good mood have been shown to be more likely to look for the best in others. They tend to be more helpful and generous, and are strikingly less selfish, all of which make for happier relationships.[20] Laughing and smiling with a friend, lover or child creates a sense of shared goals and values, as well as reflecting the reality of shared enjoyment. Playing together ensures that a relationship contains some positive ingredients, not just the daily round of washing, eating and working.[21] On a purely practical level, play has a valuable place in our relationships: joking and gentle teasing are almost always more effective ways of modifying a partner's behaviour than yelling at him; tickling a wriggling baby into helpless giggles is similarly more likely to persuade her to lie still while you change her nappy than telling, asking or begging her to do so.

It is interesting that the courtship phase of a relationship is characterised by many of the features that also define play: intense absorption, focused attention, joy, the impression that life has value and meaning, an increased capacity for spontaneity and a sense of integration and connectedness. Play in this context manifests itself through flirting and teasing, and through a particular way of touching and talking. This love-play enables people very quickly to become physically and emotionally intimate. It breaks down inhibitions and builds up bonds. The fact that the early stages of a relationship are often effortlessly playful perhaps accounts in part for why they are also often amongst the happiest.

Sex provides another opportunity for play in adult relationships. For Caitlin, who came on the Play Day, sexual play is very important. She has been with her partner for eight years. Although she often finds it difficult to play in other areas of her life, a lot of playfulness goes into her sex life. 'There's a wonderful feeling of being in harmony with somebody else in sexual play. You both know what the goal is, but you can absorb yourself in the process. And there's the inventiveness of it: thinking up sexy scenarios and games to play together, dressing up in sexy underwear, using your own special language, all that sort of thing. We have playful ways of touching each other, too. Cuddling and hugging and kissing are all part of it. Even when other things in our relationship aren't going well, sex, playful sex, is one way we can always find each other again.'

Many of the problems that arise in our relationships can be resolved through play. In *Marriage Inside Out: Understanding Problems of Intimacy,* Christopher Clulow and Janet Mattinson draw a direct connection between problem-solving in children's play and problem-solving in adult relationships. 'Throughout life', the authors write, 'a capacity to play, to symbolise and to have access to the world of fantasy can assist people to come to terms with life . . . Play can increase the extent to which people feel able to involve themselves with others, and extend the parts of their personalities they can reach.'[22]

Play For Tomorrow

As well as making us feel better in the here and now, play has important long-term implications for well-being. When psychoanalyst Erik Erikson conducted a follow-up study of children studied thirty years earlier, he found that those with the most interesting and fulfulling lives were the ones who had managed to retain a sense of playfulness.[23] I noticed this phenomenon amongst people in their late fifties when I was involved with a research project on the experience of ageing. Those people enjoying their fifties, and anticipating life with optimism, were those whose capacity for play had remained relatively undinted by the passing years. They had a well-kept store of play activities at their disposal, had a good idea of how to enjoy themselves, and were continuing to use a wide range of their faculties, whether physical, musical, linguistic or artistic. They tended to have had a rich play life as children, but they had also made leisure activities a priority *beyond* their teens and early twenties.[24]

I was further struck by the fact that maintaining both the opportunities for play and a playful attitude to life seemed to have been easier for men than women. The men's lives tended to afford more chances to play than the women's, whose spare time was so often taken up with housework. Certainly, the shock of retirement was often greater for men, bringing with it the loss of the very structure that had helped make play a legitimate pursuit. But these men were still far more likely than the women in the sample group to have some hobby or interest. For the women, on the other hand, the space vacated by their own children finally leaving home was all too quickly filled by grandchildren. While all the women who were helping to care for their children's children said it was a pleasure to do so, it nevertheless meant there was a striking continuation of the caring responsibilities that they had always had. Housework too continued to tyrannise, and only when they were widowed, or had unusually helpful partners, were the women I interviewed able to take advantage of the increased opportunities for play in later life.

Those people, male or female, who *had* managed to preserve space for play in mid-life, despite the pressures of work and family, had the best mental health and the most positive attitude towards ageing by the time they reached their late fifties. They were still able to draw on a wide range of enjoyable activities, and were looking forward to the coming years. It was not that their lives had been any easier or harder than other people's: they too had had their share of personal sorrow. The difference was that they had nurtured the skill of playing throughout their lives and it in turn had served them well. This continues to be true for people in their seventies, eighties and even nineties: Paul Thompson, Catherine Itzin and Michele Abendstern interviewed 55 men and women, aged 60 and upwards, for their book *I Don't Feel Old: The Experiences of Later Life* and their conclusions point to the beneficial role of play right to the end of one's life:

> We found at one extreme that a quarter of those who described their lives to us had very few leisure pursuits. None of them was very happy, and they included some of the most discontented. At the other extreme were those who had developed special new leisure skills in later life, such as toymaking and flower arranging and sequence dancing: activities which brought intense pleasure and meaning into their lives.[25]

It seems, then, that it is not the combined total of good or bad events in a person's life that determines the adjustment to and enjoyment of old age, but a person's resourcefulness and adaptability, the capacity for varied activities. Opportunities for play, not just those taken up in old age, but those developed and enjoyed over a lifetime, are real assurances of a rewarding third age.

The ability to play seems quite literally to help keep us alive, it is the current of aliveness that carries us through all the transformations of a lifetime: childhood, adulthood, parenthood, bereavement, love, health, wealth, sickness and poverty. Speaking at the 'Fifty Plus and Female' conference, held to mark the 1993 International Women's Day, journalist Gillian Reynolds, 57, proclaimed wisely, 'As we go into later life, we must remain game for adventure.'

Well Played

The need to continue playing throughout our lives is most clearly demonstrated in the link between play and good mental and physical health. Research from various quarters shows a clear connection between high-quality leisure and psychological well-being. Leo Hendry and his colleagues conducted a study in the late 1980s to look at the connection between health and leisure activities in a large sample of Scottish teenagers. The study revealed that where opportunities for rewarding leisure were limited or frustrated, psychological health suffered. Significantly, young women were more likely than young men to suffer from depression linked to lack of time for leisure. Amongst those with the worst mental health were young women who felt that 'they were too busy doing jobs at home to have much leisure time'.[26] Hendry and his colleagues found that it was not only the *quantity* of the leisure that determined the mental health of these respondents, but also their *attitude* towards their leisure: the teenagers with the best mental health were the ones 'who saw leisure skills as offering value to their future lives'.[27]

Eccentrics, who are often extremely playful in outlook and conduct, are twenty times less likely to visit their doctor than other people. Clinical psychologist David Weeks, who has made a study of more than 1000 eccentrics in Britain and America, found that eccentricity was correlated to creativity, above average intelligence and happiness. He also noted that eccentrics often retain a quality of youthfulness as they get older, and seem to enjoy better-than-average physical and mental health. He puts their rosy health record down to the fact that eccentrics are less bothered by the pressure to conform than the rest of us, and therefore suffer less from the stress and anxieties associated with conformity. Weeks observes that while neurotic personalities are generally over-serious and ultra-conforming, rendering them vulnerable to anxiety and depression, eccentrics revel in their non-conformity and seldom suffer from depression. Eccentrics are not usually 'mad', however unusual their behaviour; indeed, Weeks found some evidence that eccentrics may have lower rates of the psychiatric traits associated with schizophrenia than the general population.[28]

Weeks defines the true eccentric as curious, creative, non-conformist, confident in his or her own opinions, and possessing a well-developed sense of humour. It is this combination of qualities that predisposes many eccentrics to playfulness, or what Weeks terms the 'giggle factor'. In the light of the connection between the pressures on women to conform to other people's expectations and needs, and the difficulties that women have in finding room for their playful selves, it is interesting that Weeks found that in Britain in most age groups male eccentrics greatly outnumbered female eccentrics. Where female eccentrics do start to tip the scales is in later life, once they have fulfilled their familial responsibilities. Women who are unhindered by financial constraints, such as the English upper classes or wealthy Americans, or women who have grown up in cultures that encourage free-thinking, were more likely than other women to become eccentrics earlier in life.[29] Obviously, eccentrics occupy a particular place on the spectrum of human personality types, and not all of us would wish to become fully blown oddballs simply to have more play in our lives, but a mild dose of their medicine might do us some good. As Weeks concludes: 'Certain types of deviant behaviour can be healthy and life-enhancing. The condition of eccentrics is freedom; not for them the stifling habit of obedience. In an era when human beings seem more and more to be the prisoners of their culture and their genes, eccentrics are a refreshing reminder of every person's intrinsic uniqueness.'[30]

If humour is a central component of the eccentric's life tonic, we should not be too surprised to find further examples of the possible health benefits of play in the simple act of laughter. Dr Lee Berk at Loma Linda University in California maintains that 'you can laugh yourself well just as much as you can exercise or eat correctly to be well'.[31] Dr Berk has demonstrated that laughing boosts the body's supply of cytokines, the immune system hormones, and insists that 'a positive mindset and happiness have beneficial effects on physiology'. Laughter, which so often accompanies playing, is not only an effective form of physical exercise (100 to 200 laughs a day are equivalent to 10 minutes' jogging, according to American physiologist Dr William Fry).[32] It also helps people to relax, deepens the breathing, improves circulation and releases natural painkillers into the body. Just as the immune system is negatively affected by stress, it can be positively affected by laughter. Some hospitals are recognising the potential benefits and introducing Laughter Therapy into the treatments they offer. At the Great Ormond Street Hospital for Sick Children in London, clowns are brought on to the wards to give the young patients a regular dose of laughs, reflecting the hospital's recognition of the therapeutic effect of laughter. Dr Kiku, the humorologist, and Dr Leon, the laughologist, aim to induce smiles in the often desperately ill children, and are part of the hospital's formal play programme. In Switzerland, 'clown doctors' are considered part of the treatment in most children's hospitals. In New York there are clowns in eight of the city hospitals. One of the eccentrics from David Weeks's study is a practising doctor at the Gesundheit Institute in Pocahontas County, West Virginia, where he often dresses as a clown to treat people, out of a belief in the healing powers of humour.

Adopting a playful attitude to life may make it easier to see the funny side of stressful situations; this in turn will improve our outlook on events and avoid the noxious effects of stress on our mental and physical health. In recognition of the possibility of this casual relationship between play and well-being, doctors in Staffordshire, under a pioneering scheme devised by Lichfield District Council, are prescribing patients with a dose of play to cure a range of problems from hyperactivity to depression. Instead of being handed some tranquillisers, or sent off to a therapist, families are sent on day trips to amusement parks or offered free places on local play schemes.[33]

Playful work, too, seems to have a positive knock-on effect for health. Artists often live to an advanced age. This may be related to a temperamental disposition amongst artists to unconventional ways of thinking and seeing. Equally it may be connected to the opportunities that artistic work affords for creative expression. Scientists, whose work is often highly creative and playful, have greater life expectancy than non-scientists, according to a recent survey.[34] Konrad Lorenz in the 1970s claimed that 'All scientific knowledge . . . arose from playful activities conducted in a free field entirely for their own sake.'[35] American physicist Richard Feynman describes in his autobiography how the discovery that was to earn him a Nobel Prize came out of 'playing around with a wobbling plate'.[36] Corroborating this association between play and creativity in the context of work, David Weeks found that the eccentrics in his sample were clustered in certain occupations, in particular science and the arts.

Lack of play, conversely, may lead to ill-health. Ill-health occurs not only when physical needs are not met, but also when psychological and spiritual needs are unsatisfied. As well as being a consequence of unmet needs, illness may become a manifestation of those needs. Instead of allowing oneself to have a lie in, a person may unconsciously 'choose' to become ill. In this way, illness can express the way we feel: back-ache may be a way of telling others we are overburdened; urinary tract infections, a way of saying we are pissed off.[37] It is not uncommon, for example, for recently bereaved people inadvertently to hurt themselves. Bruises, cuts and even broken limbs all express the bereaved person's sensation of not being in control of his or her world, and at the same time show their inner pain in ways that other people can easily recognise. 'Illness can provide a way of meeting needs that a person is otherwise unable to fulfill. These needs may be for space or time for oneself, freedom from duties and responsibilities, or from relationships,' writes Helen Graham, author of *The Magic Shop*, a study of the symbolic meaning of illness.[38]

While illness may be a manifestation of unmet needs and unexpressed emotions, play is linked to the recognition of self and the celebration of individual needs.[39] By providing a freeway between our conscious and unconscious selves, play becomes a significant factor in good health. Many of the techniques offered by alternative practitioners, such as relaxation, meditation, guided fantasy and visualisation, are, in effect, forms of imaginative play, enabling us to access our unconscious selves.

I recently came across an account of an African community which had been transformed through play. When development workers arrived in the village, they found that morale was extremely low. There were numerous health problems (many types of worms, malaria, bilharzia), no clinic and virtually no schooling. However, when community workers asked the villagers what they felt they needed, they insisted that their top priority was to make a football field. One of the community workers was appalled by this decision, but the community development officer encouraged the group to go ahead. The villagers made their football field, started playing football together, organised a team, and began to play matches against other villages. 'The football field was a turning point in the life of the village,' according to community worker Anne Hope. 'They had gained self-confidence, a structure for communicating with one another, and a sense that they were capable of changing things. Later they tackled many other "more important" projects. But were they really more important? Was not their own intuition that they needed something that would build their sense of themselves as a community, and their confidence that they could achieve their own goals, far more important than an outsider's priority that they needed a clinic?'[40]

We do not need to go as far as Zimbabwe to see evidence of this kind of transformation in an individual's or group's self-esteem as a result of play. Cath Lloyd, a social worker, works with disadvantaged young people in Oxford. She and her colleagues use play as an important morale-booster. 'We take them to fly kites on Brill Hill, or we take them skating. Opportunities to play are an important part of our work with these kids. It helps them to think positively and creatively about how they want to live their lives.'

Learning To Play, Learning To Live

When we think of play, the images which spring to mind tend to be of *children* playing. For far too many of us, play is inextricably equated with the carefree world of childhood while the importance of play in adulthood is overlooked. Thus, a leading British sociologist, Anthony Giddens, can write about the 'more limited importance of play in adulthood', without seeming to reflect whether or not play in adulthood actually is of more limited importance.[41] In making this assertion, Giddens implies that a diminution of play is an acceptable and irreversible concomitant of growing older. Yet as Giddens writes later in the same article, play 'has important functions in the transmission of culture and the development of personality'. What

Giddens does not say is that these 'important functions' are just as necessary at the age of seventy as at the age of seven. The erroneous belief that play belongs in childhood is rooted in the widely held assumption that adulthood is a fixed point, reached at a clearly defined moment, after which all learning, experimentation, development and self-discovery are redundant: maturation is complete. In reality, the process of growing-up is a life-long enterprise. Throughout our lives, we are constantly encountering new situations that call on new skills, and adults, like children, cope best with the challenges of life when they have adequate opportunities to develop themselves through play. There may be less time for play as we get older, but there is no less need for it.

In Steven Spielberg's film *Hook*, the eternal child Peter Pan has grown up. He is now an overworked executive, who lives on his mobile phone and has no time or inclination for play. When the film starts, Peter and his family are about to fly to England for Christmas. (Significantly, in the course of growing up, Peter has not only forgotten how to fly, but has also developed a terrible fear of flying.) No sooner has the family arrived in London than Peter's children are kidnapped by Captain Hook and whisked off to Never Never Land. In order to beat his old enemy and rescue his beloved children, Peter has to learn to play again. He cannot reach Never Never Land until he has started to remember his forgotten childhood. He has to find the playful child in an adult self, and learn, literally and metaphorically, how to fly again. The turning point of the film is when Peter gets into a huge mock-fight with the Lost Boys: suddenly, his adult inhibitions fall away and he is playing again; from that moment, the audience know that he will go on to save the day. Spielberg's film is family entertainment with a serious message: play is not only a natural part of childhood, something that comes easily to children, it is also a necessary part of adulthood, without which we cannot rise to the challenges of life.

The enormously popular television series *Bewitched*, first broadcast in the United States in 1964 and one of TV network ABC's biggest hits for the next eight years, offered a similar message. The heroine of the series is Samantha, an ordinary American housewife in all respects but one: she is a witch. Domestic chores are dispensed with a twitch of the nose, leaving Samantha free to have fun. In her book *Where the Girls Are*, Susan Douglas accounts for the series' success in terms of the role model it offered: Samantha was a devoted wife and mother, whose power and influence also extended way beyond the kitchen. Samantha was a character with whom ordinary American housewives could identify in reality and fantasy. She was both subordinate and deferential, but also subversive and aspirational. As Douglas puts it, 'The show hailed young female viewers by providing, and seeking to reconcile, images of female equality . . . with images of female subordination.'[42] But the show's appeal lay also in its immense playfulness, and in its sanctioning of playfulness as an important aspect of adult life. Samantha frequently uses her magic skills to sort out other people's problems, to avert danger or disaster, and to restore happiness and harmony. In one episode, she exposes a crooked politician, in another she saves her husband from professional disgrace. Housework, tellingly, takes up relatively little time, since most of it is done (and not just 'as if') by magic.

Regular opportunities to play are as crucial in adulthood as in childhood. Play helps create a sense of balance in our lives, and helps us keep things in perspective; play 'not only prevents us from taking life too seriously, but also helps us enjoy its absurdities'.[43] Far from diminishing with age, our need for play seems to *increase* as we get older. Play smooths the often uncomfortable transition to later life, and helps elderly people retain a sense of meaning and enjoyment in their lives despite the inevitable discomforts and difficulties of old age. As the stakes are raised, we need to be more, not less, able to play in the game of life.

At a workshop organised by a national children's charity for its managerial staff, participants were asked to consider the function of play in pre-school education. Many of the people present felt that play was a way of training for adult life, a dress rehearsal for the real thing, until the workshop leaders raised the issue of severely disabled children whose life-expectancy meant they were unlikely to see adulthood. Did these children have no need to play, or were they especially entitled to it? This line of questioning unsettled many of the group members, challenging their assumptions about the role of play. Instead of regarding it as essentially a preparatory tool, they began to see that play might have a vital role not in the future, but as a means of celebrating and enhancing one's existence in the present. The implications of this realisation for adults as well as for children are important. As one group member said afterwards, 'It made me realise how much emphasis adults place on *doing*. But we're human *beings*, not human doings, and we need ways of emphasising that aspect of ourselves too.'[44]

Why Women Need To Play

When we play, we move beyond the relative facts of our doings, and celebrate the absolute fact of our being. Obviously then, play has benefits for both men and women, and both sexes need play throughout life. But, as we near the end of the twentieth century, it seems that women have particular need of the benefits of play. One of the clearest indications of this want is women's mental health record in contemporary society which is not, on the whole, very good. Women currently go to their doctor more often than men, account for more prescriptions, consume more tranquillisers and more antidepressants. In general, women are less satisfied with themselves than men and feel less in control of their lives.[45] In part, these differences between men and women's mental health are explained by normative values and expectations, which seem to make it easier for women to acknowledge symptoms of ill-health, more acceptable for them to report depression. But with women accounting for almost 80 per cent of the 5.6 million prescriptions made out for antidepressants in the UK in 1995, it would be surprising if norms explained the problem away entirely. Moreover, when we look more closely at the kinds of illness from which women typically suffer, a connection with their lack of play begins to emerge.

As far back as 1943, a group of researchers carried out a study of the effect of systematically frustrating children's desire to play.[46] The 30 children in this experiment were aged 25–61 months and were presented with a range of desirable toys, to which they had previously been allowed access but which were now taken out of their reach. The results of the experiment were striking: 22 of the 30 regressed as a consequence of their frustration, and then became less constructive in their subsequent play.

What is to say that adults do not experience similar feelings of frustration when play-deprived? The woman who constantly sees her children and partner playing, yet is herself prevented from doing so by a whole range of social and practical constraints, may react furiously to her husband returning home late after a game of squash or a drink with friends. Her anger may be a protest not only against his easy entitlement to fun, but also a display of regressive behaviour caused by a day which has allowed her no such equivalent moments for play. Her rage may be interpreted as envy or resentment, coupled with a profound sense of injustice – 'How dare he play while I work!', 'How dare he prefer their company to mine!', 'How dare he stay out, while I'm stuck at home!'

When feelings of frustration are systematically suppressed, the result is often depression. It is surely not a coincidence that depression in women is a considerable problem in contemporary society.[47] An estimated 1 in 5 young women are depressed at any one time, and 10 per cent have had thoughts of suicide. Nearly 600 people under the age of 25 killed themselves in 1990, and up to 50 times that number attempted suicide. Although 80 per cent of successful suicides are by young men, 80 per cent of suicide *attempts* are by young women. As if that were not a sobering enough statistic, there is also evidence to suggest that women become less happy as they get older, getting worse before they get better, with women aged 30–40 appearing to suffer the poorest mental health.[48]

Women, as we have seen, are far more likely to be treated for depression than men. While more severe forms of depression appear to strike fairly equally between the sexes, women seem more vulnerable than men to mild or moderate depression. While severe depression is more likely to be biological in origin (that is, it tends to be linked to genetic and chemical factors), mild to moderate depression seems more likely to be psychological in origin (in other words, it tends to be linked to external events that are stressful and thereby increase vulnerability to depression).[49] This in turn suggests that a significant proportion of women are depressed in response to external factors in their lives. Marriage or cohabiting, for example, increases a woman's susceptibility to depression. Not only are married women more likely to be depressed than single women, they also have consistently poorer mental health than married men, a fact usually explained by the likelihood that married women will have young children, which tends to be stressful and socially isolating. Most at risk of mental ill-health are working-class women with young children, no job outside the home, and an unsupportive partner. In general, housewives of all classes tend to have worse mental health and display more symptoms of stress and depression than either working married women or single women, in part because of the unrewarding nature of housework itself, but also because of the lack of recognition this kind of work receives, and the social isolation that often goes with it.[50] Depression, then, is a form of ill-health to which women seem particularly prone, and which seems to be closely linked to the social circumstances in which they commonly find themselves, and the social roles they are expected to fill, both factors depriving them of play.

Since play-deprivation results in psychological distress, as the experiment with the nursery school children showed all those years ago, many of the symptoms of psychological distress which women so commonly experience may well have some roots in the absence of play and, even before that, the restricted opportunities for playfulness. Symptoms such as depression, insomnia, anxiety, headaches, lethargy and low self-esteem may all be manifestations of play-deprivation. This is not to deny the extreme relevance to women's well-being of factors such as financial resources, physical health, social networks and emotional support, but it is to suggest that maybe we have entirely overlooked an equally relevant factor in play.

Almost certainly, lack of play is a factor in psychological distress. It is impossible to prove because no one has ever thought to study the connections directly, so there is no empirical evidence in support or otherwise. But when we look at the indirect evidence, once we are attuned to the importance of play, the connection between lack of play and ill-health stares us in the face. The connection operates in two ways: first, lack of play increases a woman's vulnerability to stress, which in turn increases her risk of suffering from depression, anxiety and other symptoms of psychological disturbance. An example of this cycle is Joanne, a single mother in her twenties, working as a secretary on a regional newspaper, hard-pressed for time, money or energy to play, ground down by the exhausting business of caring for her young son, holding down her job, paying the bills. 'My outlook on life was anything but playful,' Joanne says. 'There was never any time off. I was just living on my nerves the whole time. Sam was constantly ill. I couldn't keep taking time off work, but the nursery wouldn't take him and there was only me.' The lack of play in Joanne's life meant she never had any chance to recharge her batteries. Seriously run down, she was little able to cope when her mother died. 'I had nothing and no one to fall back on and, without really realising it at the time, I became badly depressed and eventually just collapsed.' This collapse turned out to be Joanne's salvation. A friend persuaded her to go to her doctor, who signed her off work for a month and, as well as prescribing antidepressants, encouraged Joanne to join a therapy group. The break from her job combined with attending the group gave her the chance to rethink her whole attitude to her life. 'I couldn't magic up a partner, or stop Sam getting ill, but I did realise I could approach things differently, start to value myself a bit more.' In practice this approach meant allowing herself an evening off once a fortnight to go for a swim or go to the cinema: it meant not working through the lunchbreak, but going for a walk, reading a book, meeting a friend. 'Gradually, I just started to put a bit of fun back into my life. I started valuing it, instead of just thinking, "I'm a single mother, what right do I have to enjoy myself?" These days I do enjoy myself. It's an attitude as much as anything. Enjoyment doesn't pay the rent, sadly, but it helps me cope with having to pay it.'

The second route from lack of play to ill-health is more direct. Through reduced opportunities to express frustration, creativity, physical energy and so forth, scarcity of play may actually cause psychological distress, rather than just increasing vulnerability to such distress. Conversely, introducing opportunities for play may increase resistance to physical and psychological illness. Two weeks after giving birth to her second child, Fran started a stained-glass course. 'Completely impractical, and everyone thought I was mad,' she says, 'but it kept me sane. It gave me a chance to be creative and involved at a time when life was completely overwhelming. Every week I'd think, Oh God, how can I possibly go out tonight? But I did, and I'd come back completely revitalised. I'm not joking, that course kept me sane.'

External factors lead to lack of play: lack of play leads to depression; depression inhibits the ability to play; the inability to play makes us more vulnerable to the external factors that inhibit play. The problem quickly becomes daunting in its circularity.

But just as symptoms of psychological distress may be caused by lack of play, they may also be curable through play. The encouraging evidence is that women do seem to want to play. They want to find ways of expressing and celebrating aspects of themselves that are not bound up with being daughters, partners, wives and mothers. A recent survey found that nearly half the women interviewed wanted more time to devote to themselves. Twenty-three per cent of mothers said they wanted to spend less time at home and with their families. This figure rose to 32 per cent amongst the non-working mothers in the sample.[51] Women, in short, are waking up to their need for play.

The psychoanalyst Erik Erikson developed Freud's theory that psychology mirrored physiology. During the late 1930s, Erikson conducted his classic study of pre-adolescent children at play, observing that, when given a selection of toys to play with, girls tended to make scenes of enclosure, while boys tended to build towers. In a later work, Erikson extended the idea that the topography of the body is written on the mind, arguing that the female psyche involves a sense of an 'inner space' which mirrors the physiological inner space of the womb. Crucially, this led Erikson to reject the Freudian concept of 'penis envy', and to argue instead that males are the ones to experience a lack, that of a womb. While Erikson saw the 'inner space' as a source of strength, he also wrote that 'in female experience an "inner space" is at the centre of despair even as it is at the very centre of potential fulfilment'.[52] Implicit in Erikson's words is the suggestion that we find fulfilment by filling our inner space with new life, with the growing embryo, but maybe we can just as well find that fulfilment not by creating another self, but by recreating our own, playful self, and locating it right there at the centre of our being. Through play, we can begin to fill the inner space with something other than the frustration, dissatisfaction and despair that resides there in so many women today.

What seems clear is that we cannot deny the playful self without harming other aspects of our self in the process. Women, above all, whose time is so taken up by work, and whose energy is so often absorbed by the needs of others, should be in no doubt that they are on the right track when they start to value play. Women, above all, can prosper from putting the play back in their lives, and by daring, like the eccentrics in David Weeks's study, to live playfully.

4

A Brief History of Play

'Play is older and more original than civilization.'
(Johan Huizinga, *Homo Ludens*)

Play has not always been considered the poor cousin of work, as it tends now to be; in fact, characterising play in this way is a fairly recent phenomenon. A look at the historical roots of our obsession with work reveals how this overvaluation of work on the one hand, and devaluation of play on the other, has gradually come about.

Play is not a fixed entity in culture; on the contrary, our understanding of play has altered throughout history, reflecting the prevailing concerns of each era. While at times play has been revered, at others it has been despised. With relatively little written on the subjects of either women or play, it is hard to be sure precisely what was the state of play four hundred years ago, let alone a thousand years ago. We cannot know for certain how women's playfulness found expression in the eighth, twelfth or fourteenth centuries. Much of the evidence about women's lives has come down to us in the form of personal memoirs, letters, poems and, more recently, novels. Evidence of this kind has already been filtered through the thin gauze of the literate, hardly a representative sample of the female population when illiteracy was the norm for the vast majority until the nineteenth century. Archaeological remains have helped historians to reconstruct the lives of ordinary women, and, in the last thirty years or so, great efforts have been made to correct the male bias in history, and a significant start has been made in putting women's lives back into the jigsaw of the past. From what is known of history, we can make some inferences about how play fitted into life generally at different points in the past, and, as a result of the efforts of recent historians, we can also piece together a certain amount about women's play. In all probability, women have *always* had fewer opportunities for play than men. Certainly life pre-penicillin, pre-refrigeration, pre-electricity would have been 'nasty, brutish and short' for the majority. However, for all the hardship, poverty and disease, it seems that at certain points in the past, society has been more fundamentally receptive to the concept of play than it is now, and women as well as men would have benefited from this. Despite all we know now of its many and positive effects, play is no longer a given in our lives as it was for people in the Middle Ages, the Renaissance, the Enlightenment. From the mid-eighteenth century on, as the nation industrialised, so did the individuals within it, and the spirit of playfulness came under constant attack from the spirit of capitalism.

All the great civilisations of the world have enshrined play in their cultures; it is wrought into the heart of their religious rites, their art, their literature, even in the complex rules and stratagems of their warfare. In the *Mahabharata*, the Indian epic poem, which dates back to the sixth century BC, the world is conceived as a dice-game, the seasons are represented by dice-players, and the main action revolves around a dice-game. Ancient Egyptians revelled in a visual playfulness, painting the ceilings of their tombs with vines of luscious grapes and singing birds; their fondness for the play of ornamentation survives today in the form of jewellery of the most stunning beauty. They also bequeathed to us the Sphinx, the supreme riddler and an enduring symbol of the power of word play.

In Ancient Greece, play reached its apogee in the art forms of theatre and dance, painting and philosophy. This was the culture that gave us Homer, Plato, Aristotle and Euripides, in whose words we find imaginative play at its finest. The Greek philosopher Plato is responsible for some of the most acute analysis of play in the history of western literature, and his thoughts on the subject are still powerfully resonant today. Writing in the fourth century BC, Plato described human beings as 'God's plaything' *(paignion)*, and argued that, not only is this 'the finest thing' about us, but that 'all of us, men and women, ought to fall in with this role, and spend our lives in playing this noblest of plays'.[1] By living life as play, Plato suggested in *The Republic*, we can rise above the frustrations, limitations and restrictions of the human condition; we can fall in with divine purposes, and thus aspire to the divine aspects of our own nature.[2] Elsewhere, Plato suggested that contrasting aspects of human activity – leisure and work, peace and war – are pivotally connected to one another through play.[3]

In Ancient Rome, daily life for free Romans centred around opportunities for play, embodied in the physical structures of the Forum, the baths and the amphitheatre. Roman civilisation offers us the grand spectacle of physical play, the *ludi*, the Games, as well as the literary playfulness of poets like Ovid and Catullus. In a poetic letter from exile to the Emperor Augustus, Ovid described Catullus as '*lascivus*', a word that can mean 'free of restraint in sexual matters', but also simply 'playful, frolicsome'. A new translation in 1990 of poetry by Catullus was praised in one review for successfully recreating, amongst other things, 'the wit, the lyric exaltation, the playful banter' of the original.[4] Not that this playfulness was always appreciated: Ovid's *Art of Love*, a witty and suitably ludic treatment of the amorous game, had a far from playful outcome: it led to his works being banned from the public libraries of Rome, and according to the poet himself, was part of the reason for his banishment in AD 8 by the Emperor Augustus.

For Romans and Greeks alike, there was, above all, Olympus, where the gods and goddesses who controlled human fate and fortune were themselves constantly at play. In *The Iliad*, Homer describes how the gods feast and laugh in a state of 'sublime frivolity', while humans quarrel and fight. Ovid's *Metamorphoses* is a poetic monument to the reckless and irrepressible playfulness of the gods, whose antics have such disastrous consequences for the mortals they frequently sport with. In *The Odyssey* the goddess Athene, who protects and guides Odysseus, is often described as playful, and there is something distinctly teasing about the entire course of our hero's meandering journey homewards, with its many setbacks, near misses and lucky breaks. Athene is counterpoised by the distinctly unplayful Penelope, wife of Odysseus, who virtuously weaves a tapestry and wonders when she will see her husband again. But even in Penelope's tale, there is an element of tricksiness: she tells her many suitors that she will marry one of them once she has finished her tapestry, and spends each night unpicking the threads she has woven during the day. When Odysseus finally arrives home, she disguises herself and, one can't help feeling, thoroughly enjoys the experience of teasing him before she eventually reveals her true identity.

It is important not to exaggerate the degree of play that life afforded the average person in antiquity. Life would have been extremely hard work for all but the elite, from and about whom most of our evidence derives, and in most respects women were second-class citizens wherever they fell on the social spectrum. All women in early antiquity, whether royal or slaves, would have been expected to make clothes, spin, weave, do the laundry, wash and anoint men.[5] Other tasks would have included grinding corn, reaping and fetching water. In the seventh century BC, Spartan women seem to have enjoyed more freedom than was usual, both sexually and socially, due to the prolonged absences of the men who were away fighting.[6] Heavy casualties in warfare meant that the female's child-bearing role was highly valued and in preparation for this, Spartan citizen girls were encouraged to be physically fit and were taught gymnastics and music as well as the traditional female skills.[7] Women in early antiquity wrote poetry, as we know from remnants of writing by Sappho and others, and also composed and performed songs. By the fifth century BC, Athenian women were living secluded lives for the most part, staying in the house for much of their time with the children and slaves.[8] Only poorer women went out to work, and opportunities for play were almost certainly constrained by the dark, unsanitary conditions in most living quarters, as well as by the limitations on women's chances of meeting one another. More positively, the religious rituals and ceremonies so central to Greek culture provided women with opportunities for dancing, singing and playful instruments. A cup dating from around 490 BC depicts a Dionysian ritual in which a whirling circle of women dance with great energy and evident pleasure.[9] Many public rituals involved important roles for girls and women, and some festivals, such as the Adonia, were exclusively female.[10] For wealthy Roman women in the second century BC singing, dancing, playing musical instruments and writing poetry as well as involvement in politics and other forms of public life were all acceptable and even desirable.[11]

Despite the restrictions on women's activities – and there were many – these great civilisations provided a blueprint for European culture, a blueprint in which play unmistakably had its part, and an inheritance from which successive centuries benefited. The Middle Ages were, by some accounts, exuberantly playful. If this was the age of plagues and witch-hunts, it was also the age of tournaments and pageants, of troubadours, jesters and courtly love, an age of extraordinary earthy vitality on the one hand, and ritualised ideals of honour, valour and faith on the other. The writings of Boccaccio and Chaucer open a window on to a world which, though harsh in many respects, seems also to have been, in historian Johan Huizinga's famous phrase, 'brimful of play'. In Boccaccio's *Decameron* (c.1351) ten young noble men and women take refuge from the plague in Florence, and flee to the countryside, where they entertain one another by each telling a daily story. Many of the one hundred tales that ensue are bawdy in nature, nearly all have a richly comic vein. Chaucer's *Canterbury Tales* (c.1387) are similarly rumbustious, from the little birds 'maken melodye' in the treetops of the Prologue, and

Harry Bailly, a 'myrie man' and jovial host of the pilgrimage, to the irrepressible characters who people the tales themselves. In both these works, women are depicted as accomplished participants in the game of life, narrating tales of other people's play, and well able to play themselves. The best-known example of this must be Chaucer's Wife of Bath, but she is certainly not alone.

Women would have taken part in the celebrations that marked marriages, births and christenings. They worked in the fields and, in all probability, drank in the alehouses. Courtly women would have had opportunities for visiting one another, singing, dancing, attending pageants and fairs. Contemporary illustrations depict women playing blind-man's buff and games of chess, as well as enjoying the games of love that medieval courtly life was strongly associated with. Aristocratic women were expected to patronise artists and writers, and this granted them entry into a stimulating cultural and intellectual world. Matilda, wife of Henry I (1100–1135), undertook her role of patron with enthusiasm and aplomb, causing her husband some anxiety with her financial generosity. Eleanor of Aquitaine and Queen Anne both exerted considerable influence over the artistic tastes of their day.[12] Nor did women who took holy orders necessarily relinquish all chances to play and playfulness. Monastic life in many cases freed women from the burden and fear of constant child-bearing, and allowed them to devote time to reading, writing, composition and art. Nor was monastic life synonymous with solitude, since close friendships were able to flourish in the confines of a religious order. A spirit of immense playfulness resides in the most unlikely places in medieval life: in the stories of holy quests, in the borders of sacred manuscripts, in the stone creatures carved on church doorways and ceilings.

The Renaissance, too, provides ample instances of playfulness. Huizinga maintains that 'the whole mental attitude of the Renaissance was one of play',[13] and we can see this manifested both in the wealth of its artistic output, and also in the thriving commercial and entrepreneurial activity during this period. The Americas were being explored and colonised. Music was flourishing under royal patronage. Leonardo da Vinci and Michelangelo were producing artistic masterpieces, Shakespeare and John Donne literary ones. In this rich cultural climate, women too were able to enjoy a certain amount of artistic expression. A number of women produced quality works of art and literature at this time: the French writer and courtier, Christine de Pizan (1365–1430); Marguerite of Navarre (1402–1549), who wrote love poetry, religious verse and a collection of short stories, the *Heptameron*; Francesca Caccini (1587–1640), singer and composer at the Medici court; the Italian-born portrait painter, Sofinisba Anguissola (1527–1625); Luisa Roldan (1656–1704), court sculptor to King Carlos II. Those who did not paint or write themselves were nevertheless a component of the audience who derived pleasure from the visual and performing arts.[14] Outside of elite society, ordinary women would have taken part in the local fairs and festivals that took place all over the country.

Play's The Thing

Pre-industrialisation, life certainly had its hardships and the idea of Merrie England is obviously little more than a myth, but play – no matter what it consisted of, where it took place or who did it – does not seem to have been treated as inferior to work, in the way it is now. It was not that there were necessarily more opportunities for play than there are now – hours of work were often long and conditions of work often hard – but the value of play was unquestioned, and when opportunities did arise, people took them and made the most of them.

Until the end of the eighteenth century, the majority of people across Europe depended on the land for their livelihood, and so, for most people, the seasons shaped the year, determining which agricultural activities took place at any given time. There was a strong link between agricultural activities and local celebrations: the start of the lambing season, the sheepshearing, the harvest, all were occasions for festivities regardless of one's age or class. The religious calendar, too, provided regular opportunities throughout the year for a whole range of local and regional celebrations, as it had in the Roman world. Christmas, Twelfth Night and Ash Wednesday were all marked by ritual entertainments; Candlemas meant beating the bounds, Shrove Tuesday meant pancake races, Good Friday meant pace-egging, Pentecost meant Morris dancing and Mummers plays, Whitsun meant well-dressing. The birth of a baby was marked by a 'gossiping', a celebration akin to the modern-day Christening (the word 'gossip' comes from 'god-sib', or 'relation in god').[15] Sunday itself was known as the 'revelyng day', a day of play, spent in dancing, bowling, football and dice-games. One disgruntled sermoniser in 1571 complained about the 'bulbeatings, bearbeatings, bowlings, dicyng, cardyng, daunsynges, drunkenes and whoredome' that regularly took place on Sundays.[16] Country fairs and parish feasts, mayoral processions, sporting events, music-making, plays and dancing were all familiar features of rural life right up until the end of the eighteenth century.[17] Piece-workers frequently worked a four-day week, taking 'St

Monday' off. Holidays, weekly, monthly and annual, were an important and regular aspect of the year.

Women's play, it is true, would have been circumscribed by the conventions of acceptable female behaviour, and by the responsibility for bearing and rearing children, and for managing the household. About one-third of households would have had at least one servant,[18] but even so the working day for most women was long and hard. On the other hand, people had fewer possessions and houses were far smaller, so 'housework' would not have been the time-consuming activity it had become by the nineteenth century. Kitchens were a luxury, and many people would have brought ready-made meals from cookshops.[19] Throughout this period, women were involved in a wide range of employments, from agricultural work and weaving to mantua-making and silversmithing. They would have been expected to mend clothes, provide food and tend the young and sick. A manual of good housekeeping of 1580 offers an exacting list of a woman's morning activities, including cleaning floors, spinning and carding wool, preparing ingredients for cooking and brewing, preparing breakfast, feeding cattle, brewing, baking, dairy work, laundry, malting, preparing dinner. Her afternoon was to be filled with a similar catalogue of duties. She was recommended to get up at four or five in the morning and go to bed between nine and ten at night.[20]

Where opportunities for play arose, as on feast days and at local celebrations, women would have been participants as well as providers. Smock races and maypole dances were just two of the activities particularly associated with women. Alehouses were the frequent site for celebrations to mark a wedding or christening, as well as places simply to spend time not working.[21] Evidence from court cases shows that alehouses were places where women went, usually with a spouse or companion, occasionally alone, and, once there, they would have enjoyed seeing friends, talking, singing and drinking.[22]

Between the twelfth and sixteenth centuries life undoubtedly had its drawbacks – the ordinary medieval family would have been well acquainted with poverty, hunger, disease and death; the family of the sixteenth century no less so – but there seems also to have been an integrity which afforded opportunities for both work and play; the two moved together in a dance of their own throughout the year: work was punctuated by play, and the purpose and product of labour was in turn celebrated in the various forms of recreation that people enjoyed. 'Fasts were epilogued with feasts, solemnities with sport', according to historian Roy Porter.[23] Play thus occupied a central position in everyday life, both companion and counterpart to the gruelling workload that most men and women also faced. For people of every rank, play had a respected place alongside work, rather than being entirely subordinated to a culture of work, as it is now.

Play may have been pushed aside at times of famine, or when the great plagues devastated the population, but these were always temporary adjustments. In the seventeenth century, however, play first came under serious attack at a cultural level, largely as a result of the rise of the Puritans, who regarded boisterous, unrestrained playfulness as closely aligned with sinfulness, and made strenuous efforts to suppress occasions for such wickedness. Theatres were closed, plays were censored, and, under Cromwell, the playing of football and cricket, as they then existed in their various forms, was banned for a while. In 1642, the Puritans went so far as to outlaw Christmas.[24] Easter, too, succumbed to Puritan pressure for a time. A period of celebration since the Middle Ages, Easter signalled the end of the dark days of Lent. It was the moment when light was ushered back into the church and into people's lives; on Easter Sunday, the priest was expected to entertain his congregation so that the church would be filled with the sounds of joy and laughter. Puritan reformers took exception to such levity, and asserted a more sombre approach to Easter, which to some degree has lasted to the present day.

Despite the objections, however, a robust capacity for playfulness endured. In music, literature and the visual arts, the Baroque style – flamboyant, extravagant, playful – provided a contemporary counterbalance to Puritanism. Prague, the quintessential Baroque city, is a monument to architectural playfulness, with its painted buildings and curving streets. In England, many of the traditional customs, which had for generations facilitated regular opportunities for play, were still being enjoyed in the eighteenth century, and a booming economy in the mid-eighteenth century in many ways boosted a natural proclivity for play. Musical societies, gardening clubs, pleasure gardens, public art galleries, all flourished during this period. Books were more widely available. Better roads made it easier for the well-to-do to go visiting. The novels of Jane Austen convey both the constraints on women's leisure that existed by the end of the eighteenth century and also the opportunities, with house parties providing plenty of scope for card games, amateur dramatics, music-making, singing and dancing. For the less wealthy, there were the rowdier pleasures of boxing, betting, bull-baiting, cock-fights, puppet-theatres, magic-lantern shows and waxworks. A new egalitarianism, born of the introduction of entrance fees, meant that people of all classes often found themselves playing alongside one another. Horace Walpole grumbled of the Ranelagh rotunda, 'The company is universal: from his Grace of Grafton down to children out of the Foundling Hospital – from my Lady Townshend to the kitten.'[25]

As the century progressed, influential writers such as Rousseau were arguing that play was a symbol of untainted nature, and therefore to be highly valued. The German poet-philosopher Friedrich Schiller, a contemporary of Rousseau's, regarded play as the supreme human activity.[26] Schiller believed in the profound transformative potential of play, which he regarded as the route to moral and spiritual growth. Through play, he asserted, the individual can 'combine the greatest fullness of existence with the highest autonomy and freedom'.[27] Schiller was penning these ideas at a time of great uncertainty and change. The old order was being overturned, and with it the complacent confidence of the Age of Enlightenment: technological advance was transforming the face of English society; revolution in France and republicanism in America were sending shockwaves throughout Europe; Thomas Paine had published *The Rights of Man* (1791–92). Amid these monumental upheavals, there was anxiety as well as excitement. How should the individual man and woman make sense of these changes? Where did they fit in this uncharted social and political territory? A new kind of introspection was born. Romanticism gained ground at the expense of Rationalism. Idealism posed an increasing challenge to materialism. The individual's inner state became the source of fascinated contemplation. Jane Austen, poised on the cusp of these two worlds, confronted these problems in her novels: should one be as impetuous as Elizabeth Bennet or as controlled as Mr Darcy; as sensible as Elinor Dashwood or as sensitive as her sister, Marianne? Compromise and balance, advocated Miss Austen. But the literary heirs of Rousseau, Schiller and Goethe were not rationalists, but Romantics: Wordsworth, Shelley, Keats and the Brontës.

Play was explicitly valued by the Romantics not only for its associations with childhood innocence (children at play is a recurring theme in Romantic poetry), but also because it enabled the individual to transcend the corrupting influence of society, and attain a higher level of consciousness, in the way that Schiller had described. In this new Romantic sensibility, intensity of experience was a key aspiration, and play, not least, imaginative play, an acceptable route to that end.

Play in the eighteenth century has been described as 'in full flower', both in terms of earthy realities and lofty ideals, but there were also some worrying changes afoot. As play became more various during this century, it was also more formalised and more commercialised than previously. Increasingly, it took place in specific settings at specific times. Theatres, gardens and galleries all served to cordon off the areas designated for play, even as they helped to make 'leisure' fashionable. The rules of cricket and football were formalised at this time, and both games acquired a new status as spectator sports, no longer chiefly for the participants, but increasingly an activity with an audience, who paid to watch the game, and often placed bets on the outcome. The coffee houses of the seventeenth century were gradually being replaced by private clubs. Gentlemen's clubs such as White's and Dr Johnson's Literary Club, the Spitalfields Mathematical Club, and the friendly societies which boasted 600,000 members by 1800, were just some of the many clubs that sprang up all over the country. They too were a double-edged phenomenon, both creating places and spaces for play, but also defining and regulating whom you played with, and where – for clubs led to rules governing membership, dress, age, behaviour and occupation.

Women, needless to say, were included in few of these newly formalised ways of playing. There were sporting women, however, despite the inevitable censure and ridicule they often aroused. Working-class women regularly took part, albeit in relatively small numbers, in a wide range of sporting activities, including smock races, drinking matches, foot races, horse racing and prize fights. Unusual sports, such as hot air ballooning, attracted some women. Almost as soon as the first balloon had taken flight, from Versailles in 1783, a small number of redoubtable sporting women were clambering into the basket. Madame Thible took off from Lyons in June 1784; Letitia Ann Sage flew over Harrow in June 1785, describing herself as 'infinitely better pleased than ever I was with any former event of my life'.[28] From then on, wherever there were balloons, there was likely also to be an intrepid female balloonist. In the true tradition of play, ballooning provided women with temporary release and respite from the restraints of normal life. The female balloonist could, quite literally, rise above it all. The particular appeal of ballooning was summed up over a century later by one Mrs Iltid Nicholl, co-founder of the Aero Club, in an article for *The World* magazine, written in 1901: 'What can appeal to a woman more', wrote Mrs Nicholl, 'than to rise for a season above the petty discontents, annoyances and ambitions of the daily round, into an atmosphere of sure beauty and serenity, which somehow or other seems usually to alter one's whole point of view, and is, therefore, wonderfully restful and refreshing.'[29]

The Importance Of Being Earnest

The profound change in play, both in our understanding of it and in its place in daily life, came in the late eighteenth and early nineteenth century, when a predominantly agrarian culture was replaced by a predominantly industrial one. Until the late eighteenth century, a capacity for playfulness had endured relatively unscathed in the lives of most people, but once industrialisation really began to gather pace, from the 1780s on, the old ways of living and of playing were radically altered. Romanticism may have been extolling play at this time, and enshrining a form of creative play in writing, but Romanticism took its very shape from its marginalised position, symbolised by the lonely, misunderstood figure of mad John Clare. Romanticism – and play – were set in increasingly sharp relief against two forces in particular: evangelicalism and capitalism. Singly, these elements would not have been a serious threat to play – there had been disapproving moralisers since St Augustine, and long hours of grindingly hard work had always been a feature of life for ordinary people – but together, evangelicalism and capitalism proved irresistible: the moral climate, in the words of Max Weber, 'turned with all its force against one thing: the spontaneous enjoyment of life and all it had to offer'.[30] At the same time, the demands of an industrialising economy left little inclination, energy or opportunity for play. In combination, these two forces gradually succeeded in weaning people off pleasure. Instead, they fostered a spirit of sobriety, self-discipline and seriousness, which in a remarkably short space of time had taken root at all levels of society. For the Victorians, industry was not just a word to describe a type of employment, it epitomised a way of life. By the mid-nineteenth century, the majority of people were living in urban environments (three-quarters of them in London), and 30 per cent of the population worked in the manufacturing industry, where men, women and children routinely faced a 6-day 70-hour week. Idleness had become 'the fruitful root of every vice'.

Even before the eighteenth century was out, the question of how people spent their free time had become all-important. The inclination to play, previously the pulse of life to the working man and woman, came to be seen as a dangerous tendency in need of tight control.[31] From the mid-eighteenth century, the combined interests of religious reformers, radicals, millowners and magistrates all converged on this issue, leading to nationwide efforts to restrict popular recreations. Local holidays and popular traditional pastimes were suppressed and curtailed. Over the next eighty years the number of Bank Holidays was cut from seventeen to just four.[32] Commons and greens, where people had previously met to play football or cricket, to dance or chat with friends, were sold off as private land.[33] There were even suggestions that certain forms of recreation, such as concerts, the theatre, cricket matches and horse racing, should be taxed on the grounds that they made people 'profuse, extravagant, and idle'.[34] Anyone in the business of entertaining others, it was proposed, should also be subject to taxation, including jugglers, ballad singers and actors.

For manufacturers and employers, the problem was largely a practical one: how to regulate the labouring classes. For the first time in history, it was no longer primarily women whose energies had to be harnessed and directed. The informal, unrestrained quality of traditional leisure was altogether incompatible with the demands of mechanised industry, which required human beings to resemble as far as possible the machines they operated, and now, a whole tranche of society had to be brought, literally, into line. The ideal worker was sober, sombre, predictable and tireless. Freedom and free time were inconvenient notions at best, counter-productive at worst. Working people in a wide range of employments were subjected to what historian E.P. Thompson has called 'the propaganda of time-thrift'.[35] Financial arguments about the expense of local festivities were used to support the needs of employers, who wanted a biddable, suppliant and reliable work force. Leisure activities were seen not as complementing people's work, but as interfering with it. 'Too frequent Relaxations of this kind among the Populace enervate Industry,' wrote one journalist in 1757,[36] while the *Bristol Journal* exhorted magistrates 'to lessen the number of diversions calculated to slacken the industry of useful hands'.[37] Social reformers advocated keeping wages low and prices high so that people's standard of living would be reduced, and their need to work would then, from necessity, begin to outweigh their desire to play; in this way, as one reformer of the day put it, 'constant labour may grow into a habit'.[38]

Evangelicals and other non-conformist religious groups couched their arguments in terms of moral necessity: the fires of hell were burning fiercely, and people had better mend their ways. John Wesley (1703-91), the founder of Methodism, explicitly condemned play, advocating that both children and adults pass their time in sober industry, as indeed many of them were doing in increasing numbers. By far the greatest force in this moral crusade were the Evangelicals. Their password was 'serious', their highway was duty. Stamping out godlessness wherever it occurred in society and leading people to a proper sense of their innate sinfulness was their fervent cause. Even the most innocent activities could be interpreted as opportunities for the devil.[39] Strong feeling was associated with godlessness, leisure with sinfulness. 'The soul's play-day is always the devil's working-day', proclaimed an eighteenth-century sermoniser. All forms of frivolity and liveliness were discouraged.

The Evangelicals were a mixed blessing for English society. Without doubt, they did much to improve living conditions for the working classes. They were responsible for crucial reforms, such as outlawing the forced recruitment of orphans to the cotton mills in 1802, and banning the apprenticing of young boys as chimney sweeps in 1834. They campaigned against the slave trade; they waged war on the employment of women and children under ten in coal mines, and they fought for better conditions in mental asylums. They were great proponents of charitable work, and the majority of the voluntary organisations that sprang up in the early nineteenth century were founded by Evangelicals. They set up Sunday schools and ragged schools all over the country, thus helping to raise literacy rates; they provided night shelters for the homeless, medical treatment for prostitutes, and basic clothing for impoverished children. In 1867, the Destitute Children's Dinner Society was established in order to provide free food for poor school children. Leading Evangelicals, such as Lord Shaftesbury, William Wilberforce and Henry Thornton, worked tirelessly and gave generously to improve the welfare of the country's poor. By the end of the nineteenth century, England's reputation for charitable generosity was renowned throughout Europe.

But the Evangelicals were equally effective in much less positive ways. In terms of play, their impact was profoundly damaging. At the same time as they advocated a life of diligence, duty and good works, their crusade against sin was so all-encompassing that it left no space for play. As one clergyman in 1805 declared, 'Real Christians, who diligently discharge the duties of their stations, and conscientiously fill up their places in their families, in their callings, and in the church, will find but little opportunity or occasion for amusement.'[40] Evangelicals were behind the bowdlerisation of Shakespeare, taking out many of the puns and innuendoes and other forms of word-play that had so delighted sixteenth-century audiences. (Augustan reaction to Shakespeare had been more critical, though driven by contemporary ideas about literary decorum rather than moral puritanism.) They were also responsible for the strict censorship of both the theatre and the press in the nineteenth century. They succeeded in closing down a number of London street fairs, as well as dance halls and private theatres, and were extremely influential in shaping people's reading habits, having the monopoly of railway station bookshops and running the biggest of the Victorian circulating libraries.[41]

The keystone of the Evangelical mission was reclaiming Sunday as a day of strict religious observance. To this end they ordered that the National Gallery and the British Museum should be closed on Sundays. They put a stop to military bands performing on Sunday afternoon in parks all over the country, and even brought an end to delivery and collection of mail on Sundays. Charles Dickens summed up the situation in 1855 in his novel *Little Dorrit*, describing Sunday as a day when there was 'nothing for the spent toiler to do but to compare the monotony of his six days with the monotony of his seventh'.[42]

For women, the moral climate decreed that they should be governed at all times by the imperative of innocence and godliness. The move to end the employment of women at the pit face in the coal mines was motivated as much by concerns for their moral well-being as for their physical safety. Etchings from this period tend to show women miners with torn clothing and exposed flesh. The erotic undertones of these illustrations added fuel to the fervour for reform.[43] At work and at leisure, women were to be sober, dignified, thrifty and diligent. Hannah More, a member of the Clapham Sect and one of the most zealous reformers, asserted that young people should be taught 'an habitual inner restraint, an early government of the affections, and a course of self-control over those tyrannising inclinations which have so natural a tendency to enslave the human heart'. In her book on female education, she proclaimed that women should learn 'patience, diligence, quiet and unfatigued perseverance, industry, regularity and economy of time'.[44] In short, play, and anything pertaining to play, were out.

The Church did provide a number of number of alternatives to replace the recreational actitivities that industrialisation and religious reform had eradicated. Church bazaars, pleasant Sunday afternoon outings, church choirs and Sunday schools all flourished during the nineteenth century. Culture clubs were set up to provide talks, debates and lectures for women. Many of these events were intellectually and socially stimulating, and undoubtedly offered women a much-appreciated outlet from the home, as well as a rare outlet for their physical energy.[45] Campaigning and charitable work also gave middle-class women a legitimate way to be socially active beyond the confines of the parlour and drawing room. Nevertheless, the key underlying principles of these activities were helping others, serving God and doing good. An element of play may have been present, but it was permissible only in the context of much (unpaid) hard work, which was in reality more likely to stifle play than foster it. The financial value of this work was enormous: by the late nineteenth century, many chapels were being financed by the proceeds from the bazaars and fêtes that constituted women's 'free' time.

Evangelicals alone were not responsible for the devaluation of play and the overvaluation of work, but they undoubtedly had a large and active hand in shaping the spirit of the age: sombre, serious, dutiful, hard working. Their dire influence on the spirit of playfulness could be seen right to the outer reaches of the British Empire. When Christian missionaries arrived in Samoa in the 1830s, they found a culture in which the capacity for play was still universal and valued: dancing, games and sports were enjoyed by all ages and all ranks; swimming, diving, canoeing, sailing, surf-riding, turtle-riding, sliding, fishing, hide and seek, tug of war, racing, juggling, tobogganing, boxing, wrestling, club fighting and pigeon hunting were just some of the activities which took up 'a considerable amount of time' in the everyday life of the Samoans and played an important part in their social and spiritual culture. The missionaries, however, considered many of these activities immoral and incompatible with a Christian lifestyle, and set about persuading the islanders to renounce them. As anthropologist Helen Dunlap explains:

> This was especially true of dancing, partly because some of it was of an erotic nature and partly because the early missionaries had a tendency to regard all dancing as immoral. They also frowned upon bathing and swimming on Sunday because these activities took too much time away from religious duties. Pigeon hunting expeditions, too, were discouraged as they were believed to lead to immoral practices.'[46]

By 1939, a visitor to the island noted that 'Their dances and other amusements are in a great degree abolished.' Travel to ceremonies and sporting events was restricted by government officials and, by the end of the century, many of the traditional Samoan dances were extinct.

The clampdown on play which took place in Samoa was a mirror image of that occurring back home, and in both cases the reasons were the same. It was not purely a product of Evangelical zeal, but rather a timely conjunction of a particular moral viewpoint, a supreme confidence in social reform, and capitalist fervour. In just the same way as social reformers and industrialists had restricted recreation amongst the working classes in England, the missionaries and government officials now did so with the Samoans, not because 'the officials objected to the amusements of the Samoans, but rather because of the time which such visits consumed. They thought that if they could get the islanders to stay at home more often they might be induced to develop more systematic methods of agriculture.'[47] As in England, economic requirements lent weight to moral philosophy.

A World Of Work

Throughout the nineteenth century, the process of formalising and regulating people's recreation which had begun in the eighteenth century gathered momentum. Increasingly, the world of work and the realm of play resembled one another, for both were characterised by a spirit of industriousness. While religious reformers and employers waged war on the inclination and capacity for playfulness, the cramped and insanitary physical circumstances of urban living helped further to erode the informal character of pre-industrial leisure. The lack of physical space in working-class people's homes drove them on to the streets, into the public houses, into the music halls, all of which were increasingly subjected to the kind of Evangelical 'cleansing' already described. The middle classes, meanwhile, tended to choose leisure activities to suit the moral climate, preferring sedate walks and good works to the more exuberant pastimes of their grandparents. Even the play of the upper class seems to have been more muted in the nineteenth century. According to historian Ian Bradley, 'the wild debauchery of the Regency bucks represented a final fling against the dull puritanism which they saw everywhere coming to prevail'.[48]

As work and home increasingly resembled each other in the sense of being governed by a code of industriousness, in another sense they were for the first time polarised into utterly different spheres of existence. Work entailed one set of activities and people; home involved an entirely different set. Public and private were key notions for the Victorians. Play, such as it was, belonged only to non-working time. To some extent this polarisation created new opportunities, for non-working time had to be catered for somehow. Municipal swimming baths were created in many towns; sports grounds and concert halls were built; affordable train travel meant that many working-class people could go away on holiday for the first time; while the middle classes had long frequented the towns of Bath, Brighton and Weymouth, the end of the nineteenth century saw the meteoric rise of seaside resorts such as Blackpool and Scarborough. These opportunities, however, were brief intervals in the expanse of people's working lives. For the majority of Victorians, the segregation of work and home meant also the segregation of work and play, with the monopoly of the former rapidly eroding the once sure foothold of the latter. 'The great currents of [nineteenth-century] thought, however looked at, were all inimical to the play factor in social life,' according to historian Johan Huizinga. 'Neither liberalism nor socialism offered it any nourishment. Experimental and analytical science, philosophy, reformism, Church and State, economics were all pursued in deadly earnest in the nineteenth century . . . Never had an age taken itself with more portentous seriousness.'[49]

We Are Not Amused

While the segregating of work and play that accompanied industrialisation gradually led to improved leisure facilities for men, it is less certain that women benefited in the same way. Betting and gambling, something of a national mania from the eighteenth century, were frowned upon for women; sports were played and watched predominantly by men; the many clubs and societies that sprang up were invariably only for men. Middle- and upper-class women, throughout the nineteenth century, were to be found engaged in hunting, shooting, skating and archery, but the press frequently condemned and mocked these 'modern amazons'[50]: Mrs Thornton, who not only raced, but beat top jockeys in her races, was known as 'the Yorkshire folly', and journalists paid as much attention to her daring clothes and want of morals as to her skills as a horsewomen.[51]

In general, though, few of the new forms of leisure were enjoyed by women. The world of institutionalised play was predominantly aimed at men, and available to men; it took little account of women's needs.[52] This change came about in tandem with what can be called the masculinisation of the work-place. As the technological advances of the eighteenth century began to transform the systems and structures of manufacture, the value of women's work, as well as women's play, was gradually obscured. Women came under pressure not to work for money, but to content themselves with their 'natural' sphere, the home. For the many women for whom this was not possible, there was considerable hostility to be endured, as working women were increasingly subjected to criticism for their moral laxity and neglect of their domestic responsibilities. Whereas, a century before, women had been praised for their skill at combining the work of looking after children and a home with the necessity of making money, women who worked outside the home in the nineteenth century were increasingly castigated. Not only was their work becoming more arduous, more stressful, less compatible with the other demands on their time and energy, it was also being devalued, becoming a cause of condemnation. Slowly and surely, women's work was being pushed into the realm of the private, the domestic, the obscured, the unpaid. Their equality with men, in terms of the value of their productivity, was coming to an end. And as their productivity was devalued, so, inevitably, was their play.

It is a telling coincidence that the nineteenth century not only presided over a marked decline in women's opportunities to play, but also witnessed a sharp increase in mental illness amongst women.[53] Records up until the 1850s show that there were more men in lunatic asylums than women, but from the 1850s women inmates began to outnumber men. Although men and women were roughly equal in number in the general population, by 1872 54 per cent of certified lunatics in England and Wales were female, and this figure continued to rise.[54] Anorexia nervosa was first identified as a clinical syndrome in 1873, and there was also a sharp rise in the reporting of other behavioural disturbances, such as depression and hysteria. Victorian medics were much intrigued by women's proneness to 'hysteria' (one or two made a fortune from it), but generally attributed it to physical causes, rather than cultural ones. A few enlightened doctors connected hysteria in adolescent girls to their enforced passivity and dependency: the neurologist Horatio Bryan Donkin, for example, pointed to the 'barriers to the "free play of her power" as a central cause of mental and emotional instability in young women.[55] But the usual treatment for hysteria resolutely failed to take social or psychological factors into account. It ranged from bed-rest and seclusion at best, to removal of the womb, ovaries or clitoris at worst.

As the Great Exhibition of 1851 was busily celebrating England's achievements, Queen Victoria's novelists, poets and artists were dwelling on a less upbeat theme: that of female insanity, a potent symbol of the uncertainty behind the confident façade. Mrs Rochester in Charlotte Brontë's *Jane Eyre* (1847), John Everett Millais's 'Ophelia' (1852), Miss Havisham in *Great Expectations*

(1861), Wilkie Collins's *The Woman in White* (1860), Bathsheba in Hardy's *Far From the Madding Crowd* (1874) – all are women imprisoned in some way, physically and emotionally: in attics, in grief, in loveless marriages. They have dangerous yearnings and impulses that threaten the order and stability of those around them. In real life, Elizabeth Barrett Browning in the 1840s and Florence Nightingale in the 1850s were two of the most notable Victorian women made ill by the lack of outlet for their creative energies. Florence Nightingale, writing about the stifling restrictions on women in an autobiographical novel, took the persona of Cassandra, the Trojan princess from Greek mythology, who is cursed with the gift of prophecy which no one will believe. Cassandra is driven mad by the refusal of those around her to hear what she is trying to tell them. The same could be said of countless Victorian women, whose veiled pleas for 'free play of their powers' were also consistently ignored or misunderstood.

Out Of Play

Play itself came under attack in the nineteenth century in a way that it had never done before. There had always been sections of society for whom play was more possible and plentiful than for others, and within each section of any given society it was probably always the men who had easier access to play than women. But in the nineteenth century something new was occurring, something from which we have not yet recovered at the end of the twentieth. The nineteenth century represented a challenge on an entirely new scale, quite different from, say, the existential challenges of medieval life. The combined forces of evangelicalism and capitalism meant that for the first time the assault on play was felt throughout society. The attack on play was no longer merely an effective way of controlling or oppressing certain groups of individuals within the general population. Instead, it was a culture-wide phenomenon which brought about a fundamental shift in the place of play in our cultural mindset.

In the course of the twentieth century, the substitution of various types of 'leisure' in place of the old spirit of 'play' has continued, marked by the rise in organised recreation and formal leisure activities. This has not been wholly negative: in the early part of the twentieth century, the Girl Guides movement helped to break the stranglehold of Victorian notions of propriety on exercise for women, and made it acceptable for girls to be physically energetic and expressive. D.H. Lawrence's robust heroines, with their penchant for diving into cold rivers, reflect this increased range of physical expression allowed to women; the frenzied wrigglings of the Charleston would have seemed horrifying even twenty years before.

Despite these areas of positive change, the overall trend has not been so encouraging. In recent years, even as a vast market has sprung up to cater for our spare time, opportunities for real play have been squeezed out of our lives. Leisure has become a commodity. No town is complete without its fair share of shops selling snazzy leotards, hi-tech trainers, fishing rods, videos, computer games and hi-fis. The bookshops overflow with manuals on every conceivable form of leisure from gardening and cross-stitching, to hang-gliding and fly-fishing. On Sundays throughout the country, people head for the sheds: the DIY stores and garden centres, those national monuments to the commodification of leisure.

Paradoxically, in the attempt to make leisure as different as possible from work, the former has become more like the latter. Like work, leisure often requires a uniform, a specific location, a period of training, special skills; it often mimics work in its tendency towards goals, rules, competitions, rewards. Leisure, in this way, 'strives to re-enter the world of labour from which it is supposed to offer relief'.[56] Like work, leisure has become an economic product, and an indicator of economics: it not only divides up people's time into neat, productive portions, it also segregates them by class and sex. On the basis of people's leisure activities, we can – and market researchers constantly do – make assumptions and draw conclusions about their class, age, sex and occupation. Conversely, the type of work a person does also provides a fairly reliable indication of the types of leisure activity he or she is likely to enjoy.

All this is a very, very long way from genuine play.

Men's opportunities for play-time have been, to a large extent, formalised and institutionalised. Women can, and increasingly do, partake in these kinds of formal play, or their own versions, such as netball and hockey. But the *value* of female playfulness has remained debased. Women, if they do find ways to play, are no longer considered, by themselves or anyone else, as equally *entitled* to play. The football pitch and the pub have became symbols of a man's right to time off, counterpointing the increasing demands of work, but where are the equivalent spaces for women? They can be found, to some extent, in the church hall of the 1890s, the cinema of the 1940s, the coffee morning of the 1950s, the aerobics class of the 1980s. In the last twenty years, a growing number of women have also determinedly made their way on to the traditional playing fields of men, the football pitches, racing tracks, sailing circuits. But for women, opportunities for play have always been, and still are, circumscribed by domestic responsibilities and financial dependency.

William Blake, writing his visionary verse on the eve of industrialisation, with revolution rumbling on the continent, conjured a world in which 'the voices of children are heard on the green and laughing is heard on the hill', yet Blake also heard and conjured with awful clarity, a world of 'delight chain'd in night' and 'mind forg'd manacles'. It is Blake's latter vision that remains relevant to us now, and which applies to women more than any other social group. Many of the anti-leisure statements and sentiments of the nineteenth century still apply to women's leisure today; industriousness still characterises many of women's leisure activities, limiting the chances of that leisure being in the least bit playful. In the late twentieth century, women are still the labourers who must be kept in line. The inclination to play is there, but it is undermined, undervalued and under pressure. The ability to play is there, but it has been pushed to the very margins of our lives.

This chapter's concern has been to describe the cultural devaluation of play, but this is not the only alteration to have occurred since industrialisation. In the last hundred years other changes have taken place that have profoundly altered the position of women in society. This makes it less acceptable than ever that we should continue to feel so unentitled to play, that we should continue to be so disadvantaged in this crucial area of our lives. The challenge now must be to identify the ways in which we can put play, perhaps for the first time in history, right at the centre of our lives, where it properly belongs. Perhaps in another two hundred years, our current obsession with work will appear an historical oddity, a blip; meanwhile, it is time to make real progress in women's lives by heralding in a new age of the playful self.

PART TWO

5

The Leisure Myth

'Now with women it is supposed that they can amuse themselves or live without amusement.'
(Anthony Trollope, *The Last Chronicle of Barset*)

Before a new age of the playful self can begin to emerge, the impediments to women's playfulness need to be addressed. One of the main reasons why play is not more present in women's lives is, quite simply, because they do not have time to put it there. The old saying that a woman's work is never done holds true for many of us. A great deal of women's time is taken up with work of one kind or another and, even when women are not working, the leisure time they have is often strikingly unleisurely. The combination of relentless work and unleisurely leisure makes barren ground for play.

Leisure Under Pressure

The vast majority of women work hard, and the growing number of women who are also employed outside the home are working especially hard. According to the Humphrey Institute of Public Affairs, women constitute half the world's population, but do two thirds of the world's work. The 1989 Labour Force Survey showed that 66 per cent of British women of working age were in paid employment, and the trend since the late 1980s has been upwards.[1] An increasing proportion of women are in employment, and an increasing proportion of the work force is female. Women now make up 45 per cent of the labour force in Britain, and official figures show that even amongst the group traditionally least likely to work – women with very young children – an increasing number are now doing so.[2] By the late eighties, 40 per cent of mothers of children under 5 were in paid work of some kind.[3] The number of women working part-time has gone up by more than a fifth since 1984 and, by 1994, 86 per cent of British part-timers were women.[4] Women now also represent 25 per cent of the self-employed. A survey by Income Data Services in 1993 revealed that, in some parts of Britain, there are now more women than men in paid employment.[5]

Increasingly likely to work outside the home, women are continuing to shoulder the bulk of the work in the home. They still take the lion's share of responsibility for childcare and matters relating to children, regardless of whether or not they have a partner, regardless of whether they or their partner are working. The World Conference for the United Nations Decade for Women stated that, once housework is accounted for, 'Women around the world end up working twice as many hours as men'. A survey by the National Council of Women of Great Britain found that even amongst women in full-time paid employment outside the home, one-fifth said they still spend most of their energy on domestic matters.[6] These are European-wide trends, according to a survey by the Henley Centre for Forecasting. Even though British women fare better than their counterparts in Germany and Italy, they still spend over double the time that men do on domestic duties, and where children and food are concerned the differential is even greater.[7] Although the majority of people agree in principle that household chores should be shared, in reality analysis of 1993 data from the National Child Development Study found that 85 per cent of the laundry is carried out by the women, 77 per cent of the cooking, 75 per cent of the cleaning, and 66 per cent of the shopping.[8] In addition, women often have unpaid responsibilities for people outside their immediate family, caring for the elderly, sick and disabled.

When you add together the amount of time that the average woman gives to paid employment outside the home and the amount of time she gives to unpaid domestic chores, the total sum of her working time is daunting.

This situation is not new: as we saw in the last chapter, even where a spirit of play was more evident than it is now, women have always had to work hard. The range and extent of their work may not always have been documented, but there is well-supported evidence that a woman's working day started early and ended late. Historian Rosalind Miles has estimated that in prehistoric societies women did five things where men did one: 'The labours of early women were exacting, incessant, varied and hard.' This pattern repeats itself throughout history. Women in medieval England would combine work in the fields and making items to sell at market, such as clothing and blankets, with childcare, cooking and cleaning. Spinning, weaving, sewing, candlemaking, mining and brewing were all jobs traditionally done by women, in addition to childcare and housework, up until the late eighteenth century. In the burgeoning factories of nineteenth-century England, women were indispensable for the long hours they worked for low pay – as they are still indispensable today. Many of the unions formed during the nineteenth century to protect and advocate the rights of the worker refused membership to women, leaving them vulnerable to further exploitation of this kind.[9] By 1900 there were a quarter of a million women working in the cotton mills of Lancashire alone. Wages were low and working hours were long, yet women continued as before to be responsible for child-care and food preparation. In their account of the growth of the women's suffrage movement in the north of England, Jill Liddington and Jill Norris reveal a world far removed from the Victorian myth of 'the angel in the house', a world in which, for decades, women had worked outside the home, in the factories and mills of Yorkshire and Lancashire. These women knew all about the 'double shift'. As one of their elderly interviewees recalled, 'No cause can be won between dinner and tea, and most of us who were married had to work with one hand tied behind us.'[10]

Betty Boothroyd, the first woman to become Speaker of the House of Commons, began her life, too, in the industrial north and remembers clearly how hard life was for her mother, and the many other women like her, who during the 1930s worked long hours in the textile mills of west Yorkshire, then came home to start work again:

> Women had a very, very hard, very difficult life. My father would set the boiler going to do the washing when Mother got home on a Monday night. On a Tuesday night, it would be the ironing. On a Wednesday night, it would be the bedrooms that had to be done. On a Thursday night it would be the house. On a Friday night, it would be the baking for the weekend. It was really a full-time job for women. They had a very hard time indeed. Many of them were the only breadwinners of the family. When I was a child, my father spent a lot of time being unemployed. My mother used to say to me, 'You know, I am not employed for my sex appeal, I'm employed because my rate of pay is lower than that of your father's. That's the only reason.'[11]

The majority of women, especially if they have children, still work this 'double shift' that Betty Boothroyd witnessed during her childhood. Liz, a 36-year-old journalist and mother of two, speaks for many women today when she says, 'Play? What's that? There just aren't enough hours in the day. By the time I've done all the things I have to do, it's time to go to bed. I don't think I've played for years.' Once you start to ask people what their lives are like, what the lives of their parents and grandparents were like, it quickly becomes apparent that the traditional view of paid work as the man's job and family as the woman's is grossly inaccurate: while men may have had relatively little to do with the family, women have always had plenty to do with work.

Not surprisingly, in view of the amount of work they do, women have consistently less leisure time than men. Even in areas where there is high male unemployment, and even when women are the primary wage earners, men still enjoy more leisure time each week than their female counterparts. On average women have 15 hours a week less leisure time than men.[12] According to a survey by the Henley Centre for Forecasting, the average man in full-time employment has 4.8 hours of leisure time each weekday, while the average woman in full-time employment has only 3.3 hours. At weekends, he gets 11.4 hours of leisure time, while she gets 9.2 hours.[13] While working part-time increases the amount of leisure time for men and women, it does not do so equally: government statistics show that the average man working part-time gets 7.8 hours of leisure time a day during the week and 10.8 hours of leisure time at weekends, while the average woman working part-time gets only 4.7 hours off each weekday and 8.6 hours off at weekends.[14] Even full-time housewives, who are cited as having 7 hours of leisure time each weekday, still get at least two hours less leisure time at weekends than the average man. Detailed analysis by Richard Layte of Oxford University of the way that 387 couples spend their time revealed that, although weekends in theory offer men and women equal opportunities for leisure, in practice, men get consistently more leisure time than women, regardless of employment status.[15]

Alarming as these figures are, they do not show the whole picture, since the fundamental matter of what constitutes 'leisure time' is very much open to debate. Standard ways of measuring leisure are usually based on the assumption that there is a clear demarcation between leisure and work, but women's leisure, as every woman knows, is seldom organised so neatly. A report by Mintel reveals that 98 per cent of men and women watch television and videos in their spare time, but it fails to tell us how many of each sex will be doing the ironing at the same time. Women of all ages, all classes and all occupations do far more of this kind of doubling-up of their time than men. Richard Layte's analysis found that women in full-time employment spent well over twice as much time as men doing domestic jobs during their leisure time, while women in part-time employment and unemployed women are *three times* more likely than men to be working while they apparently rest.[16] In addition to this hidden bias, the enjoyment derived from a given activity varies according to the gender of the person involved. An activity as apparently gender neutral as getting washed and dressed in the morning may be a more anxious enterprise for a woman than a man in a society that has far more exacting standards about female appearance. It may well be that men's and women's leisure time are simply not quantitatively comparable, and studies which attempt to make quantitative comparisons without taking adequate account of these qualitative differences will always risk giving a distorted view of the real situation.

The Growing Burden Of Work

A constantly overlooked fact, and a cause for considerable concern, is that *the proportion of time that women spend working is increasing*. Not only do the growing number of women who are in paid employment have less leisure time than men, they are also spending far more of that leisure time doing domestic chores. A British survey in 1993 found that only one man in 100 did an equal share of the housework. A recent study of newly married couples found that the majority of the young wives interviewed expected to do most of the housework, even though most had full-time jobs. Furthermore, they felt that cleaning should be performed as unobtrusively as possible, and went to great lengths to fit housework in around their day-time jobs without it impinging on their leisure time with their husbands. They felt guilty if their husbands did help more, and accepted that they should do housework even when their partner was using his equivalent 'spare' time in a leisure activity.[17] Although I am neither newly married nor particularly young, I recognise this syndrome from my own life: if my husband is reading the paper while I am washing up, I feel resentful; if I am reading the paper while he is washing up, I feel guilty.

Despite labour-saving devices, despite more women choosing to do paid work outside the home, despite changes in men's attitudes towards domestic chores and childcare, the amount of time the average woman spends working is growing. This trend has been emerging for the past forty or fifty years. In 1952, an employed woman in the US spent an average of 4 hours and 6 minutes per day on household chores; by 1968 she was spending over 5 hours on household work. That same period, 1952 to 1968, saw a narrowing of the gap between the amount of time spent on household work by employed women on the one hand and by housewives on the other. In other words, the theory that going out to work released women from the shackles of domesticity was simply not being borne out in practice. Figures for the UK reveal the same trend. British sociologist Carolyn Vogler found that even in households where both the man and the woman were in full-time employment, the woman still took ultimate responsibility for housework in 85 per cent of cases.[18] Only when the man was unemployed and the woman was employed full-time did she begin to relinquish some responsibility, although even then, when she was working full-time and he was working not at all, the woman was still responsible for housework in half the households in this employment situation.[19] Although women who work outside the home put in fewer hours of housework overall than unemployed women or full-time housewives, there is actually very little change when you look at the housework they do as a proportion of *available* time. Paid employment may provide women with some of the things they need – company, money and variety, for example – but it does not seem to offer time off from housework. A survey by *She* magazine in 1992 found that 90 per cent of the 1000 women respondents felt their unpaid work was not sufficiently acknowledged. This work, underpaid and undervalued as it is, is actually of enormous value to society. As Naomi Wolf puts it in *The Beauty Myth*, 'The economics of industrialised countries would collapse if women didn't do the work they do for free.'

Class was once a determining factor in the amount of time that women spent on domestic chores, but this is no longer the case. In the 1930s, middle-class housewives did half as much housework as working-class housewives, but by 1961 the difference between the two groups was insignificant, with the middle-class women doing far more than before.[20] This is in part explained by the decline of the servant class during and after the Second World War, which led to many middle-class women doing their own housework for the first time. Despite the extravagant claims of advertisers and the high hopes of housewives, the labour-saving devices that became household items in the fifties and sixties, such as washing machines and vacuum cleaners, in fact brought about only the slightest reduction in the time spent on household work. By the mid-1970s, men were spending about one-fifth of their total work time on domestic work, while women were spending about half their total working time.[21] By the late 1980s, women accounted for over two-thirds of the time a couple spent on housework, regardless of her employment status.[22] In America, the workload for employed mothers has risen 165 per cent in the last 25 years.[23]

Children, of course, exacerbate the problem. One in five women with dependent children now works full-time in Britain, and twice that number are in part-time work.[24] Yet research has shown conclusively that, once she has children, the amount of unpaid work a woman does rises steeply, while remaining virtually unchanged for men, with obvious, negative implications for the woman's leisure time.[25] In 1975, an average British couple, both in full-time employment with no children, did roughly the same total amount of paid and unpaid work: around 8 hours per day. When children appeared on the scene, the picture changed dramatically: the man's time was relatively unaffected: his total unpaid work went down very slightly, by five minutes, and his paid work went up very slightly, by eight minutes. But the woman's unpaid work rocketed up by more than an hour a day, while her paid work total fell by only 35 minutes.[26] The situation has worsened in the last twenty years. Today, men are likely to experience a 37 per cent drop in their free time when they become fathers, from 50.1 hours to 31.6 hours a week, but women's free time drops by 52 per cent when they become mothers, from 46.6 hours to just 22.5 a week.[27]

Why are we spending so much of our precious free time on housework? Are our houses bigger? Cleaner? *What* is going on? The answer may lie in a parallel situation that arose in the 1960s, when changes in the world of fashion coincided with the phenomenal growth of the dieting industry. It has been argued that once heavily corseted clothing no longer physically restricted the female body, women were then confined by cultural pressure alone to make their bodies 'fit' the fashionable shape. The skimpy, skinny look of the 1960s demanded a skimpy, skinny body without the aid of sturdy corsetry. The physical tyranny that fashion had for several centuries exerted over women was finally exposed as the even greater cultural tyranny it has always been. Similarly, perhaps, the tyranny of housework is one facet of how women's time and energy has always been manipulated and constrained. Now, however, with increasing numbers of women in paid work, and declining numbers of women whose 'job' it is to do the housework, the tyranny of housework is made manifest. Paid work strips the pretence to the bone, revealing housework for what it is: something that women do because no one else wants to. When fashion no longer restricted us with bones and laces, we bowed to its strictures in other ways; when lack of paid work no longer justifies the burden of housework, we take it on all the same on top of the paid work we do. Just as so many of us still do not feel entitled to choose the shape we want to be, so we do not yet seem to feel entitled to choose the work we want to do. We burnt our bras – metaphorically at any rate – but found other ways of controlling our shape; we are increasingly rejecting the full-time role of housewife and mother (almost no one stops work when they marry these days), but we still take responsibility for housework and childcare all the same.

Industrialised Woman

The amount of time women currently spend working undoubtedly restricts the amount of time they have available for leisure. But women's leisure is *itself* part of the problem. Although leisure time is potentially a key opportunity for play time, in reality women's leisure is very rarely playful.

Men not only have more leisure time than women, they also do a wider variety of things with their leisure. On average, they will play more sport than women, have more hobbies than women, go out to pubs and restaurants more often than women, listen to music more than women. By contrast, women's leisure presents a dismal prospect: outside the home, a large proportion of women spend their time shopping or doing charity work (not very playful), while at home, they're to be found knitting, sewing and watching television (still less so).[28] Small wonder, then, that while women crave time off, they often feel unsatisfied by it when it comes.

Katherine, 37, is a film editor for an independent production company. She has a large circle of close friends whom she sees regularly, and in many respects has a fulfilling professional and social life, but she came on the Play Day because of 'a sense of dissatisfaction with daily life'. Katherine summed up the problem for many women when she described her feelings about her leisure time:

> I want to find ways of relaxing, rather than flopping, but it's hard to use free time properly. I find my mind turning round and round, needing to be released into something, to be absorbed completely by something, but it's hard to relax and really lose yourself when there are so many things that have to be done in a day. I have this dream of a life in some magical cottage doing all those wonderful things and the day just unfurls. But why can't I do these things in the here and now, why do they have to take place in some imaginary world? I get glimpses of play in my life every now and then, but there's not enough of it. I want to find ways of concentrating on something that doesn't exhaust me by concentrating on it! I suppose it's the difference between swimming lengths in the pool and building a sandcastle on the beach.

Swimming lengths in the pool is typical of much of what passes for leisure in women's lives. A year or two ago, I was dutifully swimming up and down the local pool one afternoon when a noisy and exuberant group of foreign language students plunged into the water and proceeded to splash about with a great deal of merriment and a total disregard for the lane dividers or the orderly calm of the lane-lappers. But it was they who were playing, not I. Though there was a time when I would not have dreamt of going swimming to swim lengths, now I was there for earnest exercise. Pleasurable to a degree, because it gave me time to think, to relax, to stretch tired muscles, to boost a sluggish circulation, and because I did feel better afterwards. But *playful*? No.

Women are under constant pressure to be busy and to use their time productively, and this inevitably impinges on the way in which women spend their time, with direct and deleterious implications for their ability to play. Instead of doing things for the sheer enjoyment of doing them, there is an overwhelming tendency amongst many women to do things only if 'a good reason' can be found first. The sandcastles that we secretly long to build would be washed away by the next tide, but swimming lengths will make us fit, tone our muscles, burn off a few unwanted calories. No matter that swimming lengths is boring as hell, nor that the delight of building sandcastles survives the turning tide.

Throughout history, the industrious woman has been praised as virtuous, while the woman who neglects duty in favour of pleasure has been held up for rebuke. Literature provides examples in plenty, from the patient Griselda to the pleasure-seeking Wife of Bath, from dutiful Elaine to adulterous Guinevere, from obedient Little Dorrit to wilful Emma Bovary. Idleness in a woman has been portrayed as worse even than talkativeness: Jane Austen's muddle-headed heroine Emma is set against the garrulous Miss Bates, and it is clear which of the two is the more blameworthy. Emma is portrayed as a young woman lacking proper employment, as a result of which she busies herself in unsuitable matters – romantic matchmaking – and soon finds herself out of her depth. The day is saved by the serious, hard-working Mr Knightley. In complete contrast to Emma is Pamela, the eponymous heroine of Samuel Richardson's novel (sub-titled *Virtue Rewarded*), who is so committed to doing what is dutiful and good that she can seem absurd to a modern reader. But when the novel was first published in 1740, it was an instant and huge success, and Pamela was heralded as the ideal of moral rectitude. The novel traces the story of a beautiful, innocent and hardworking maid-servant called Pamela whose life is thrown into disarray when her kind mistress dies, and Mr B, her mistress's son, becomes head of the house. Mr B can think of little else but his lust for Pamela, and seems to have little else to do but devise ways of satisfying it. Pamela, however, persistently and determinedly wards off his advances. In fury and desperation, Mr B abducts and imprisons her, attempts to rape her, and even sets up a false wedding ceremony to trick her into submission. All to no avail. Pamela's steadfastness is eventually rewarded by the transformation of Mr B's self-serving lust into genuine love and a proposal of (genuine) marriage. Throughout the book, Pamela's virtue is highlighted by her industriousness: being unemployed is as intolerable to her as her master's unwanted advances. During her imprisonment, she permits herself the 'amusement' of reading and writing, but only because she has 'no work given me to do'. From the books she reluctantly allows herself to read, she nevertheless hopes 'to receive improvement, as well as amusement'.[29]

By the mid-nineteenth century, a woman who was not conscientiously occupied risked moral censure. The pressure on women to use their time productively and virtuously was extreme. An article in the *Saturday Review* in 1868 attacked young women 'whose sole idea of life [was] plenty of fun and luxury'.[30] Prostitutes were the demons, and the demonised, of Victorian society, reviled not only for their immorality, but for their rejection of the acceptable contemporary models of feminine behaviour. So powerful and pervasive was the ideal of wifedom and motherhood that unmarried women were regarded as a social problem and the cause for considerable concern.[31] No matter what their achievements, single women were seen as 'superfluous'. Newspapers printed articles on the subject, social commentators debated it: how should these women best occupy themselves in the absence of husbands and children? According to historian Martha Vicinus, 'If the prostitute symbolised the extremes of unbridled passion and evil in woman, the spinster had thrust upon her absolute purity and goodness. She was supposed to remain virginal and utterly self-sacrificing for all who need her.'[32]

This is the legacy that we have inherited and largely accepted. A spirit of industriousness imbues the way in which many women spend their time. The industrialised woman is compelled into a state of chronic busy-ness that not only mitigates against genuine leisure, but is contrary to the very spirit of play.

Cursed With Practicality

Alison, an editor in her thirties, married with one child, attended the Play Day workshop in 1991. She had no difficulty identifying in herself the phenomenon of the industrialised woman.

> My desk at work is covered in little stickers saying, 'Reheel shoes', 'Send birthday card to so-and-so', 'Buy bread, milk and cheese'. I have to think about those things as well as the ten things I'm trying to do for work. Women may be better than men at holding six things in their head at once, but it's not good for them, it's terribly, terribly tiring. There are all these things in a woman's head that aren't in a man's. They clutter up your mind, and if your mind is untidy with all this clutter, it's difficult to be absorbed in any one aspect of your life. It militates against being able to lose yourself in play.

Women's so-called 'talent' for managing the practicalities of life is nothing short of a curse. We learn to be very organised in order to cope with the myriad tasks that fill our days; in turn, we are praised for our organisational skill, our ability to think about several things at once. But is there a price to pay for this practical genius? Are we not striving to make a virtue of necessity, when necessity serves us as a vice? The sheer quantity of women's work obliges us to be efficient, practical and busy, but should we not be concerned by the extent to which we have accepted this pressure to be usefully occupied, internalising it as somehow quintessentially female? Might this utilitarian talent not simply be a coping strategy which women have had to learn but which men have neatly side-stepped? Might it not limit us even as it marks us out as admirable? Vera Brittain neatly observed that 'The majority of potential women philosophers have been unable to find time or energy for problems in the abstract because they have been faced with so many awaiting solution in the concrete.' Is it really so praiseworthy, this practicality? Are we not rather like the force-fed geese whose burst organs make the delicacy *foie gras* – valued for our capacity for deformation?

The 38-year-old daughter of a well-known sculptor described how when her father died she found his studio was full of unfinished bits of sculpture. Much of what he did, she said, was unfinished, perhaps never intended to be finished. Part of his creativity was his ability to forget about the finished product, and instead to become wholly involved in the process of creating. 'When I paint or sculpt,' she said, 'however much I try to enjoy the process, I'm still always conscious of wanting to have finished something. I'm too practical to be really playful and creative. It's the same with sewing or knitting: I'm too goal oriented to ever play fully, my mind is always fixed on the end product and I'm too interested in getting there. I think that's why there are so few women visual artists. Women find it hard to play because they're so used to thinking in terms of the usefulness of their activities. Degas never thought of anything as finished.'[33]

Creativity and playfulness have little to do with usefulness, yet our minds being full of the latter, there is little room left for the former. When Virginia Woolf in 1930 wrote, 'How any woman with a family ever put pen to paper I cannot fathom, always the bell rings or the baker calls', she was lamenting the constant infringement of practical tasks and chores on women's creative space and energy. When a man says, with a charmingly apologetic smile, 'I'm so sorry, it entirely slipped my mind to collect the dry cleaning/hang up the washing/feed the cat/sterilise the baby's bottles (sigh). You're so much better at remembering all these things than I am, darling. I don't know how you do it', make no mistake: he is protecting his right to mental space, emotional space, leisure space, play space. He is refusing to be crowded out by the mundanities of everyday life. If we are to enjoy the fruits of genuine playfulness, women need to start refusing too.

The Busy Lizzy Syndrome

A few years ago a leading women's magazine ran an article entitled 'Me-Time'. It began with the promising injunction: 'Rethink your priorities and you will learn that the ironing can wait, but that the time to take care of yourself is now.'[34] The article described 'an insidious cycle of deprivation', in which women are so busy meeting everyone else's needs that they forget their own. Furthermore, women feel guilty if they take time out for themselves: 'Faced with a pile of laundry in one corner and a partner looking for companionship in another, a woman has to have a very strong sense of self to announce that she is off to apply a face mask instead.' The article then encourages women to take their needs seriously, and to try scheduling in time in their week for themselves.

While the problems that it outlines are real enough, the article has little to offer in the way of solutions, apart from suggesting a weekend in a health farm every now and again, and citing one woman who found 'Me-Time' by paying a beautician for a regular home-facial. More troubling though is the additional text tacked on to the end of the article, which gives the following advice: 'Once a week, lock the bathroom door behind you and treat yourself to a dose of private time . . . Run a warm bath and add to it a relaxing and soothing aromatic oil . . . Make time for a quick pedicure too.' Just when the reader thought she might be able to act on some of those 1500 words of wisdom, urging her to forget all the things she *should* be doing and take some time to do what she *wants* to do, she finds herself back in the world of imperatives: 'Always tackle feet immediately after your bath when skin and nails are at their softest'; 'Remove hard skin from heels with a natural pumice stone, then rub in a little almond oil'; 'Trim toenails straight across using clippers, never scissors'; 'Make a point of rubbing over each toenail with remover lotion to get rid of any oil'. And this was supposed to be time off! Not to mention the lost lunch hours spent searching for the aromatic oil, pumice stone, nail clippers and remover lotion. Lock the bathroom door, by all means, but take your obligations in with you.

This article provides a particularly blatant, though far from solitary, example of the way in which, even when women are seemingly taking time for themselves, they are frequently under pressure to be using that time 'usefully', in this case by softening their skin and beautifying their feet. Just as that vital change of mindscape that would enable us to play begins to seem a possibility, it is snatched out of our reach once again. The article's underlying and all-too-familiar message is that Me-Time is only justifiable when it is time used productively. In this case, the product is the woman herself.

The pursuit of physical beauty devours women's time, money and energy, as Naomi Wolf has described very well in *The Beauty Myth*.[35] Millions of pounds are spent every year on dieting foods, dieting magazines, dieting books. Millions more go on cosmetics. Cleansing lotions are marketed as modern-day healing potions; water, the chief ingredient in most of these products, is as holy today as it was for Christian pilgrims in the Middle Ages. The quest for physical beauty is double-edged: on the one hand, it provides a justifiable way for women to pamper themselves, and a much-needed respite from the demands of daily life; on another level, it is directed towards self-improvement, rather than self-indulgence. In every city in the country there are women leaping up and down in aerobics classes, not having fun, but working hard; you will see them later in the changing rooms, some wafer thin, some apologetically plump, their faces not relaxed, but grim. 'If I look better,' you can almost hear them thinking, 'I'll feel better, and if I feel better, I'll cope better.' Exercise classes, work-out gyms and swimming pools are part of the vast weaponry that many women employ in a battle against their shape or weight. Exercise is another item on their Must list, genuine play the last thing on their mind.

A legion of Shoulds and Oughts march through women's leisure time, and women's magazines are a source of constant reinforcements. While magazines present themselves as a woman's best friend, her confidante, confessor and advice-giver, they simultaneously convey powerful messages that undermine, belittle and devalue. An article designed to help you love your body is accompanied by a picture or advertisement of a model whose body is more likely to make you hate your own. An article designed to help you prepare for Christmas is full of 'useful tips' that can only make you feel overwhelmed by your own lack of forethought and inefficiency. Women's magazines are a paradoxical phenomenon: they offer women a carrot with which to beat themselves, they simultaneously feed our hopes and punish us for them. 'You want to feel good about yourself?' they lisp down from the racks at us. 'Of course you do. Just buy me, read me, and I'll tell you how. But first, let me remind you how very imperfect you are . . .' Despite conjuring an image of the relaxed female reader in her tidy, tranquil home, they impart an urgent message: 'Don't sit around, you've got to get fit, get thin, get laid.'

A tension exists at the very heart of women's magazines, mirroring the tension that exists also in the reader. This inner conflict between what we are, what we dream of being, and what we fear becoming, is encapsulated in the pages of the magazines we read: they reflect reality at the same time as they both offer solutions to it and provide temporary escape from it. 'Believe in yourself!' proclaim the articles, while the flanking advertisements add, 'But only if you eat this, wear this, look like this.' Reading magazines is an allowable luxury because, for the price of the magazine, you get recipes, knitting patterns, ideas for birthday presents, tips on childcare, not to mention advice on your hairstyle and sex life. Reading magazines is an allowable luxury because it promises to help women cope with their unrelenting responsibility for others. Reading magazines is an allowable luxury because, although it looks like leisure, it is actually a form of work.

Earn It Or Spurn It

The pressure to be busy influences how women spend much of their time, both their working time and their leisure time. It has become so powerful and pervasive that many people today feel that enjoyment must be earned through some kind of work. We have long since forgotten Thomas Aquinas's maxim that 'Not everything that is more difficult is necessarily more meritorious'.[36]

Earning enjoyment may take the form of running five miles before allowing yourself the pleasure of delicious food, or doing the washing up before feeling entitled to sit down with a book. 'Naughty but nice' was one of the most successful advertising slogans of all times, and the agency that coined it really did. At the heart of the campaign's success was the way it traded on the unspoken understanding that we ought to earn pleasure. Go on, indulge yourself, was the slogan's powerful message, a message that could only work in a culture that usually enjoins people to do the very opposite: hold out against their instincts, urges and desires.

Guilt about pleasure is only fully assuaged in our culture by work. This even applies to children: as a head teacher of a state school in London proudly proclaimed recently, 'We don't talk about play. We always use the word work.' The 29 children in her school are not yet five years old, but already they are being well versed in the prevailing ethic of our culture.[37] Unless we have earned leisure – and often despite the fact that we have more than earned it – we feel 'guilty', 'selfish', 'naughty' or 'lazy' when we permit ourselves some time off.

This creates considerable problems for unemployed women. How do you earn leisure in the absence of the framing, legitimising context of work? The familiar caricature of the leisurely suburban housewife, flitting from one coffee morning to another and doing a bit of dusting in between, is a very far cry from the reality. *The Women's Room* by Marilyn French became a best-seller in the seventies because it gave voice to the frustration that many women felt as they faced the repetitive monotony of household chores and free time restricted to seeing neighbours. Hannah Gavron's sociological study, *The Captive Wife*, first published in 1966, similarly exploded the myth of the happy housewife, by revealing the misery, loneliness and depression suffered by many women in this position.

Unemployed women, more than any of us, have to prove through their unpaid work that any leisure they take is well-earned. But this is not easy when it is in the very nature of unpaid domestic work to be unending. A woman's work is never done in part because housework is never done. A further complication is that, for a great many women, work and leisure have to take place in the same physical space: the home. The traditional refuge of the man at leisure, the garden shed, was not just geographically separate from the house, but symbolically so. For the housewife – indeed, for anyone faced with responsibility for domestic work, and that is most women – there are no external markers for clocking off. Paid work has its problems, but it does provide a useful structure, some guidelines, for legitimate time off (although even 'time off' is often loaded with awareness of the very activity that we are taking time off from).

The pressure to earn leisure affects all women, whether they are in paid work outside the home or not. One way we try to get around this conflict of interests is by taking up hobbies that involve an element of work. Operating on the assumption that a change is as good as a rest, many women use certain kinds of work, paid and unpaid, to justify taking time off from other kinds of work. Church and charity are obvious examples, but this kind of industrious leisure crops up in many guises: the lunch hour is more likely to be spent tracking down fabrics for new curtains than wandering through the park sniffing roses; women are far more likely to enrol in an evening class in cookery or dress-making than macramé or trampolining. At the Oxford College of Further Education, the class enrolment for 1996 bears this out: three of the most popular courses with women were dress-making, assertive communication and introduction to counselling. On the other hand, only four women had signed up for woodcarving. Even in our leisure time, we tend to do things because they are useful, rather than for the pure delight of doing them. Sometimes the two can come together though. On the Play Day, Caitlin insisted that, for her, going shopping *was* genuinely pleasurable: 'I don't go to buy, I just go to look. I love wandering round the big department stores, seeing all the different things on offer, especially those rows and rows of beautiful fabrics, and all the buttons and different coloured cotton-reels. It always makes me feel like a little girl in a wonderful toy shop, mouth open, marvelling at everything!'

More typical, perhaps, is Penny, 29, who decided she needed to take up a hobby to counteract the pressures of her job. 'I took up the guitar, something I've always wanted to do, but even though I wanted to play for pleasure, I found it hard to enjoy. I think I approached it in the wrong way, and ended up treating it like a second job. I was too worried about practising and playing and doing well. It became a real chore, not at all relaxing, and certainly not play. I gave it up after a couple of months, because I was finding it so stressful!'

The pressure to earn leisure through work of some kind is felt by both men and women in our culture, but given the particularly complex meaning of female employment, it is not surprising that earning leisure creates especial problems for women. When exactly is enough enough? When precisely is one allowed to stop? Add to this the emphasis in women's lives on self-sacrificing service (about which more in Chapter 6), and it becomes clear that a woman's work is a full-time undertaking that leaves little room for play. The pressure to be usefully employed even when we are at leisure is a constant droning in the background of our minds, drowning out the inner voices calling us to play. Even when we do begin to play, that same droning sound is always there, threatening to overwhelm it, and all too often succeeding.

Exploding The Leisure Myth

The Leisure Myth is the myth that leisure is freely and equally available to all; the myth that women who are not in paid employment are not working and are therefore at leisure; the myth that leisure is a straightforward entity that exists in time not taken up with work. Whichever way you choose to look at the issue of how women spend their time, whether from the perspective of work or leisure, the picture that emerges is one of women as a profoundly un-leisured class in modern society. Like a flower struggling to bloom under a ton of cement, women's leisure is under pressure. Wherever the constraints and expectations are coming from, whether from children, parents, partners, friends or from the individual woman herself, the evidence suggests that giving priority to one's own leisure needs is often very hard for women. Since leisure is a key context for play, leisure under pressure is also play under pressure. It is hard to see how women can be genuinely, regularly playful when their lives offer only occasional, restricted opportunities for play.

The work ethic is thriving in women's work and leisure activities alike. Dutiful leisure is paramount. Regardless of whether it takes the form of knitting in front of the TV, making chutney for the church fête, or burning up calories in the multi-gym, women's leisure is largely predicated on the concept of utility. Usefulness and busy-ness characterise much female leisure, and as a result snuff out the opportunity for much female play. The preoccupation with exercise and dieting is only partly a response to cultural pressure to be a certain physical shape, be it thin or fit or muscular; it is also a product of a more fundamental cultural prerequisite, namely that women should not be at ease. Women are seldom at ease, nor are they encouraged to be, for society is far better served by women being in a perpetual state of busy-ness; by women who have accepted that their work is never done; by women who have forgotten what it is to play and be playful, and who, even when they remember, have not time to do much about it.

6

The Imperative of Service

'She rose to his requirement – dropped
The playthings of her life
To take the honourable work
Of woman and of wife.
(Emily Dickinson, *Selected Poems*)

Watch a small, contented child looking about, taking in the shapes, colours and noises of the objects and people all around her, endlessly inquisitive; that child is firmly located at the centre of her world, all things emanate from where she is; play is possible precisely because the child occupies that central place. The story of play in women's lives is too often a tale of *displacement*, of how they become lost to themselves as the beings at the centre of their own existence.

One of the chief causes of this displacement is the tendency to put other people first, to let other people take the central space while we orbit around them. This tendency is itself the result of cultural pressures which insist that we find fulfilment and meaning through the happiness of others and that, even when we don't, we should nevertheless continue to put their needs before our own. 'Selfishness' is a word with very different connotations when applied to men and women. Call a man 'selfish' and in a sense you are affirming his maleness: the adjective implies determination, single-mindedness, ambition – not all good, but not all bad either. Call a woman 'selfish' and you are making an unreservedly derogatory comment about her: that same adjective now implies meanness, unnaturalness, dereliction of duty. Selfishness can affirm masculinity, but it only ever indicates a want of femininity. Selfishness has a place in a man's life, but no place in a woman's. Any act of self-assertion, however small, brings with it the risk of censure for a woman. Not that we are all as saintly as Mother Teresa (nor would most of us want to be), but the yardstick against which our thoughts and actions are measured is still that of self*less*ness; the fact that we fall short of the mark only serves to reinforce the ideal we should be aiming for; the inescapable sense of failure and guilt that we feel when we do put our own needs before those of others creates a kind of mental confusion that undermines the benefits of the action: if we sit down with a book rather than clear the table; if we drop in on a friend and let the children arrive home to an empty house; if we stay in bed on a Saturday morning and let someone else hang up the washing, have we done something good or bad?

Assertiveness training, which became so popular in the eighties, was an interesting product of this dilemma, setting out to eradicate the 'white noise' of our confusion by assuring us that we were entitled to have, and meet, needs of our own. Yet even though the numerous books and courses on the subject provided a vocabulary and a set of techniques for doing so, a great many of us still feel a residual unease as we resist the temptation or pressure to put other people first. Ros Coward argues in her book *Our Treacherous Hearts* that many women in the 1980s attempted to resolve the dilemma by meeting their own needs *and* trying to fulfil the traditional role of meeting everyone else's. As a result of the ambivalent feelings, not to say the exhaustion, which arose from the monumental effort this required, many of the women Coward interviewed were retreating into the private world of home and family – returning, that is, to the old, straightforward world of 'others first'.

This pressure to put other's needs before one's own is one of the key reasons why so many women have such difficulty when it comes to finding either the inclination or the opportunity to play. Susie Orbach has called this the 'imperative of service'. In a recent newspaper article, Orbach wrote that 'One of the crippling requirements for contemporary femininity, wherever women are located on the class or cultural map, is an imperative of service, of giving, of midwifery, of doing for others. In doing this, we understand that the psychological price of focusing on the needs of others might produce a discomfort with recognising one's own.'[1]

The imperative of service runs directly counter to the impulse to play and, like other aspects of female socialisation, it conditions, not to say infects, our play from an early age, making it increasingly difficult to play as we get older. The Russian novelist Vladimir Nabokov relates an account of an ape which, after months of coaxing by a scientist, produced the first picture ever drawn by an animal: the picture showed the bars of the animal's cage. The imperative of service is similarly a prison whose bars dominate our field of vision, yet we have grown so accustomed to them doing so that we tend to take it for granted that they should; we can scarcely imagine a life without this prison, these bars. If we are to move beyond this state of captivity and reclaim both the right to play and the freedom that comes from playing, we need to understand how we came to be thus secured. We need to understand how the component parts of the imperative of service inhibit play in our daily lives, and how, as a whole, the imperative of service has turned many of us into profoundly *un*playful adults.

Sugar And Spice And All Things Nice

A central pillar of the imperative of service is the strong cultural pressure on girls to please and be pleasing to others. Little has changed since Rousseau declared in the eighteenth century that 'the woman is expressly formed to please the man: if the obligation is reciprocal also, and the man ought to please in his turn, it is not so immediately necessary.'[2] Mary Wollstonecraft condemned this as 'the philosophy of lasciviousness',[3] yet it has proven a hard habit to break and continues to inform a great deal of female behaviour today. Pleasing others, however, can often negatively affect our ability to please ourselves.

A study of young school children by Jane White in 1989 found that girls were far more likely than the boys to sit still, behave and try to please the teacher by carrying out instructions as well as possible.[4] Boys on the other hand, were more likely to move about and not pay attention. They talked more, and were more active than girls, who tended to be passive and reactive. Furthermore, teachers actively encouraged the girls to behave in this way, praising them for their obedience and politeness. White also observed that while the girls enjoyed winning the teacher's approval, there was a price to be paid as it involved the constant suppression of responsiveness to their own internal directives. 'Good' behaviour earned them social approval, but it seemed to inhibit their freedom of thought and action. Other studies have found that while a level of 'bad' behaviour is tolerated as normal in boys, girls will be more swiftly and severely chastised for behaving in the same way.

Not being 'good', girls learn, causes distress to other people, and this we are told is to be avoided at all costs. To upset someone else by failing to take sufficient account of their needs or feelings, or, worse still, by considering and then dismissing their needs or feelings, is to commit the cardinal female offence of selfishness. Instead, we learn to adapt ourselves in myriad ways to the needs and requirements of others.

Tape-recordings of conversations between teenagers has revealed that in single-sex groups girls and boys talk very differently, but in mixed groups girls tend to modify both their way of talking and their subject matter to blend in with the boys.[5] This seems to set the pattern for life. American linguist Deborah Tannen has spent many years analysing how men and women take or yield space in conversation. She concludes that men and women have distinctive conversational styles, but that, while men's conversational style remains largely unaffected by whom they are talking to, women in a mixed-sex group will modify their conversational style to fit in with the men present. As a result, women tend to speak consistently less often in mixed groups, and when they do it is for shorter lengths of time.[6] This phenomenon can be observed in action every day of the week in the Houses of Parliament. The Labour peer Baroness Ewart-Biggs, in an interview a few years before her death, laughingly complained about the long-windedness of her male colleagues in the House of Lords. She was struck from the first day she took her seat in the Lords not only by how long the men spoke for, but by how little they seemed to worry about whether what they said was of any interest to their listeners. The women, on the other hand, took great care and effort to be both relevant and succinct.[7]

We also accommodate others in non-verbal ways, as Elizabeth Aries found in her comparison of the body postures of young men and women. Aries discovered that, regardless of whom they were with, men tended to take up more physical space relative to their size than women. Their body postures were not affected by being in a single-sex or mixed group. The women, on the other hand, tended to sit in relaxed, sprawling positions when alone with other women, but when they were in a mixed group they confined their physical postures to neat, tidy, small spaces.[8]

Where women do not bow to the pressure to accommodate others, they risk criticism for being 'pushy', 'bossy', 'loud' – in short, unfeminine. A study of teenagers in a London school by psychologist Sue Lees and her colleagues showed how this pressure on girls to yield space to boys operated even at the level of who got a go on the ping-pong table during the lunch hour. While most of the girls sat back and let the boys monopolise the table, a few did not. These more assertive girls were seen as trouble-makers by their peers.[9] In learning to accommodate themselves physically and verbally to others, girls learn also to relegate their play-needs to second place.

Intolerance of self-oriented behaviour in girls has some worrying repercussions. Research in the USA has looked at the way children handle conflict that arises during play and found that, while boys tend to settle the dispute and then continue playing, girls tend to stop playing the moment they encounter conflict. If play is one way in which we learn how to manage feelings of aggression and hostility towards others, what are the consequences for girls whose play brooks neither? Girls' play provides few opportunities for learning about these 'bad' emotions, either in others or in themselves, still fewer opportunities for expressing them.

On the basis of her study of women in business, Jane McLoughlin, author of *Up and Running: Women Mean Business*, argues that this tendency to avoid conflict, rather than learn to manage it, will later hold women back in the work-place. 'In our traditional domestic role, "good" women did not compete with each other,' McLoughlin says. 'Women's survival depended on nurturing and keeping the peace. They operated from a position of weakness, both physical and economic, and naturally enough they saw direct competition within their ranks as an attack on their security . . . The same fear of conflict still colours many adult women's response to each other at work. Most successful women over the age of around thirty-five still find it easier to compete with men than they do with other women.'[10]

If play is a valuable way to learn how to handle conflict and aggression, we must pause here to ask why, when boys' play allows them more opportunities to learn precisely this, are boys still more inclined to violent, aggressive and socially deviant behaviour than girls? The answer may lie partly in gender differentials in levels of the hormones and chemicals linked to these types of behaviour – in other words, boys are from the outset predisposed to be more aggressive than girls. But there may also be an explanation in the aspects of the self that boys' play does not acquaint them with, such as empathy, co-operation and verbal communication. It could well be that both boys and girls suffer from the gender bias in their play. With play as with food, an imbalanced diet is bad for us.

The chief consequence of the insistent emphasis on co-operation and conflict-avoidance in girls' play is that it fails to encourage boundary-building between self and other. The individual – so girls learn – must bow to the communal. Research on play in childhood and adolescence shows very clearly the importance of innovation, exploration, independence and risk-taking, yet all of these are antithetical to the co-operative endeavours towards which girls are guided and for which they are praised in their play. This creates a form of 'negative competition', with girls banding together to undermine and exclude anyone who eschews the interests of the group in favour of her own (a tendency borne out by the ferocious intensity of girls' friendships).

Women, too, will compete as a group against those who seem to threaten the group.[11] In the context of play, a woman who chooses to value her individual needs above the needs of others risks censure, not only from men, but from other women. It thus becomes very difficult for a woman to fulfil her play-needs when the overarching message she has received all her life is that to be female means to be caring of and pleasing to others.

The pop star Madonna is an interesting, and exceptional, case of a woman who has become phenomenally successful by violating traditional notions of acceptable female behaviour. Indeed, she has found increasingly extreme ways of rejecting these norms, graduating from displaying her underwear to displaying that she is not wearing any – *most* unladylike! Madonna exploits the philosophy of lasciviousness, exposing the hypocrisy of the virgin/whore dichotomy, whereby some women must be pleasing to men by renouncing their sexuality, while others must please by exaggerating it. But although Madonna claims to challenge conventions and explode myths, it remains questionable how far she herself actually manages to escape the constraints she mocks. The paradox of Madonna's success is that while she parodies the 'good girl'/'bad girl' dilemma, her success nevertheless depends on pleasing others: she may please women by offering them a role model of acceptable 'bad' behaviour, but her appeal, at least as far as men are concerned, is the age-old allure of titillation.

Mother's Little Helper

Another of the pillars upholding the imperative of service is the pressure to be helpful, whose clearest manifestation is perhaps the assumption that girls will help with domestic chores. A recent Canadian study found that 85 per cent of girls were regularly expected to do household chores and half were taking major responsibility for housework.[12] The same is true in Britain, where housework impinges on female leisure time from an early age. In adolescence, domestic jobs may take as much as sixteen hours a week of a girl's spare time, while seldom infringing at all on a boy's leisure.[13] Typically, a boy might have to tidy his room occasionally, but a girl will be expected to put in regular time on the housework front. While there is some evidence that boys are having to help more with domestic work than they used to, they rarely help as much as girls of their age and class.[14] A study of 50 teenage girls in

Yorkshire by Vivienne Griffiths revealed that the majority had daily chores, including childcare, washing up, cooking and cleaning.[15] On the whole, the girls in these studies accepted domestic duties as a fact of life, even if they did grumble about it, and even when they were aware that their brothers were not equally encumbered. 'Their experience was preparation for unpaid domestic work as well as maternal duties,' concluded Griffiths. 'They were already learning to sacrifice their own time and interests to others' needs.'[16]

The requirement that we be available to help, regardless of what we may have planned to do, makes it increasingly hard to be self-directing in our activities. Our time is not our own, either in theory or in practice; it is a commodity to be used by others. Aware that something is not quite right, but unsure what to do about it, we subside into frustrated acquiescence. Eliza, a language student at Sheffield University, describes how irritated she is by her mother's engrained habit of helpfulness: 'I love it when we're alone together and can sit and talk and just be ourselves. But the moment my father comes home or one of my brothers walks into the room, it's: "Oh, darling, can I get you a drink? What would you like? Are you hungry?" It drives me mad. Our time, our enjoyment, is always so *interruptible*.' Eliza's annoyance in part reflects her recognition that in helping others her mother denies herself and denies Eliza too. Their autonomous, self-sufficient pleasure is obliterated by the arrival of family members whose requirements take precedence – a demotion that Eliza clearly resents. And so she should. For how can we take ourselves seriously when we show so little regard for ourselves? How can we discover and develop the things that make life pleasurable when our pleasure is of so little value?

The helpfulness habit undermines our sense of self by constantly knocking us off-balance, demanding that we be available and responsive to others. We are like skittles that are never left standing for more than a few moments at a time, and no sooner are we upright than the needs of loved ones, friends and colleagues scatter us in all directions once again. The damage thus done to our self-esteem and self-confidence in turn damages our sense of entitlement to play and, eventually, our fundamental ability to play. Perhaps it is possible to be helpful *and* playful – playfully helpful, maybe, or helpfully playful. For most of us, though, neither of those possibilities seems to come too easily and, in the meantime, the accumulating habit of a lifetime, the habit of helpfulness, continues to push our playful selves further and further underground.

Made To Care

Caring for others is a key aspect of the imperative of service and an extension of the helpfulness that is expected of girls and women. The role of carer has been assigned to women for so long that it has come to define much of what is considered appropriate behaviour in women. In Britain today women represent a major portion of the country's carers. In 1990, there were 3.5 million women carers in all, and 40 per cent of women over the age of 45 were working as carers in some capacity.[17] In all probability the real figures are far higher than this, because women typically under-report caring duties (a case of taking those cage-bars for granted again). Women vastly outnumber men in the so-called 'caring' professions, as well as in the huge range of voluntary activities that provide care for others. There are 25,000 volunteers running Oxfam shops up and down the country, 90 per cent of them women. The figures are similar for Meals on Wheels, the British Red Cross, the Samaritans and countless other charitable organisations. One study found that as many as 48 per cent of professional-class women are involved in voluntary work of this kind.[18] Society is financially dependent on the work that this army of women does for free: looking after the elderly, the disabled, the sick, and providing childcare for grandchildren. This is not to say that charity work and other forms of unpaid work are not a source of genuine enjoyment to those people who do them, but leisure activities that are so clearly self-less rather than self-full, care-full rather than care-free, will seldom be the source of genuine play. Leisure time for many women is an extension of, rather than a break from, the caring they do all day every day.

Women throughout history have been the carers in society. They have been persuaded into this role through a combination of practical considerations, economic pressures, political exigencies and, of course, plain bigotry. In his exhaustive catalogue of the faults of women, Semonides, a poet-philosopher of the seventh century BC, likened different kinds of women to different animals. The only woman worthy of praise was the one who resembled a bumble bee in her ceaseless care for others:

To her alone no blame is attached,
But life flourishes and prospers under her care.
She grows old cherishing a husband who cherishes her,
After she has borne to him a lovely and distinguished group of children.
Among all women her excellence shines forth,
And a godlike grace is shed about her.[19]

Some two thousand years later, the tone was more complacent, but the message was unchanged. 'All a woman has to do in this world is contained within the duties of a daughter, a sister, a wife and a mother,' asserted Richard Steele, the eighteenth-century dramatist and essayist. By the nineteenth century, the view epitomised by Steele had been marginally reshaped by sentimental notions of 'naturalness'. An influential journalist of the day, W.R. Greg, expressed the opinion of the majority when he described woman's natural role as one of 'completing, sweetening and embellishing the existence of others'.[20] As recently as 1963, the role of carer was being unselfconsciously enshrined in official policy recommendations. The Newsom Report had this to say on the education of girls: 'In addition to their needs as individuals our girls should be educated in terms of their main social function – which is to make for themselves, their children and their husbands a secure and comfortable home and to be mothers.'[21] While it is unlikely that a government report today would get away with the phrase 'main social function', it is less certain that the attitude underlying it has been entirely vanquished.

Despite the rhetoric suggesting that women are 'naturally' fulfilled by caring for others, the role of carer is designed not to liberate or maximise female energy and talent, but to contain it. Whenever the role of carer has brought with it any significant degree of power or autonomy, it has either been wrested from women's hands or redefined in such a way as to render it once more an inferior social position. Midwifery commanded both respect and even influence in ancient civilisations, but since then it has gradually been marginalised and stigmatised. By the fifteenth century, it had become a debased and precarious profession, left in the main to poor, illiterate, often elderly women with no other means of support. By the nineteenth century, the tasks performed by midwives had been sufficiently limited to ensure that male doctors, not midwives, were seen as the real authorities on childbirth, a situation that continued well into the twentieth century. In her book *Woman As Healer* Jeanne Acheterberg argues that the art of healing has always been associated with women, and that their presence in the caring professions is an ancient one. What has changed over the centuries is the prestige attached to women's caring activities in this sphere. Only in the last thirty years, with the growth of the natural birth movement, has midwifery begun to reassert itself as a distinguished and skilled profession.[22] Social work is another profession in which women's caring has been demoted, paradoxically, as it has acquired more status. Until the Second World War, it was customary for middle- and upper-class women to carry out informal, unpaid social work. They visited schools, homes and hospitals, providing both financial and practical assistance. By the late nineteenth century, as many as 200,000 people, the majority of them women, were doing district visiting. In 1946, with the creation of the National Health Service, social work was established as a proper career, with a professional hierarchy, salary scale and public status; the next twenty years saw the women who had once led this army vanishing into the ranks, while the top jobs went to men. Helen Brook, founder of the Brook Advisory Centres and a leading campaigner for women's right to free contraception, recalls with some indignation how rapidly this process of marginalisation occurred in the sphere of family planning: '[At first] the doctors were women who couldn't have a full-time practice because of being married. The male doctors really despised the family planners. They thought it was just pin money for lady doctors. It wasn't until the sixties that they saw there was money and a career and some prestige in it and they started jumping on the bandwagon. And then, of course, bossing us all around!'[23] Local government changes in the 1970s brought about the same marginalisation of women in housing management, another profession which had developed from women's caring, and had originally been run by women on a voluntary or low-paid basis.[24]

Where women have resisted the role of carer altogether, they have been punished and castigated. Many of the women who were burnt as witches during the fifteenth and sixteenth centuries had challenged social convention simply by remaining single, and therefore relatively independent. They were not hidebound to the same extent as other women by the ceaseless job of caring for men and children and, though they would very likely have paid a price in terms of poverty and loneliness, they nevertheless enjoyed a degree of autonomy that other women did not. However, by resisting the role of carer that society ordained for them, they were labelled eccentric and during the height of the witch hunts even mild eccentricity indicated wickedness. A woman out alone after dark was off to meet the devil. A woman stirring a pot of something late at night was casting spells. Any mishap could be easily laid at her door, and with no husband, child or parent to serve as an alibi, who could defend her against such charges? A respectable but slightly maverick individual could be transformed into the scapegoat for a community's petty grievances. The extraordinary phenomenon of the witch hunts can be seen, from this perspective, as collective social punishment of women who refused to conform, a punishment meted out in many cases by other women.

In contemporary society, the preassigned role of carer determines much of what women do with their time by directing them towards certain kinds of work and leisure. The ability to override the dictates of self in favour of the requirements of others is a fundamental prerequisite of the caring role. A pattern of heightened awareness and responsiveness to external cues, combined with the suppression of internal cues, is encouraged in girls, but not boys, from a young age. While boys tend to play games that develop motor skills, provide organisational skills and involve competition with others, girls tend to play games that teach sensitivity, consideration and empathy. By the age of three, these differences are clearly noticeable, with boys more likely to play active and aggressive games, with more hitting and pushing, while girls are more likely to be found having pretend tea-parties, brushing each other's hair, playing with dolls and dressing up.[25] Nancy Chadorow has said that 'In any given society, feminine personality comes to define itself in relation and connection to other people more than masculine identity does.'[26] This pattern or tendency has been termed 'otheration'. It stands in direct contrast to play, which is about responding to one's own impulses and instincts, rather than denying them.

Elizabeth, a full-time housewife in her mid-fifties, came on the Play Day because she was searching for ways to let go of a lifetime of caring.

> I married young and had my family young, and from then on I never did anything for myself. I always did whatever my husband or my three children wanted me to do. Even now the children are grown up, I still drop everything if ever they need me. I immediately put myself on one side to help them. It's taken me fifty-six years to feel that I'm worth something in my own right, and I still can't really tend to myself until everyone else is taken care of. The best times of day are still when no one else might need me – at midnight, or very early in the morning. But I am changing. I'm fighting for my time now, taking myself seriously enough to play. On Monday, for instance, I took the day off and spent it with a friend. That's unheard of! The other day I was talking to a friend on the telephone, and my husband came in and said, 'I've got a very important call I'm waiting for, can you get off the phone?' 'No,' I replied, 'I've got a very important life to lead on this phone, so you'll have to wait.'

Play starts with and celebrates the self. In being made to care, women are being denied access to play; as a result of the caring they do, they are losing – in many cases, *have lost* – the ability to play, with all its attendant benefits.

Responsible Girls And Big Strong Boys

At the heart of the imperative of service is the habit of taking responsibility, a habit instilled in girls from an early age, certainly long before adolescence. Without a well-developed sense of responsibility, women would be much less inclined to take on the all-pleasing, all-helping, all-caring role that they do; as it is, pleasing, helping and caring are socially acceptable ways of expressing this underlying habit of responsibility. Once again, however, it is a 'skill' that curbs the impulse to play, making women overly sensitive to the requirements of the people around them and less inclined to respond to their own needs and interests.

One of the recurring themes of my own childhood was the teacher's request for 'responsible girls' and 'big strong boys'. How come, I wondered, it was always the boys who got to shift the tables and chairs, while we girls were being sent off to the staff-room bearing slips of carefully folded paper between earnest fingers? Shifting furniture looked much more fun and made a lot more noise; bearing messages was boring. It was the same in the Brownies: you earned your badges by taking mother a cup of tea in bed on Sunday morning or by ironing the tea-towels. As a Scout, you got to learn Morse code and make camp-fires – or so it seemed to me, and I knew which I preferred.

Looking back, I can see how little time was wasted in loading us girls with responsibilities. However light the early loads were, we were being trained up for greater things – responsibility for children, for husbands, for elderly parents, for lonely neighbours. Long before we would have actual responsibilities, we were being trained to have a *sense* of responsibility. We were learning to gauge others' needs, to gain our sense of self-worth through helping other people. We were learning these things not only from our parents and teachers, but from a complex and pervasive web of overt and covert messages, coming at us from every quarter.

When American psychologist Carol Gilligan and her colleagues interviewed teenage girls at the Emma Willard School in America in the early 1980s, the word 'responsible' cropped up regularly. Asked about the sort of woman they admired and sought to become, all thirty of the girls interviewed by Janet Mendelsohn included 'responsible' in their list of key attributes.[27] As well as being responsible for themselves, the girls anticipated that one of their key responsibilities in the future would be combining family and work. Becoming and being responsible was intricately bound up with how these girls perceived womanhood. They did not equate responsibility with the subjugation of their own needs, but rather with the acquisition of personal influence. Responsibility was not usually seen as a burden, but as 'the glue that holds the pleasurable aspects of life together'.[28] Several of the researchers on the Emma Willard project were keen to emphasise the positive construction that the girls themselves placed on the notion of responsibility for others. However, in the context of the other qualities the girls valued and to which they aspired, this looks suspiciously like plastering over unsightly cracks since, alongside responsibility, the girls repeatedly emphasised self-control, independence and self-sufficiency as important and admirable attributes. Becoming a woman was seen by these girls as a process of simultaneously reining in their own needs and reaching out to encompass other people's.

Reading the collection of articles that came out of Gilligan's research project, I was continually struck by how much these girls – all middle-class, sheltered and privileged – expected of themselves. The majority seemed to accept, or at least not to foresee any difficulties with, the prospect of entering an adult society that would make little provision for their own needs. Indeed, remarkably few of them seemed to envisage *having* any particular needs of their own, and combined this startling oversight with considerable naivety about what 'being responsible' would actually entail. Only a small minority of the girls consciously articulated anxieties about what becoming a woman might mean for them personally. For the most part, they were earnestly, eagerly, uncritically preparing for the role of superwoman: she who would understand, anticipate and fulfil the needs of everyone else, without having any of her own. Teenage girls in London, interviewed by psychologist Sue Lees, were more realistic: while they too anticipated a future that would allow little space for their own needs, they nevertheless were able to foresee that this might be a problem. Many of them talked of wanting to 'live their own life' before getting married and having children.[29]

While *actual* responsibilities fill up time that might otherwise be available for play, the *sense* of responsibility that women feel so keenly engenders a state of mind which is inherently inimical to play. Responsibility is essentially referential, but play is the act of justifying and celebrating one's existence *without* reference to other people. It may involve other people, as in the case of a team sport or a game, but it is not fundamentally about those other people, it is about *you*.

They are simply your co-players, they facilitate your pleasure, *not* the other way round. Playing in an orchestra can be profoundly fulfilling even when you have little personally in common with the other musicians. Angela, a 30-year-old woman who describes ballroom dancing as her favourite form of play, is not friends with any of the people she dances with for several hours a week – 'we have absolutely nothing in common apart from ballroom dancing' – but her immense enjoyment is not in the least diminished by that.

Angela is single and childless; her responsibilities are comparatively few, and she has little trouble listing several ways in which she plays: dancing, walking, going to the cinema. For women with partners, and particularly those with children, daily responsibilities for others, combined with the engrained habit of feeling responsible, create genuine practical and psychological obstacles to play. Recognising how this habit of responsibility robs us of both the ability and the opportunity to play is one of the first crucial steps towards reclaiming some play time for ourselves.

You Were Made For Loving Me, Baby

The habit of taking responsibility looms especially large in women's personal relationships. So often it is the needs and expectations of children, partners and parents that limit play in a woman's life. Almost unthinkingly, we take on responsibility for the day-to-day running of the lives of our loved ones. You know where his wallet is, even when he does not (and he *relies* on you knowing); you make sure your daughter's games kit is clean on a Wednesday morning and your son's recorder is in his school bag on a Friday. 'I can hardly leave the house for an hour without issuing my partner with a long list of instructions, covering everything from how many nappies and bottles the baby will need, to what time the meter man's expected,' says Jenny, harassed mother of fourteen-month-old Freddie.

Equal parenting remains an ideal, rather than a reality. Children are still seen as primarily the responsibility of the woman, at all levels of society. Even when a woman has the financial resources to employ someone else (invariably another woman) to do this work for her, it remains her responsibility.[30] In upper-class families, the appointing and overseeing of nannies has always been seen as part of the wife's housekeeping duties. Amongst middle-class couples, even where both the man and woman are in paid employment, childcare may to some extent be shared, but responsibility for it nearly always remains with the woman; it is she who places the advertisement, phones agencies, interviews potential minders, investigates local nurseries and crèches. And when these arrangements fall through, as they frequently do, it is usually the woman who takes time off from her work to fill in.[31]

Even women without responsibilities for children will often have their free time restricted by responsibility for others. Grown men can be as constraining as small children in this respect. One woman, reflecting on this, described how her mother's occasional days off are still bound by responsibilities: 'The only time she really gets some time to herself is when my father goes off to play golf for the day. But even then she has to get up at the crack of dawn to cook his breakfast and make up a packed lunch for him. And she has to be there when he gets back to run him a bath and make him some supper. And then there's all his clothes to wash. It's not much fun for her.' A retired man whom I interviewed a few years ago complained bitterly about having his aged in-laws to stay at Christmas. By his own admission, his wife would be taking time off work to look after them, but he was nevertheless cross that they were going to be there at all, spoiling his holiday. I could not help thinking how much more of a burden it was likely to be for his wife, who seemed set to get no holiday at all.

Wherever there are other people around with competing needs, it will be hard for a woman to take time for herself. 'It drives me mad,' one woman said, after her accountant husband retired. 'I'm used to just grabbing a sandwich at lunchtime and getting on with whatever I'm doing. Now Peter's retired, I'm expected to make a proper meal. He comes down to the kitchen looking expectant, and waits for me to produce something. He's been spoiled by forty years of canteen lunches, and it's driving me berserk. It's such a waste of my time. I don't even want to eat at that time of day, but on the dot of one o'clock, there he is!'

Helen, a 22-year-old language student in Glasgow, feels she is to blame for not putting her own play needs first, and is exasperated by her inability to do so. 'I nearly always wait for my boyfriend to decide what he wants to do in the evening before deciding what I'll do. It's such an engrained thing. If he's gone out with friends, then I might do something with my friends, but I almost never go out on my own if that means he'll be left at home by himself.'

Sheila, a retired school teacher in her early fifties, describes how her leisure has been affected by her husband being made redundant:

> When we were first married, he was [out] every day, so that I did things in those times. Since he was made redundant, apart from his golf, he is around, if you know what I mean. That sounds an

> awful thing to say, because, you know, I love doing things with him, but it means I must plan what I want to do around what he's doing, because that's only fair. There are problems sometimes over how much time I spend at [the local hospice], or helping with various church activities which I enjoy. I've got a number of friends round about and I like seeing them, but, as I say, I don't go round to their houses or invite them over for coffee or lunch in the way that I would perhaps if he wasn't at home all the time.[32]

Sheila's situation is typical in many ways: not only does her husband make it difficult for her to see friends at home, he also discourages her from going out to the places where she could meet them away from the home. Theirs is not an unhappy marriage. She is not an unduly submissive wife, nor he an unkind or overbearing husband. Nevertheless, in a variety of subtle and not-so-subtle ways, he makes it clear that her first responsibility is to him. Particularly telling is her throw-away remark, 'because that's only fair'. It may be normal for women to fit their leisure around other people's. It is anything but fair.

We also take responsibility for our loved ones' relationships with *their* loved ones. Who is it who remembers his mother's wedding anniversary, his sister's birthday, his friend's important job interview? A 1992 survey by the National Council of Women of Great Britain, found that 88 per cent of women take the main responsibility for maintaining contact with family, friends and neighbours.[33] In many sections of society, it is still the woman who is expected to write thank-you letters, and even in the most enlightened couples, the woman is often the unofficial social secretary, the one responsible for developing and nurturing friendships and relationships. Emily, 41, resents but accepts this responsibility. 'I'm the one who reminds Adrian to ring his mother. I'm the one who suggests he ought to see his friends. If people want to come and stay, or ring to invite us out, Adrian just hands the phone to me, or tells them I'll call when I get in. We have a joint diary, but I'm the only one who ever looks in it or writes in it. I honestly think if I didn't make arrangements to see friends and relations, we'd never see anyone.'

As if all that were not enough, we also take on the responsibility for the *well-being* of our relationships. Time with friends is often seen by women as a chance to sort out problems in their relationships with men; men, on the other hand, tend to see time with friends as 'time off' from relationships, time to talk about everything but personal difficulties. Their concept of responsibility in and for a relationship is quite different from that of their partner, more related to what they bring in than what they put in, more related to what they get out than what they sort out.[34]

Pauline Naber's study of working-class woman in Britain found that time spent 'having fun' with friends dropped off dramatically after marrying or moving in with a partner. Friendships were quickly reduced to shopping trips or talking on the telephone, and much of that time was spent sorting out difficulties in their relationships, rather than actually enjoying themselves.[35] This is a tendency that cuts across class. Thirty-five-year-old Maria, a solicitor, is married with a three-year-old son.

> Last weekend, my best friend and I decided we wanted some time alone together, just looking round the shops and having fun. So we left the children with our husbands and set off, but the whole time we were away all we talked about was our children and our husbands. It was ridiculous. Even though we weren't with them, we were thinking about them, about their various problems at school, at work. Every time we changed the subject, it just circled back round to them again. By the time we got back, I wasn't at all pleased to see John or Alex, I just felt cross with them for having dominated my precious morning off.

With one eye on the other person's enjoyment, women are constantly diverted from their own. From adolescence on, women tend to fit their leisure needs around those of their partner, modifying and adapting their preferences to his. This often means spending free time doing things they simply do not find very enjoyable. Relinquishing this sense of responsibility is extremely difficult. Not only is no one else leaping forward to take those responsibilities from us – as the figures on who does what around the house make only too clear – but play time itself is often not seen as something a woman is entitled to, but something she must fit around her responsibilities for others. She must be seen to deserve what play time she takes, and, frequently, she must negotiate for it. Doing so may well rouse hostility and disapproval from her children, her partner, other women, and even her own mother. There are also those disapproving inner voices to contend with. A friend of mine looks after her son full-time apart from the one morning a week when she employs a childminder so that she can go out for a swim and afterwards sit in a café and read the paper from cover to cover. She takes this time for herself, but still feels faintly guilty as she does so. One morning a week! Yet, for so many women, even that would seem an impossible indulgence. And, for as many again, it actually *would* be an impossible indulgence.

Beyond The Service Sector

In reality, in all sorts of ways, we *are* bound to the imperative of service. Like it or not, you simply do not have the option of lying on a beach reading a good book when your three-year-old is heading off into the waves; you simply cannot put off shopping until tomorrow if that means your elderly, house-bound mother will have nothing to eat tonight. We cannot turn our backs on others who need, and have a right to expect, our help, by dint of their youth or age or helplessness. We cannot, as a matter of fact, play when and how we want. But nor should we accept the role of servicer, provider and carer unquestioningly. Instead, we can aim for a playful attitude which allows us at the very least to take those opportunities to play when they do arise. And, at best, this playful attitude may show us how many opportunities for play do exist in the midst of our responsibilities for others.

The imperative of service makes it hard for a woman to take her own needs seriously enough to put them before the needs of others. This applies whether we are talking about our need for decent education, for equal job opportunities, for fulfilling sex, or for proper leisure and genuine play. Women know they are losing out somewhere along the line, yet the tendency to ignore our own needs in order to meet the needs of others is so engrained that many of us still tolerate an extraordinary degree of imbalance in this respect.

We carry the imperative of service with us at all times, we wear it like a second skin. If, increasingly, we are aware of how restricting it is, we still feel strangely lightheaded, uncomfortable, even guilty, when, for a moment, we dare to shrug it off. The implications of the imperative of service for play are wide-reaching: how can we respond to our own needs when we are so finely tuned to the needs of the people around us? How can we find time to respond to our own needs when there is no time left over? How can we ignore the disparaging, critical voices that we have been trained always before to listen to? Even when we sincerely wish to recognise our own needs, we scarcely know what they are, so bound up are they with the needs of others. Even when we do make a start on responding to our own needs, there are considerable internal obstacles of uncertainty and guilt to be overcome.

The imperative of service is like the wall of a dam, holding back the waters of our needs; behind its rigid strength, the inner conflict builds up. Orbach and others have identified this inner conflict in their work on the symbolic meaning of eating disorders, which, as Orbach has said, reveal 'an internal struggle between restraint and entitlement, between desire and denial, between appetite and negation, between yearning and restriction, between wanting and inhibition, between freedom and enslavement, between private and public'.[36] It would be naive to expect to avoid altogether the complexities and ambiguities of adulthood. Compromise is an integral part of the package. Life, we inevitably learn as we get older, is not about choosing between black and white, but about distinguishing between different shades of grey. It is about learning to navigate a route through irreconcilable entities, both in the world around us and the world within ourselves. But, for women, 'compromise' too often means capitulation, the 'internal struggle' which Orbach describes too often leads to self-sacrifice.

The problem is by no means an insignificant one.

The imperative of service imposes a considerable strain on women; accommodating others and adjusting constantly to their needs, verbally, physically or emotionally, *is* taking its toll. 'I just want some time to be myself', 'I'd like ten minutes in the day when I don't have to think about anyone else', 'Sometimes I lock myself in the bathroom, just for some peace and quiet', 'What I'd like is a room, some corner of the house, where I know no one will disturb me' – phrases like these crop up again and again in women's conversations, regardless of class or age, articulating a deep and unfulfilled need for sacrosanct space and time, somewhere to be able to sink into oneself, lose for a moment the pressing awareness of others that seems to be the inescapable condition of a woman's existence, and experience once again the pleasure of self-absorption, self-sufficiency, self-fulfilment. Play could meet these unfulfilled needs, ease this barely articulated dissatisfaction, at a stroke.

Play provides a vital means of bridging the gap between these polarised states of being. Through playing, we can experience the pleasures of self, we can explore and redefine our boundaries, we can taste the forbidden fruit without fear of reprieve, we can rediscover the delight of self-absorption. Play, uniquely, offers us a realm in which reality can be safely tested, rearranged, even rejected; it both leads away from reality and feeds back into it. It offers precisely the experience of selfness (as distinct from either self*ish*ness or self*less*ness) that so many of us crave. Deprived of play, whether by internal or external codes of behaviour, we find ourselves deprived of an invaluable way of reconciling dissonant aspects of ourselves, left only with brittle choices.

Play puts the player at the centre of the universe. It is a way of saying 'I exist! I have the right to enjoy the sensation of existing! I am fully in the world and of the world! I am entitled to be here!' For women, whose sense of entitlement to exist is so bound up with enhancing other people's existence, play offers not only a source of vital self-affirmation, but also a way of redressing the balance in their lives. There is undeniably an element of self-centredness in play that may make many of us feel uncomfortable for it goes against the grain of our conditioning, but for precisely that reason it has the capacity to mitigate many of the malign effects of our conditioning.

So far, 'progress' as applied to women has too often meant increasing women's responsibilities, rather than reducing them. Perhaps we have accepted this as the price we somehow have to pay for a little independence, some money in our pocket, the right to buy a house, the right not to be raped by our husbands; perhaps it expiates some of the guilt we may feel, however unconsciously, as we turn our backs on thousands of years of tradition. But tradition is often the institutionalising of one individual's privilege at the expense of another individual's freedom – think of the Turkish harems, the black slave trade, child-labour in the coal mines. However much it is dressed up as 'natural' or 'inevitable', the tradition that a woman should take responsibility for the people around her is the enshrining of others' privilege at the expense of her freedom, and one of the most significant freedoms it deprives her of is the freedom to play. If we are serious about progress, serious about overturning outdated and harmful traditions, serious about improving the quality of life for women, then we must be equally serious about our right to be playful.

Real responsibility is not only about responsibility for others; it is about taking responsibility for ourselves. We tend to forget this, as we allow ourselves to be subsumed by the wishes and needs of children, partners, parents and even friends. Maybe we forget our responsibilities to ourselves because it is easier to forget them. It takes considerable effort and determination to stand firm against the great current of other people's needs, with its powerful undertows of social expectation and cultural norms. Yet being subsumed in this way is an abdication of our responsibility to ourselves. Remembering how it is crucial to take the initiative for our own happiness is the major step towards rediscovering our playful self.

7

Eve's Legacy

'Men look at women,
women watch themselves
being looked at.'
(John Berger, *Ways of Seeing*)

When Eve succumbed to her curiosity and plucked the apple from the Tree of Knowledge, she could never have guessed how high the price for doing so was going to be. The Book of Genesis relates how, in the very moment of eating the apple, she and Adam were suddenly ashamed of their nakedness and quickly made loincloths out of fig leaves in order to cover themselves. God, who is taking an evening stroll round the Garden, finds them lurking nervously in the undergrowth and realises what has happened. The disgraced pair are promptly despatched from Eden. Pausing only to receive a few curses and some warm clothes, they are banished for ever from earthly paradise.

The price Eve paid for momentarily indulging her curiosity was a lifetime of self-consciousness. It is a price that women all over the world have been paying ever since. Adam was also afflicted with self-consciousness after eating the apple, but that is the last we hear about it; for the daughters of Eve, however, self-consciousness became a condition of existence. Centuries of misogyny reinforced the message that women were weak-willed and easily tempted, that they should watch themselves, and be carefully watched over, lest they go the way of their fore-mother. St Clement of Alexandria claimed in AD 190 that 'Every woman should be filled with shame by the thought that she is a woman.' St Ignatius Loyola, founder of the Jesuit Order, declared in 1548, 'The spiritual direction of just three women is a task more arduous than the administration of an entire Order.' And while women have persistently attracted critical attention for their spiritual failings, their bodies have been subjected to even closer scrutiny.

Even when the aesthetic beauty of women is praised, the underlying current of feeling about female physicality has often been hostile. Attitudes towards menstruation and childbirth are in stark contrast to the glorification of women found in poetry and art. Traditionally, the pains of childbirth were considered a punishment that all women had to bear for Eve's transgression. Menstruation, too, became a way of regularly pointing out to women their sinful, contaminated state. Myriad strictures about what menstruating women should and should not do have made countless generations of women painfully self-aware, month in and month out.[1] In Ancient Rome, contact with menstrual blood was thought to turn wine sour, destroy crops, drive dogs mad and kill bees.[2] The Old Testament specifies that a menstruating woman is 'unclean' and instructs men not to have sex at this time of the month, an injunction still obeyed by Orthodox Jews today. In western Europe of the sixteenth century it was thought by many people that children conceived while the woman was menstruating would be born deformed, and a late-sixteenth-century poem by the French poet Quillet refers to the menstrual flow as the 'foul Pollution' that caused such birth defects.[3] The fact that men would not be there were it not for women's bodies has failed to stem the tide of vilification. Perhaps it has even increased its force.

Even when women are described favourably, their presence is still seen as disruptive. Pliny, writing in AD 50, mentions a brilliant female medic, who was so beautiful that she had to lecture from behind a curtain, rather than distract her students; another had to dress as a man to disguise her gender and so be able to get on with her work unhindered.[4] In 1990 the Chief Rabbi Jonathan Sacks explained on BBC Radio 4 that allowing women to sit with the men in synagogue, rather than being seated separately in an upstairs gallery, would put men off their prayers.[5] It is a wonder men ever get anything done with all these distracting women around.

More importantly, what of the women themselves on the receiving end of all this attention? What does it do to one's sense of self to be constantly scrutinised in this way? How is it ever possible to reach the self-absorbed state necessary for play when one is the constant object of other people's, and one's own, regard? Amanda Lear, known chiefly for her eighteen-year love affair with Salvador Dali and her rumoured transsexuality, recently described in a newspaper interview the kind of objectification that is to some extent familiar to most women. Asked about her age, she replied, 'Today I feel about forty-five, yesterday I felt sixty. It is the way I feel people's eyes on me. If I see desire in the eyes of men when I go in the street, then I feel young.

It's like a mirror.' We are so used to being looked at that many of us have come to define ourselves according to how we look, and how we look determines how we feel. A wolf whistle from the guys on the building site may be an annoying intrusion, but it is also a required confirmation of something that we do not even like to admit to ourselves: that we frequently rely on other people's reactions to enforce our sense of self. Whether we like it or not, the fact remains that many of us are chronically, constantly self-conscious.

This is Eve's legacy: the curse of self-consciousness. Together with the imperative of service, it is in direct conflict with the spirit of playfulness and it is a key factor in the disappearance of play from women's lives. By inhibiting spontaneity, and demanding instead a high degree of self-vigilism, self-consciousness diminishes both the ability and the inclination to play.

Here's Looking At You

Women are used to watching themselves being looked at. They are used to being assessed on the basis of their appearance. They are used to the continual awareness of others' scrutiny, but not *so* used to it that they are not bothered by it.

Take the case of the Single Woman Abroad. Waking up in her hotel room on the first morning of her holiday, she looks out of the window at the blue sky above and blue sea below, and is filled with a pleasurable sense of anticipation. She gets dressed and goes downstairs for some breakfast. In the dining room, she is the only person breakfasting alone. She wants to look about the room at the other guests, but does not want to give people the 'wrong message', so she keeps her eyes on her plate instead. Even so, she is aware that the middle-aged man on the other side of the room is watching her. As this is beginning to make her feel uncomfortable, she quickly finishes her coffee and goes back upstairs to her room. In any case, she tells herself, she does not want to waste any time in getting down to the beach. Walking along the promenade a little later, she feels again the sense of freedom and excitement that she experienced earlier that morning. She is looking forward to a lazy day, sunbathing and swimming, shrugging off the tensions of her daily life back home. She is here to enjoy herself. She finds a good spot, not too near the other people, but not too far from them either, and begins to lay out her things: towel, book, sunglasses, sunhat, suntan lotion. She takes off her shorts and T-shirt and settles down for a quiet morning. Mmmm, this is nice, she thinks, as the sun warms her skin and the breeze from the sea cools it again. She begins to drift off into sleep. Ten minutes later, the Single Woman Abroad opens her eyes, aware that someone is moving about near to her. A stranger has placed his towel parallel to hers a few feet away. He is closer than she wants him to be, but she can hardly tell him so. He looks over at her. She is glad she is wearing her sunglasses, so that he cannot tell where she is looking. Feeling rather cross, she closes her eyes and tries to go to sleep again, but she can feel the stranger watching her. The sun is getting hot and she needs to put more lotion on. She sits up and begins to rub sunmilk on her legs and stomach. The man watches.

Most of us know the scene. How many women have not experienced the frustration of being approached or scrutinised by 'friendly' males while trying to sunbathe on a beach or read a book in the park? Sometimes it is appreciated, usually it is irritating, intrusive and strangely demoralising. Even when women are out with a friend or group of friends, the social and sexual freedom that they could, in theory, enjoy is often reduced by this kind of unwanted attention, not to say harassment, from (usually male) strangers, for whom the fact of a woman or group of women being without a male escort is frequently taken as an indication of sexual availability.

Women watch each other too. Ever-mindful of our own appearance, we scrutinise other women to see how *they* look, to check out their shoes, their thighs, their complexion, their hairstyle. We are constantly monitoring our own and other women's appearances to try to see who has got it right, or got it wrong.[6] 'I am never judgemental about how other people dress,' actress Joan Collins recently told *Hello!* 'If Michelle Pfeiffer and Jodie Foster want to go around in a sack, that's for them to decide.'

It is not just Joan Collins making it clear to us that appearance matters. Images on every side tell us how we should look, behave and respond. For every pornographic magazine implying that we are not sexy enough (or why would men need to read them?), there is a diet magazine telling us we are not slim enough. Immaculate models gaze out at us from billboards, magazines and TV ads, presenting us with a physical ideal to which we are encouraged to aspire; page-three pin-ups present a very different but just as powerful image for us to try and match up to. And we *do* try, oh *boy*, do we try! Thousands of women throughout the western world slavishly follow miracle diets, obsessively memorise calorie counts, closely monitor their weight and shape, are made jubilant by irrelevant weight losses, made wretched by minuscule gains. According to one estimate, half the adult females in the US are dieting at any one time. In the UK, a recent study has found that 1 in 4 women aged between 16 and 35 are on strict diets, while 50 per cent of women exercise regularly to control their weight or shape; 7 per cent have a significant eating disorder, such as bulimia or anorexia.[7]

From infancy girls learn that attention is focused on tidy eating, pretty clothes and hair. A girl is more likely than a boy to be praised for her appearance and, in some countries, girls as young as three or four years old are entered for beauty contests.[8] By the time they reach adolescence, girls are more critical of their bodies than boys, and more likely to overestimate their size: an American study found that by the age of 13, 80 per cent of girls had tried to lose weight, compared with 10 per cent of boys.[9]

Millions of adult women feel anxious, ashamed and despairing of their bodies, despite the fact that the much-paraded models comprise the minutest percentage of the female population. Go into any changing room in any public baths or clothes shop in the country and the reality of the female form is almost shocking in how little it resembles the ubiquitous images of femaleness. Hips, breast, thighs, stomachs do things you would never imagine in a month of women's magazines; they hang out, droop down, flop, bulge and burgeon – *that* is what real live women's bodies are like. But we forget. Even women without a 'weight problem' are seldom entirely free from the burden of physical self-consciousness. The way we dress, the way we do our hair, the make-up we put on (or don't), all these private decisions transform us into public property. And what is more they are treated as matters for public discussion: 'Why don't you wear high heels?', 'I prefer you with your hair down', 'That colour doesn't suit you at all.' Where women have rejected the party line, chucked away their depilatory creams, trashed the bathroom scales and donned clothes for comfort, they have simply attracted more attention still, from the much-maligned women at Greenham Common to the (Armani) be-sacked Mss Pfeiffer and Foster.

Mirror Mirror On The Wall

In *Snow White and the Seven Dwarfs*, the unselfconscious beauty of Snow White – so beautiful she does not need to think about it – is set against the obsessive self-regard of the Wicked Queen. We see her watching herself, and know that however beautiful she may appear she will never be truly beautiful, for her wickedness renders her morally ugly. This association of ugliness and wickedness is standard fare in fairy tales, the message being that reprieve from the torment of self-consciousness is only for the superlatively good, while the rest of us must just hope that if we are good enough, we may also become beautiful. Most of us, like the Wicked Queen, are prey to anxieties about appearance, most of us seek confirming reflections of ourselves, most of us know what it is like to experience ourselves from the outside in, instead of the inside out. We are watched and we watch ourselves.

The requisite of self-consciousness makes it hard for women to feel at ease in their own physical space, whether on a towel on a beach, at a table in a restaurant, or even inside their own bodies. On the Play Day, the problem of self-consciousness was a recurring theme. People talked wistfully of losing themselves in play, forgetting themselves, becoming totally absorbed. According to 38-year-old Beth, 'Play combines spontaneity and unselfconsciousness. It's about taking risks. You have to have faith that you can do it, not be frightened of failing. You have to allow yourself to become fully involved.' Remembering the deep absorption of her childhood play, Elizabeth, 56, commented, 'I could get right away in a fantasy world of my own. I wasn't at all inhibited then.' Ella also mentioned inhibitions as a block on playfulness: 'Being able to play requires trust and a lack of inhibition. I've been quite inhibited by other people's judgements in the past, and that has made it difficult to play.'

Both our appearance and our behaviour are subject to constant though not always overt critique. The Roman poet Ovid advised young women of the day:

> *Don't open the mouth too wide, control those dimples, Keep your*
> *Teeth concealed behind your lips.*
> *Don't split your sides with endless hilarity, but rather*
> *Laugh in a restrained, a ladylike way –*
> *Some women distort their features with lop-sided guffaws, some*
> *Get so cross-eyed with mirth*
> *You'd swear they were weeping. Others utter a harsh unlovely*
> *Braying noise, like a she-ass hitched to the mill.*
>
> (The Art of Love, Book 3, l. 280-290)

Long before Fats Waller was teasingly complaining, 'Can't love yer, cos yer feet's too big', the tale of Cinderella was driving home the message that, without a light tread and a dainty foot, a girl stood little chance of love, happiness and marriage. When the ugly stepsisters fail to squash their huge feet into Cinderella's tiny glass slipper, their wickedness is symbolically revealed along with their unsuitability as marriage partners.[10]

Uncontrolled, noisy, flamboyant, boisterous, expansive activities are on the whole discouraged in women, whatever the context.

Today, at active birth classes round the country, women need to be taught to do what might once have come naturally. All those years of being trained to do the opposite, and now they have to be *told* that it is OK to spread one's legs, grunt, sweat and bellow. They are having to unlearn the physical lessons of an entire lifetime. Scary stuff. Small wonder so many opt for medically unnecessary epidurals and caesareans. 'The whole idea of being so out of control scared and appalled me,' one woman told me. 'I certainly did not want my husband to see me like that.'

Throughout our lives, throughout history, we have been taught that we must not shout, yell, argue, snore, fart, burp, thud or stamp, we must not move our bodies with abandon, we must not roar with laughter, grief or rage; we must eat quietly, move quietly, speak quietly, climax quietly and, afterwards, sleep quietly. We must, above all, *play* quietly. Ballet dancing is deemed better than wrestling; life drawing classes are considered more acceptable than joining a women's rugby team; chatting softly is preferable to loudly debating.

Not that women always subscribe to these normative values. Classes and courses in flamenco, Salsa and Arabic dancing are attracting increasing numbers of women who have had enough of restraints on weight, noise and shape. In sport, the recent fashion to have a female cox of a rowing eight has provided an opportunity for women to raise their voices in a full-bodied shout; boxing and weight-lifting, too, are being taken up by women, though still in very small numbers. Women's attendance at football matches is also on the increase: they now account for one in eight supporters, and one in four spectators at Premier League matches.[11] In 1996, Football Cindy arrived on the shelves in a splendidly lurid pink-and-lime strip, just in time for the European Soccer Championships, a robust indication of the levels of interest in football for the current generation of young girls. In Swansea schools, girls are now playing the game in equal numbers to boys.[12]

These are encouraging signs, but such instances are still the exceptions that prove the rule. Where women do find abandoned, boisterous ways to express themselves, they are usually regarded askance. The Ann Summers party and the outing to the Chippendales may be all the more enjoyable for the censorious curiosity they arouse in others, but generally speaking, if women want to let their hair down, they are still more likely to have a bath than test-drive a vibrator; if they want to raise their voices, they are still more likely to join choirs than cox boats. From the office to the kitchen to the bedroom, we are pursued by what Elaine Showalter calls the 'hectoring spirit', which 'delivers a running critique of [our] appearance and performance',[13] making it difficult to be truly guided by our impulses and instincts, whether we are getting dressed, making love, giving birth or simply having fun.

No wonder that the absorption of genuine play proves for so many of us an elusive goal. No wonder that it can be difficult for women to be really playful in the company of others, when the self-consciousness which accompanies femaleness is so hard to shrug off. No wonder that, while men tend to play in packs, women on the whole prefer more solitary forms of play. When women do play in groups, there has usually been a prior agreement, explicit or implicit, to forget, suspend or override self-consciousness. The exhilaration of the gang of teenage girls setting out for the town centre on a Saturday night has its roots in their sense of defiance: they are out for a good time on their own terms. Older women too enjoy the buzz of an 'evening with the girls', going out for a drink or to a restaurant, and here again the buzz derives in part from the sense of being temporarily unconcerned about other people's opinions, the sense of being able to say and do just what one wants for a while. But if the group can sanction a degree of unselfconsciousness, it is just as likely to do the opposite and monitor behaviour, ensuring that the bounds of acceptable behaviour are not transgressed. It is still often the case that the only time we can truly forget ourselves is when we are by ourselves.

The Unofficial Curfew

The sense of being watched creates in many of us a feeling of physical vulnerability. Even in spaces specifically designated for safe public use, women often feel exposed and afraid. One study showed that two thirds of park users were men; women felt too vulnerable to go to parks alone.[14] Solitary walks, day or night, are a luxury that few women dare allow themselves, despite the fact that for women in particular, time and space to oneself is an infrequent and precious occurrence. Sensational reporting of tragic but rare incidents like the murder on Wimbledon Common of Rachel Nickell, or the savage killing of teenager Naomi Smith, whose battered body was found by her best friend in a local recreation ground in Northamptonshire, augment anxiety about personal safety, without increasing measures to alleviate women's concerns. When the Secretary of State for the Environment John Gummer announced the City Walks in London scheme in 1995, aimed at encouraging people to walk in the city, he seemed to take no account of the fear that already prevents thousands of women from walking through the quieter streets of their towns and cities.[15] No matter that these fears are largely unfounded, that women are far less likely to be attacked by a stranger in the street than by a husband, boyfriend or partner in the privacy of their own home, the threat of attack is still perceived as real enough to keep a significant proportion of women indoors after dark.[16]

The feeling of physical vulnerability and fear of physical attack are the dark faces of the self-consciousness that we all experience daily in our lives. I know for myself the profound frustration of housebound November evenings, wanting nothing more than to get some air, clear my head, be alone for a while. A friend of mine, a man in his late thirties, told me recently how he had found himself unable to sleep one night and, after listening restively for twenty minutes or so to the dawn chorus starting up outside his window, he had decided to get up and walk down to the river near his home. The sky was lightening over the water, birdsong filled the air, the grass was heavy with dew. As he stood quietly on the river bank, absorbing the tranquillity of the dawn, a pair of swans floated by, and a lone grey fox stole out of the undergrowth and crept past him. While I vicariously shared the pleasure of his experience, it was hard not to feel also a tinge of envy, knowing that it was an experience barred to me by a million messages, direct and indirect, which I had received in my life telling me that a woman alone is at risk. However often I have countered these messages by telling myself that the greatest risk is from my own fear, that young white males are more likely to be physically assaulted than women of any age, that the media distorts the prevalence of attacks on women by disproportionate coverage, nevertheless, I am bound by my culture, by its unease and vilification of the woman who refuses to stay home. In the Middle Ages, women who walked alone, lived alone, sought their pleasure alone, were burnt as witches. Today, they are 'asking for it', 'deserve what they get', 'have only themselves to blame'.

We are shocked when Israeli soldiers impose curfews on Palestinian villages or when South African governments impose curfews on Black townships. But the great majority of women in apparently civilised western countries live under unofficial curfew every second of their lives. It impinges on women's working lives (Susie Lamplugh's disappearance while doing her job seemed to highlight the potential dangers of ignoring the curfew); it compounds the practical problems that many women already face in managing their daily lives (who is going to save thirty minutes off the trek home by cutting up the back lane, when a woman was murdered in just such a place only last week?); and, just as importantly, it amounts to a policing of women's freedom to enjoy themselves. The fear of standing and waiting for a bus at eleven o'clock at night; the fear of walking back from the bus stop at half past eleven; the fear of returning to your car in an unlit and deserted car park – these are all real enough considerations for women, who may decide it is easier just to stay at home and catch up on the ironing.

Self-consciousness directly curtails our ability to play by making a whole range of places off-bounds. The unofficial curfew dictates that we play in places and at times that have been designated 'safe'. Churches, cinemas and swimming pools are OK; nightclubs, pubs, a peaceful wood or a street corner are not. These restrictions are prevalent from adolescence on. While boys can hang around the streets with impunity, girls are far more likely to be censured for doing so, labelled 'slags' and 'tarts', their behaviour interpreted by others as an indication of sexual availability, and similarly, while clubs and pubs are seen as the rightful stamping ground of young men, young women have to pick their venue and their company with care.[17] In her study of the leisure activities of teenage girls, Vivienne Griffiths found that even youth clubs could be considered by parents too 'rough' for their daughters.[18] Those youth clubs which the girls were allowed to attend still tended to give more space to the activities preferred by the boys, such as football, pool, space invaders and table tennis, and the girls frequently found themselves being the audience to the boys' play. Griffiths describes a phenomenon of 'seasonally adjusted leisure', in which many teenage girls were as likely as boys to hang about in the streets in the summer, but were hardly allowed out at all during the winter months.[19]

One reason why bingo has for so long been such a popular activity for women is because it has been considered 'safe': men know where their wives are, and what they are 'up to'. They also know they will be in the company of a great many other women, which both removes the sexual 'risk' of a woman being out alone, and also ensures that there are plenty of witnesses to any untoward behaviour. Women, meanwhile, can enjoy an evening out, without being vexed by suspicious or anxious husbands. When younger women in a working-class community in Leeds began rejecting bingo precisely because of its 'safeness', they confronted the double bind of the unofficial curfew. Perceiving and resenting the element of control in the legitimate activities on offer, they instead preferred to go to discos or the pub, which they saw as allowing a greater degree of freedom. The downside was that precisely because these activities gave more freedom they were also more likely to be frowned upon by their parents.[20] Three million people currently play bingo on a regular basis, 80 per cent of them are women, a figure that reflects both the need for and the curbs on play in women's lives.

To experience daily, as so many of us do, these kinds of constraints on our physical freedom, is necessarily to experience a curtailment of the degree of play that will be possible, a severing from our playful selves. When so many options are automatically ruled out, we are obliged to approach play not with a sense of its expansive capabilities, but mindful of the severe limitations which are its context. In girlhood, our capacity for play is constantly triggering warning bells: you must not play with the gypsies in the wood; you must not get your clothes dirty; you must not stay down at the park alone; you must not go out after dark. In adulthood, the messages have modulated to a different key, but it's the same dismal tune: you may not go out if anyone else has need of you; you may not stay out after others are in; you must not wander alone out of doors after dark; you must not go out without first checking it is all right with everyone else. Women who do seek pleasure outside of these culturally determined containers are seen to be stepping over the mark, and society will not be held accountable for the consequences. However lovingly these dictums are expressed, whether they are uttered by internal, external or eternal voices, the outcome is the same: we, and our play, are under surveillance.

Forbidden Fruits

Eve's punishment for eating the forbidden fruit of the Tree of Knowledge was two-sided: she was burdened with self-consciousness, and she learnt the terrible cost of curiosity. Eve's legacy is similarly double-edged: women ever since have not only been plagued by the requisite of self-consciousness, they have also been taught to curb their curiosity. Pandora brought evil into the world by failing to control her curiosity; Lot's wife was turned into a pillar of salt for indulging her curiosity about the fate of Sodom; Bluebeard's wives were killed for wanting to discover the contents of the mysterious locked room they were forbidden to explore (a room which turned out to contain their own punishment for their curiosity). A whole range of limits are imposed on girls' play that teach us that ours is not to reason why. From an early age, we are taught to suppress our desire to explore, doubt our capacity for risk, stifle our longing for more, dread our delight in appetite, and deaden our urge to conquer. Instead, we learn to watch ourselves, and to watch for other people's responses to us.

One of the tragic realities of women's earliest experiences of play is that it is often the very means by which they learn how *not* to play. If little boys often learn through play that the world of feeling and relating is closed to them, the lesson for many little girls is that the world of exploring and inventing is off-bounds. Through play, we learn about ourselves and our world, and we also learn to use play to enact what we have learnt. It is both tutor and mirror to our tutoring. The simple, devastating message which women learn and enact, from childhood on, is that self-consciousness is encouraged and curiosity is discouraged.

Learning To Be Different

One sunny spring morning, a few years ago, in the second century BC amphitheatre of Tlos in rural western Turkey, my husband and I stumbled upon a group of thirty young school children having an on-site history lesson. They sat in five neat rows on the ancient stone seats, their school uniforms forming a block of brilliant blue against the grey stone, listening attentively to their teacher's words. After a while, the lesson came to a close, and the teacher left the children to play for half an hour while he adjourned to the nearby village for a drink. Within moments of his departure, the tidy block of blue had dispersed as all the children ran down into the grassy circle in the centre of the amphitheatre. They soon formed two quite different groups: while the boys chased around in an anarchic fashion, fighting and wrestling each other to the ground, the girls all joined hands in a circle and began to dance and sing. One of the girls, bolder than the rest, moved into the middle of the circle and performed a coquettish sequence, imitating a dance she had seen the older women do perhaps, watching us all the time. The others clearly thought her very daring, giggling behind their hands and looking up at us for our reaction. While the girls were very aware of their audience, frequently glancing up at us and smiling shyly, the boys, in striking contrast, took no notice of us or anyone else, oblivious to everything but their opponent of the moment.

Boys and girls behave differently from infancy. Girl babies eat less, cry less, smile more and sleep more;[21] by the age of three, they are less physically energetic and make less noise than boys;[22] by the time they reach nursery school, little girls make more effort than boys to co-operate, obey and please;[23] by the age of seven, boys are 'more egotistical, enterprising, competitive, aggressive and daring' than girls.[24] But children do not develop in a vacuum. They learn to behave differently because from a very early age they are *treated* differently. Infant girls are handled more gently, fed for less time at each feed, weaned sooner, potty-trained earlier, more frequently discouraged from playing with their food, and more often encouraged to eat tidily and keep clean whilst doing so.[25]

Infant girls are also *perceived* differently. In 1975 a group of British psychologists conducted a now famous experiment that revealed how many assumptions we bring to our interactions with children.[26] A group of adults were given a three-month-old baby to play with for three minutes each while being observed through a two-way mirror. The baby was dressed in a yellow babygro. One third of the adults were told the baby was female, a third were told it was male, a third were not told either way. Clear differences emerged. The adults were more likely to give the child a doll when playing with a 'girl' and a train when playing with a 'boy'. When the baby's gender was not known, the adults guessed on the basis of the boy's firm grip, or the girl's softness. The baby was in fact in all cases a girl.

Pregnant for the first time while writing this book, I was astonished by the regularity with which I was asked, 'And do you know what it is?' No, I didn't, and didn't want to, being much less concerned by its sex than that it should be whole and healthy. But I was very struck by the depth of other people's need to know. It was not only one of the first questions they asked, but also the single most frequently asked question. They badly needed to attach a gender to the baby, even *before* it was born. Without that crucial label, a tidal wave of assumptions and preconceptions was held at bay. Had its sex been known, each hearty kick would have been interpreted as a sign of its glorious future in rugby union, each gentle flutter taken as an indication of its assured fame as a ballerina. I began to feel that as well as providing a safe physical environment for the baby, my womb was providing also a precious gender-free zone in which, for the only time in its life, this child could remain unshackled by its sexual identity.[27]

Gender stereotypes are reinforced by the toys that we give to children, the clothes we dress them in, the way we cut their hair, as well as through the way we respond to different kinds of behaviour. Typically, behaviour that is seen to 'fit' the child's gender is noticed, encouraged and praised, while behaviour that contravenes convention is ignored, discouraged and even punished. Boys are encouraged to show curiosity, aggressiveness and tenacity, but discouraged from behaving in ways that are deemed 'feminine', while girls are encouraged to be compliant, kind and cheerful.[28] Even when boys and girls behave in the *same* way, we interpret it differently. Charlotte, a language teacher in her early thirties, overheard her three-year-old daughter, Lily, playing in her room one morning, and was disturbed by what was taking place: 'I couldn't believe my ears! She was saying to her doll, "If you don't stop that at once I'm going to smack your bottom, you naughty doll!" We've never smacked her, or said anything about smacking to her, and I can't think where she got the idea from. But when I think about it, she's often quite aggressive with her doll. She pretends to drown it, and pulls its hair.'

Charlotte's embarrassment at admitting to her daughter's harsh treatment of her doll reflects the generally held view that this is in some way *unnatural* behaviour in a girl. Yet no one would worry about a boy throwing his Action Man over the banister or plunging it headlong into a pond. They would be more worried, however, were he to start pretending to breast feed it, cuddle it and sing to it. Charlotte's discomfort reveals the strength of our socially conditioned preconceptions about what is appropriate behaviour for girls and boys. When the four-year-old son of friends of mine announced that what he really wanted for Christmas was a ballerina outfit like his best-friend Alice, they found themselves caught between their liberal beliefs and the strength of their own conditioning. 'We just couldn't do it in the end,' admits Sian. 'I was worried about what the other children might say to him. In the end we compromised and bought him a bumble-bee outfit.'

It remains unclear whether there are innate psychological differences between boys and girls, or whether they emerge as a result of socialisation.[29] Nevertheless, while there may be no definitive case for nature or nurture, assumptions about how children should behave and be treated are still based on deeply held convictions about the differences between males and females. Girls and boys *are* treated differently from an early age, and an invidious facet of this differentiation is that children are directed towards different kinds of play, regardless of any innate play-preferences they may have. The power and pervasiveness of gender stereotypes is such that, from a very early age, they are shaping the way we play.[30] Even before the play-impulse in girls is inhibited, it is being carefully channelled and directed.[31] Children as young as three-and-a-half show a preference for sexually stereotyped roles in games, with girls playing wives and mothers and brides, and boys playing fathers, sons and brothers. A small number of the girls may resist conventional sex roles, but boys almost never do: they *want* the male roles![32]

Furthermore, this kind of gendered play appears to be cross-cultural. Health worker Janie Hampton spent twelve weeks observing more than a hundred children at play in rural communities in Zimbabwe. Beyond the age of six, boys were explicitly discouraged from playing 'girls' games and from assuming female roles in acting games: a girl could act the part of the groom in a play-wedding, but boys would never act the part of bride. Hampton also found that boys' and girls' games were of very different *types*. While girls' games centred largely on pretend cooking, feeding, child-care and other domestic activities, the boys were more exploratory in their play. From a young age, they made intricate and ingenious vehicles from bits of wood, wire, tin, string, cardboard and anything else they could find. Their games took them further away from home, and involved a degree of inventiveness and creativity that was largely lacking in the girls' games, which were more based on mimicry of their mothers. While both boys and girls played ball games, the girls were less active and less competitive than the boys; the girls played ball games that encouraged co-operation and co-ordination, the boys' games were more likely to encourage speed, strength and competition. Hampton also found that boys enjoyed a wider *range* of play activities than the girls. As in the west, girls' play and boys' play were valued differently: parents praised creativity in boys and rewarded imitation skills in girls. The mothers in particular took their daughters' play for granted, seeing it as a vocational training. 'Dolls help them to be good mothers,' said one. 'Playing helps children for their futures, especially girls with cooking,' said another. Perhaps the most striking feature of these gender differences in children's play was that from as young an age as four, girls' play contained a great deal of work, both pretend and real, such as cooking, cleaning, and child-care. For example, in three hours of 'play', Sweetie, a little girl of five, spent 73% of her time in pretend cooking, pretend washing and real sweeping. In contrast, boys' activities contained more elements that might genuinely be termed 'play'.[33]

As a direct consequence of the kinds of play we engage in as children, we develop different skills and mental abilities, and certain aspects of our personality take precedence over others. For girls, this usually entails learning to play in ways that are oriented towards self-consciousness, self-restraint, co-operation, obedience and passivity.[34] In a study of nursery school children conducted by Corinne Hutt, a group of 3–5-year-olds were watched as they played with an unusual object. On the basis of their response, the children were categorised into three groups: *non-explorers*, who looked at the object, but did not inspect or investigate it any further; *explorers*, who looked at and investigated the object, but then did little else; and *inventive explorers*, who, after investigating the object, used it in many imaginative ways. Girls were over-represented in the first category of non-explorers by a ratio of three to one, while boys were over-represented in the third category of inventive explorers by a ratio of four to one. A few years later, the researchers re-interviewed the same children, now aged 7–10. They found that although the gender gap had diminished there were still twice as many non-explorer girls as non-explorer boys, and twice as many inventive-explorer boys as girls. The researchers also found that 'inventive play was positively associated with creative and divergent thinking, but particularly so in boys.' Of the five girls who fell into the inventive-explorer category, two were regarded as behaving in a way their parents and teachers considered 'undesirable', in other words, non-conforming.[35]

Children who are encouraged to go that little bit further from their parents' side, to test their physical strength, or sense of balance, or lung capacity, are being allowed to have influence, to affect the world. Through play, they are able to explore and discover the nature and extent of their influence. The child who is repeatedly restrained and curbed in her efforts to explore will gradually lose faith in her ability and sense of entitlement to take an active part in the world about her. Discouraged from experiencing the world at first hand, girls are orientated towards experiencing it through others: in this way, girls are predisposed towards the needs of others. Thus, the requisite of self-consciousness and the imperative of service, sooner or later, join forces in the female psyche. Curbing curiosity on a continuous basis inevitably leads to an impoverishment of an individual's capacity for playfulness, which in turn limits that person's scope for creative self-discovery and self-expression. It is little short of a tragedy that a willingness or a reluctance to explore should be one of the most striking differences between boys' and girls' play.

Undoubtedly, boys are *also* limited by gendered play, but the consequences for girls are particularly restricting and, ultimately, damaging, as the joys of exploration and inquisitiveness are gradually weeded out of girls' play, to be replaced instead by an overarching emphasis on appearance, obedience, relationship and service. Exploration, which is a fundamental aspect of play, becomes increasingly absent from female experience. Self-consciousness, which is perhaps the greatest single inhibitor of play, becomes increasingly present.

The Watershed Years

If our play is girded about by notions of femaleness from infancy, in adolescence the belt is tightened further still as we learn that we must measure up to notions not just of femaleness, but of womanhood. For many women, adolescence is a crisis point, a time when the wealth of their childhood play is eclipsed by the pressing consciousness of the Three B's: Boys, Breasts and Blood. By the time the average girl reaches puberty, she has internalised the fundamental rules from her childhood about which kinds of play are appropriate and which are not. Until adolescence, this has directed girls' play, but it will not usually have violated the girl's sense of entitlement to play itself. Her playful self at this stage is still relatively intact. In adolescence, however, as girls confront all the complexities and contradictions of what adulthood will mean for them, this internalised knowledge about what behaviour is and is not allowed, begins to have an increasingly negative effect on her ability to play, as well as drastically limiting her opportunities to do so. It is deeply ironic that the very activity that could offer freedom from the constraints of gender becomes instead one more way in which gendered behaviour is reinforced.

For some teenage girls, ambivalent feelings about adulthood are acted out in symbolic gestures of revulsion or revolt. 'Unwanted' pregnancy may be a way of speeding the passage through the perilous straits of adolescence; anorexia may be a way of holding off the dreaded moment of embarkation; bulimia may simply be a way of saying that the whole thing makes you sick. For most teenagers, though, the symptoms of distress are less dramatic, but still visible. A substantial body of research indicates that girls tend to develop psychological problems in adolescence; they are more likely than boys to experience depression; they make more disparaging comments about themselves than boys of the same age, and they have a more distorted self-image. Teenage girls interviewed by psychologist Carol Gilligan and her colleagues often prefaced their answers with the phrase 'I don't know', an indication, according to Gilligan, of their diminishing sense of certainty about *themselves*: 'Teenage girls and adult women often seemed to be caught on the horns of a dilemma: was it better to respond to others and abandon themselves, or to respond to themselves and abandon others? The hopelessness of the question marked an impasse in female development.'[36] Gilligan argues that adolescence for girls marks a crisis of realisation that one is stuck between two conflicting truths, 'the psychological truth that relationship implies the presence of both self and other, and the social truth that caring for others requires resources but is associated with economic disadvantage'.[37] A

1991 survey commissioned by the American Association of University Women found that while the majority of nine-year-old girls were confident, assertive and had good self-esteem, less than a third felt that way by the time they reached high school.[38] Psychologist Margo Maine has described this as the shift 'from confidence to confusion, and from self-assertion to self-denial'.[39]

Another American feminist, Christina Hoff Sommers, strongly contested the findings of the AAUW survey in her book, *Who Stole Feminism*. She disputes the AAUW's conclusions on the basis of the survey's own data, and is also highly critical of the conceptual and methodological basis of the survey. Sommers also queries the reliability of Carol Gilligan's research, pointing to its 'anecdotal' nature, and the lack of tabulated data to support its findings.[40] While Sommers's case against Gilligan and the AAUW is cogent and convincing, she does not provide sufficient alternative data to support the case that there is *no* psychological fall-out in adolescence amongst girls and, in view of existing research on gender differences in rates of depression, eating disorders, self-criticism and self-image, it is therefore likely that Gilligan's work, anecdotal or otherwise, nevertheless contains an important general truth about the experience of adolescence for girls.

It is in adolescence, then, that the playful self comes under concerted attack in women's lives. Once again, we see the combined effects of the imperative of service and the requisite of self-consciousness playing their part. Not only does the acute self-consciousness of adolescence take much of the freedom out of girls' play, it also rules out many of the forms of play she might previously have enjoyed. Ann, a housewife in her mid-fifties, vividly described to me the transition from the carefree play of her childhood to a paucity of play in adolescence:

> When I was young we used to go picnicking; we used to build dens out of twigs. I would climb trees, rip my dress, fall in the stream, all sorts of things. As long as we were back for lunch, nobody seemed to bother a lot. The restrictions came in the teenage years, when I had to be in at a certain time. I didn't go out a lot during the week. I didn't have any transport, and the public transport didn't take me where I wanted to go. We used to go dancing at the Regal in Alderly Edge on a Saturday night, but my parents took me and came for me. During the summer I played tennis at the local club, and we'd go to the pictures, but there really wasn't all that much to do.[41]

Compared to the fluency and exuberance with which Ann recalled her childhood play, the hesitancy that creeps into her descriptions of her teenage activities is striking. So too is the contrast between the unbounded, outdoor world of her childhood, and the enclosed spaces in which her teenage play took place: the dance hall, the tennis club, the cinema.

On the Play Day, many of the women recalled their teenage years as a watershed, in which their ability to play had been overwhelmed by growing awareness of the serious and, for some, menacing presence of impending womanhood. They spoke wistfully of 'a time before'. Thirty-eight-year-old Alison summed up the experiences of many when she described what happened to her ability to play during her own teenage years:

> Things definitely changed around puberty for me. Everyone started talking about periods and boys and bras, and all the fun stopped. Suddenly there was nothing to do. You were too young to date, and there was just nothing. A void. And that void was self-consciousness. I remember standing in the playground at the age of eleven, and suddenly feeling self-conscious. Everyone was very competitive about sexual changes. For those who started their periods early, it was a status symbol. It got written up on the blackboard: 'So and so's started!' But becoming a woman was frightening. What is a woman? A mother? Someone responsible and sober? From all sides there were messages that you had to be ladylike and behave in a different way from before. Even the silent messages, the disapproving looks, were clear.

Declining play is not a universal symptom of adolescence. Boys' play may change, but it is altered in form, rather than in quantity or quality: they may swap Meccano kits for car engines, football cards for CD collections, but what they retain, crucially, is a sense of *entitlement* to play. For teenage girls, however, play goes underground in a way that simply has no equivalent amongst boys of similar age, rage and class. Leo Hendry and his colleagues concluded from their study of Scottish teenagers' leisure that in mid-adolescence 'broadly comparable male and female lifestyles were found. By late adolescence, however, our results suggest a much greater differentiation of life-style patterns between the sexes.'[42] While young men maintain a degree of continuity with their childhood play, adolescence for girls often marks a cessation of childhood play. One illustration of this is that girls stop playing with toys sooner than boys. Hendry's study found that among 9–10-year-olds boys and girls played equally with toys, but among 11–12-year-olds girls were significantly less likely to play with toys.[43]

In her account of her teenage years, historian Sheila Rowbotham poignantly recalled 'the me who cried because I couldn't play bar football, who had periods and watched the sun sink, who longed to return to before puberty, splashing through puddles in the mud, who did handstands in the park before men bothered to look at your knickers.'[44]

The enormous physical changes of puberty result in a growing self-consciousness for *both* sexes, with some research showing that young men tend to place *more* emphasis than girls on physical shape and 'looks' generally.[45] But adolescent self-consciousness has very different meanings for boys and girls. The self-consciousness of the average teenage girl tends to be associated with a host of negative emotions ranging from mild ambivalence to intense shame. It has little to do with a sense of growing physical power, sexual possibility or increasing autonomy, as it does for boys. Though boys too are prone to self-doubts and anxieties about their changing appearance, they do not have to contend with the same sense of physical awkwardness, sexual restraint and diminishing freedom. The teenage girl is painfully aware that her breasts bounce when she runs, that her sanitary towel may show when she bends over, that other people may smell her menstrual blood, that her body is attracting sexual attention. Teenage boys often exacerbate a girl's self-consciousness with derogatory comments, jokes and innuendoes about menstruation, sex, and female appearance in general.[46]

Even when boys are not present, girls are still intensely self-aware, as well as highly conscious of how they look in relation to one another, commenting frequently and often critically on the appearance and behaviour of other girls.[47] At the mixed comprehensive school in West Yorkshire which I attended for two years, the most agonised displays of self-consciousness were in the girls' changing rooms after games lessons, where we performed contortionist feats in our attempts to undress, shower, dry ourselves and dress again behind the skimpy shields of the regulation towels. Anything but be seen naked. Fascination and prudery went hand in hand.

While the *need* for play does not diminish in adolescence, for boys or girls, the *prevalence* of play for girls certainly seems to. Self-consciousness is a chief culprit. There is an unselfconsciousness in boys' play, in particular a physical unselfconsciousness, which continues from childhood, throughout adolescence and into adulthood. The same is simply not true of girls.[48] While the concerns and anxieties of the teenage years make genuine playfulness increasingly difficult for girls, the diminution of inclination and opportunity to play simultaneously exacerbates the crisis of confidence and self-esteem that so many girls experience. The degree of self-policing which is required of girls of every class and race makes uninhibited playfulness difficult at best, impossible at worst. The struggle to accommodate the conflicting requirements of parents, teachers, friends and boyfriends leaves many teenage girls with little time or space for responding to their own needs. Psychologist Sue Lees argues that 'Both girls and boys see considerable advantages in being a boy in terms of their greater autonomy, their lack of responsibilities and the double standard of morality.'[49] Lees points out that 'The very concept of adolescence is a masculine construct at odds with femininity as constructed in present society. Girls cannot behave like typical adolescents – moodily, recklessly, selfishly rebellious – without infringing the dictates of femininity.'[50] Even when they conform to these dictates of femininity, girls are still open to criticism, for being old-fashioned, dull and sexually unresponsive. Small wonder then that girls' play tends to go under cover at this stage. With so many places and activities deemed out of bounds, teenage girls spend an increasing proportion of their spare time at home. Visiting and being visited by friends becomes a central part of their leisure activities (as it is also in adulthood for mothers at home with small children). British sociologist Angela McRobbie has termed this the 'bedroom culture', from which boys, adults and unwanted girls are all excluded.[51] This 'bedroom culture' is a way in which girls can create an empowering alternative to the pervading culture that is so disempowering. It is, in other words, a space in which they can be what and how they like.

Nevertheless, most of the time, for most teenage girls, the pressure to behave in a certain way, to conform to a certain look, to respond to others' needs and wishes, combine to restrict the degree of genuine play in their lives. For a great many teenage girls, adolescence is a process of un-learning, of de-knowing, of erasing aspects of the self that seem increasingly inconvenient, uncomfortable and inappropriate. Too often, the ability and impulse to play is the baby that gets thrown out with the bath water.

Reclaiming The Garden

We learn through our earliest experiences of play that boys are the ones who are allowed to explore, test, push back the boundaries, make new things from the old, while girls are the ones who respect limits, maintain order, uphold the status quo. In adulthood, we see these lessons enshrined in the fact that the home, symbol of security and safety (in theory if not in reality), is still the prime responsibility of women, while exploration, invention and genius are still the preserve of men. Women maintain, men challenge. But maintenance is seldom a playful role. It is motivated by caution, rewarded by stasis; it is serious, rooted in the everyday, built upon the needs of others.

Self-consciousness is not always antithetical to play: the artist is self-conscious, the sauntering teenager is self-conscious. Self-consciousness can be a doorway to self-assertion and self-recognition, or it can be a gateway to the prison of self-denial, self-restraint and self-repression. Self-consciousness can be an aspect of playfulness, as anyone who has ever enjoyed dressing up knows well, but it can also make playfulness impossible. By the time we reach adulthood, most women have been socialised in the ways of self-denial, self-restraint and self-repression, in other words, in ways that direct us *away* from play. We have been taught and encouraged to have a view of ourselves as women that is largely incompatible with a view of ourselves as players. Instead, we have learnt that we are to inhibit our impulse and our need to play as we have learnt to inhibit other impulses and needs that are deemed inappropriate. We have learnt that we are to be, in the main, the facilitators of other people's play. From infancy, from the very moment of birth, the imperative of service and the requisite of self-consciousness do the utmost damage to our capacity for play, waging war on the playful self wherever they find it. These two elements take root and flourish at the heart of female identity, to the detriment of genuine play. Adolescence may be the moment when our play reaches crisis point, but the seeds of that crisis have been sown long before, in the pre-fall of pre-pubescence. Like bindweed, these two aspects of female socialisation gradually prevail until, by the time we reach womanhood, their thickening stems and spreading leaves have taken over. So insidiously pervasive are these very elements which stifle what is truly creative in so many of us that they have become culturally enshrined as the identifying signs of femaleness. To seed genuine play into lives, we need to hack back to the very roots of these inner growths that threaten to overwhelm us. Only then will we be in a position to tackle the external pressures and expectations that make play such an elusive aspect of our lives.

8

Man-Made Play

'One half of the world cannot understand the pleasures of the other.'
(Jane Austen, *Emma*)

The playful self is, we have seen, at odds with the social and economic conditions in which many of us currently live. In addition, women must contend with a process of socialisation that leaves them psychologically ill-equipped to play. But a further obstacle to play exists within language itself, within the actual words that we use, and the ways in which those words shape our perceptions of the things they signify. Before we can look at some solutions to our lack of play, we need to consider this linguistic impediment, since it is a key way both in which the playful self is devaluated, and also in which play can be re-admitted into our lives.

Play has been the subject of enquiry for well over two thousand years. Virtually every great writer and thinker in the western cultural tradition has given some thought to the matter: Plato, Erasmus, Montaigne, Shakespeare, Schiller, Rousseau, Blake, Bentham, Dickens, Nietzsche, Freud, Jung, Winnicott – the list is long and impressive, and overwhelmingly *male.* Almost without exception play has been discussed and defined by men. Throughout history, play has come to us through the cipher of male minds, tinted with the hue of male perception, shaped according to male experience, and transmitted through the medium of male language. Play, in other words, has been man-made. Men, of course, need to invent play in their own image and for their own purposes, but women's experiences may be very different. We cannot, and indeed *must* not, assume that they are the same. In the first part of this chapter, we see how the word 'play' has come to be associated with male rather than female activities; how a man-made language inclines us to think 'male' when we think 'play', and how language is often a means of downgrading women's play while giving value to men's play. Of course, language is not only a system for designating play, it is also itself a source of play – the riddler, the joker, the story-teller, all play with language – and so, in the second half of the chapter, we see how language as a play material is often colonised by men, and how women for generations have been given clear 'keep off' signs when it comes to playing with language. But we will also see how women have frequently found ways of circumventing these prohibitions in order to claim their right to verbal playfulness.

Shaping Language, Shaping Play

Over and above the general neglect of the play-concept in contemporary society, discussed in Chapter 4, there has also been a specific shift in the way the word itself is used, how and to whom it is applied.

One of the ways in which female experience of play has been discounted has been the gradual dissociation of the word 'play' from women's activities. Despite its many applications in contemporary western culture, the word 'play' is no longer so readily associated with women as it is with men. The *Oxford English Dictionary* runs to ten pages of definitions of the word 'play', and makes revealing reading. First, it shows how there has been a gradual shift away from the early non-gendered applications of the word.[1] Until the fifteenth century, for example, 'play' could mean 'enjoyment; pleasure; joy; delight', a gender neutral usage now obsolete.[2]

Secondly, while a great many of the current usages of the word 'play' are linked to traditionally male activities, very few relate to specifically female activities. 'Play' may be applied to sport (as in 'to play a game/match/shot'), to racing and hunting (as in 'to make play'), to angling (as in 'to give play to a fish'), to battle (as in 'to play a round of ammunition'), to making music (as in 'to play an instrument'), or to business (as in 'to play the market'). Although all these expressions may apply to women, they are far more commonly associated with activities done by men. One of the few uses of the word 'play' given in the *OED* which does apply specifically to women is the phrase 'to play the harlot/strumpet' – the negative connotations speak for themselves.

The word 'play' sits more easily with male activities than with female ones. No one ever talks of 'playing knitting' or 'playing talking'. But why should running round a muddy field in sub-zero temperatures be 'playing', while sitting in a warm room chatting and laughing with friends be denigrated as 'gossiping'? Football, after all, is no more inherently playful than gossiping; the difference is only in the value attached to it, yet the former commandeers over 300 million square metres of national land, while the latter has none; it must take place where it can – on the telephone, at the school gate, by the coffee machine, over the garden fence.[3] There are 38,571 sports pitches in England, and over 75 per cent are for football and other predominantly male games. Lacrosse, hockey and rounders, the sports most likely to be played by girls and women, account for 25 per cent of playing pitches, but they will be also played by men.[4] Less than 6 per cent of sports space is given to women's events in national newspapers.[5] Even where women play in exactly the *same* way as men, the activity is valued differently. When Christine Spreiter, the UK's top-ranking woman windsurfer, notched up her best result in five years of world cup racing in 1994, the result went unreported. Like Nik Baker, her male equivalent, she came second in her division: his success was celebrated in the press, hers was not mentioned.[6] These examples show how disproportionate is the physical space given to male and female play. The discrepancies in turn embody the relative values attached to these activities. As British sociologist Jennifer Hargreaves points out: 'Gender relations in sport and in sports writing and theorising are examples of the general social patterning of relations between men and women.'[7]

Australian feminist Dale Spender coined the phrase 'man-made language' to describe the way in which the words and phrases we commonly use take male experience as the norm, and thus often devalue and discount female experience. Until very recently collective humanity has been designated by the word 'man', and while on one level we may understand that the meaning of 'man' in this context is in fact 'human being', on another we do indeed see *men*. As Spender has pointed out, the extent to which we 'think male' when we use masculine words is easily demonstrated by substituting the word 'woman' for 'man' in a sentence which then becomes culturally unacceptable or absurd, for example, 'Man is one of the few animals to breastfeed her young.' Using a masculine noun effectively obliterates all those it describes who are not male. Thus the language we use tends to establish a male perspective of reality as the norm; a female perspective, where it differs, is seen as abnormal.[8]

When we use words that evoke corresponding mental images that are male, we employ a language which effectively denies an independent, or distinct, female reality.[9] This applies whether we are talking about women's experience of work, sex, hunger or, indeed, play. When a man writes or talks about play, he tends to assume that the person playing is a *man*; the subject of male-authored play is invariably *male*. (According to the German philosopher Friedrich Nietzsche, the subject of play is always male, for women, being the *plaything*, are necessarily the objects of male play.)[10] A woman reading about play, where the player is male, inevitably feels a degree of disqualification from the activity described: to identify with the player is that much more difficult for her than it would be for a male reader. Once again a clear example of this comes from the sporting world, where the idea of playing football or rugby or cricket is unproblematic as long as it is men and boys who are doing the playing; when women and girls start to trespass on these male playgrounds there is considerable unease because they do not match the preconceived image of the (male) players who accompany these activities in our mind's eye. The quality of the female footballer's game is often ignored by onlookers who can't quite get over the fact that the player is a woman. Commentators, too, can find it hard to concentrate on the game, frequently focusing instead on the femaleness of the players.

By talking always about the play of man or men, women's experience of play has tended to be discounted. Woman's play is relegated to the 'negative semantic space' that Spender describes. This is not particularly surprising: history after all has been largely interpreted through male eyes, from male experience, and for male edification. Recent efforts to open up the reality of history as women have lived it have exposed how insufficient the male-centred view of the past has been. So it is with play: while much of the thinking and writing on the subject has assumed that it encompasses women's experience, its fundamental male bias, both linguistically and historically, has meant that the specific role of play for women has been consistently neglected, and women have no real bank of mental images of themselves playing on which to draw.

Visual images of men and women at play invariably enact the lessons of language, since we 'read' them in the same way we 'read' the messages of the written or spoken word. Films and advertisements frequently reinforce the invisibility of women's play, or else portray it as inappropriate or irrelevant. That said, there *are* films that celebrate playfulness in women. *Passion Fish* and *Fried Green Tomatoes*, both films made by women as well as about them, chart with great tenderness a woman's gradual decision to loosen up, abandon her efforts to please others, and start doing things to please herself. Both these films are located in small, isolated communities; their heroines are physically distanced in some way from the world of men; their central focus is the internal world of and between women.

In *The Piano*, Jane Campion takes this to extremes: her heroine is profoundly isolated through her inability to speak, as well as imprisoned geographically in the swamps of the New Zealand rain forests (the black tree trunks dramatically evoke the bars of a cage). Her silence both frees and traps her, and, as if to escape from and to resolve this contradiction, she plays the piano, furiously, passionately, articulating experiences and feelings that man-made language cannot express. *The Piano* can be read as a metaphor of suppressed play, as much as suppressed sexuality. When her husband discovers her with another man, he vents his fury by cutting off one of her fingers. He attacks directly and symbolically her ability and right to play – physically, sexually, emotionally.

While a spattering of films, such as the three just described, implicitly question the male appropriation of play, popular culture in general tends to emphasise rather than challenge the idea that play is out-of-the-ordinary for women, and liable to lead to trouble. Films that purport to show women playing often carry a warning message to the women watching. *Beaches* chronicles the changing friendship between two women. The heroine, acted by Bette Midler, is constantly seen behaving playfully: she jokes and teases, she dances on the beach, she pulls silly faces. She is also seen as selfish and ambitious. Her commitment to herself is set against her loyalty to her best friend, played by Barbara Hershey. When the best friend discovers she is dying of cancer, the conflicting requirements of self and other are set on a collision course. Her transformation at the end of the film into the selfless mother-substitute for her best friend's little girl is poignant precisely because it is precariously placed alongside her dedication to having a good time. *Heavenly Creatures*, based on a true story, is about two girls whose play spirals out of control as they give free rein to their murderous fantasies. Again, the meta-message is ambiguous. On the one hand, we are seeing that girls are not all 'sugar and spice', that they are capable of malice and destruction; on the other, we are seeing the appalling consequences of girls' play when it breaks free of the conventions that normally bound female behaviour. In *Boys on the Side*, three women travel across America together. At the start of the film, their playfulness is permitted expression, but the plot gradually reels them in towards anguish, grief and death. Even in the much-acclaimed *Thelma and Louise*, the outcome of women's play is shown to be devastation and tragedy; yes, the women successfully cast off the constraints on their lives, but ultimately the price of liberty is death. It is as if we must never be allowed to forget that women are there to care, to endure, to sustain;

however hard they try to shrug off these roles, to let go, to fly, life itself will conspire to bring women back to earth again. Since *Thelma and Louise*, a number of spin-off advertisements have been made which feature young women setting out to have fun. (Interestingly, almost all these adverts are for cars, the traditional symbol of *male* power and freedom.) As with the films, the message is double-edged: the girls get the car and the good time, but always at a cost, which is usually paid by an abandoned boyfriend, humiliated husband or stupefied pump attendant. Let loose, *her-play* is shown to be lethal.

Downgrading Women's Play

Man-made language not only familiarises itself with male forms of play while leaving women's play in a kind of linguistic darkness, it also frames women's play as negative by attaching to it a host of castigating epithets. This verbal onslaught against women's play is particularly pronounced in relation to women playing in groups. From darts tournaments to gentlemen's clubs, opportunities for men to gather in groups for the purposes of play are instituted in the fabric of contemporary society, but the prospect of a group of women getting together in large or even relatively small numbers still gives rise to consternation and disapproval. Women-only events are routinely demeaned, ridiculed and criticised.[11] All-women's sporting events are an especially easy target, treated by many journalists (and spectators) as a bit of a joke: reporting in 1994 on Britain's top women's rugby team, Saracens WRFC, the *Daily Telegraph* gave way to laddish guffawing and comments such as 'when not busily employed trampling opponents under ladylike foot' and 'the only loose-head prop ever to be seen carrying a Gucci shoulder-bag'.[12] Alongside this article was an item about Denise Annett, one of the world's top woman cricketers, which devoted five lines to Annett's sporting achievements, and 42 lines to her quarrel with the Australian Women's Cricket Council over the issue of her sexual orientation.[13] Coverage in *The Times* newspaper of Tracey Edwards and her all-women crew of *Maiden* similarly focused on the women's personal difficulties and differences, confirming the fondly held myth that women are 'bitchy' and 'backbiting' and generally unsuited to teamwork of any kind.[14] It is ironic that in another sphere, the work-place, precisely the opposite myth is invoked: that women are *better* team-workers than men, evidence which is readily seized upon as a justification for promoting women into positions where they are responsible for human management, rather than into positions where they are responsible for creative thinking and planning. In the world of work, too, the playful element is seen as male territory, to be reserved for men. The fact that women's participation in sport is on the increase indicates that women themselves are daring to trespass on this male play territory, thereby offering a very real challenge to the sexism implicit – and not so implicit – in these attitudes. In the forefront of this challenge are the Doncaster Belles, Britain's premier women's football team. Pete Davies's book about the team, *I Lost My Heart to the Belles*, is mercifully free of the usual sniggering asides and put-downs about sportswomen: Davies takes them as seriously as they take themselves, and makes it clear that they fully deserve to be taken seriously. It is not a carefree world that Davies depicts, but alongside the accounts of aching muscles, torn ligaments, missed opportunities and ferocious determination, there is an overwhelming sense of these women defending their right to *play*. As one of the players put it: 'She had work, money, relationships, the back wall of her bathroom so raddled with damp it was falling off into the yard, a wagonload of hassle all week – and she had ninety minutes on a Sunday when she didn't have to think about those things, when she was dead good at what she did, when no one got past her, and it was all she really cared for in the world. She said, "All the problems you have, you don't think about them. So whatever else happens, I have a lovely ninety minutes every week."'[15]

Despite these heartening challenges, the female group, particularly a group directed towards the possibility of play, is still likely to be treated with suspicion, derision or even contempt, and the most effective vehicle for these hostile or contemptuous reactions is often language. A vast array of activities that women experience as play are denigrated through the language associated with those activities. In the 1970s, consciousness-raising groups were frequently greeted with hostility by ruffled men, who responded with angry words of their own, or with resentful silence; in the 1990s, many of the women who flocked to see the Chippendales encountered verbal disparagement from partners; even the harmless Tupperware party has long been the object of mirth.

Before they can get on with enjoying themselves, women of all ages and backgrounds, embarking on all kinds of activities, from an evening course in silk painting to a weekend away with friends, are obliged to overcome, resist and ignore multiple and often extremely subtle messages opposing their play. Sometimes the messages are not even very subtle. In Gilda O'Neill's *A Night Out With the Girls*, there is a moving and very humorous account by one woman of her son's outraged discovery that his aged mother was belly dancing in her spare time, and, worse still, planning to be photographed doing so for the local paper. The woman, who described belly dancing as 'the first good laugh I'd had in ages', was momentarily stopped in her tracks by her son's vehement disapproval. She eventually decided to drop out of the photograph, but resisted her son's pleas that she should stop dancing altogether.[16] Negative words attach themselves to female pleasure like fleas to a dog. Spending time on one's self is called 'vanity', 'fussing', 'selfishness', 'frivolity'. Playing sport is 'butch', 'unfeminine', 'aggressive'. None of these words is applied to these activities when enjoyed by men.

Girls' Talk

Nowhere is the linguistic attack on female play more evident than in the case of women who show an appreciation and enjoyment of talking together. 'Gossiping', 'nattering', 'blathering', 'tittle tattle', 'chin-wagging', 'gassing': these are just some of the words used to describe finding pleasure in talking – if you're female, a point well made by poet Liz Lochhead in her poem, 'Men Talk':

> *Women*
> *Rabbit rabbit rabbit women*
> *Tattle and titter*
> *Women prattle*
> *Women waffle and witter*
>
> *Men Talk. Men Talk . . .*
>
> *Women gossip Women giggle*
> *Women niggle-niggle-niggle*
> *Men Talk . . .*

By labelling women's talk as 'gossip',[17] it is trivialised, and the occasions when women get together to talk are framed as time-wasting.[18] Telephone adverts routinely satirise women's talk, even as they strive to cash in on it.

In this way, women have not only been unaccounted for in the language of play, they have also been actively discouraged from playing with language. This play with and through language may take the form of telling jokes or making people laugh, or it may be the exchanging of news and views, equally it might be writing, having ideas, thinking along free, unfettered lines. The writer Michèle Roberts, for instance, has described writing as a form of play. 'Another definition of writing has to do with play: something I thought women had to give up at puberty in exchange for dedication to the needs of others. Play: making a mess, moulding mud into pies and sculptures, tearing up bits of paper and reassembling them into patterns, mixing water paints and splashing them around, digging for treasure, fishing, exploring unknown places, finding out how things work, exploring the bodies of other children. I enjoy writing tremendously, though it often terrifies me.'[19]

Injunctions on women's word-play are older than the Bible. From Sophocles ('Silence gives the proper grace to women') to St Paul ('Let the woman learn in silence with all subjection') to Shakespeare ('Her voice was ever soft, gentle and low, an excellent thing in woman'), on and on, down the generations, women have been enjoined to leave the talking to men.[20] Early Christian teaching held women's speech directly responsible for man's fall from grace, since it was Eve who conversed with the serpent and was thereby persuaded into eating from the Tree of Knowledge. In medieval art, the serpent is often given a woman's face to emphasise the connection between evil, speech and femaleness. In Orthodox Jewish homes on Friday nights it is still the custom for the husband to recite the *Eshet Chayil* to his wife. Intended as a token of his appreciation, the words are double-edged, admonishing even as they praise:

A woman of worth who can find her,
for she is more precious than rubies.
Her husband trusts her in his heart
and has no loss by it.
Every day of her life
she does him good, not harm . . .
When she speaks, it is with wisdom
and on her tongue is the guidance of love.
She looks after her home with care,
and does not idle away from time.
(from Proverbs 31)

Such a woman deserves praise indeed, but, truly, who *can* find her?

During the witch hunts which spanned Europe and parts of America from the fifteenth to the seventeenth centuries, women's talk was commonly cited as evidence of witchcraft. The witch hunters' bible, *Malleus Maleficarum*, published in 1486, and continuously in print for the next two hundred years (republished as late as 1928 with an astonishingly misogynistic preface by the Reverend Montague Summers), specified women's 'slippery tongues' as 'the third reason' why witches were more likely to be women than men.[21]

In literature, garrulous women have been universally mocked, while happy endings are often predicated on the silencing, or training, of women's tongues. Kate in *The Taming of the Shrew* is 'transformed' from 'an irksome, brawling scold' into a compliant and subservient wife, whose advice to other women is 'place your hands below your husband's foot', and who has learnt that the best way to conduct herself is by quietly agreeing with whatever her husband says, however absurd. Beatrice in *Much Ado About Nothing* is one of Shakespeare's most irrepressibly articulate and witty heroines, and is celebrated for her verbal alacrity, but even she is finally silenced by Benedick with the words 'Peace! I will stop your mouth' and a kiss. It must be said that some of the unkindest portraits of garrulity in literature have been drawn by female authors: Jane Austen's Mrs Bennet in *Pride and Prejudice* and Miss Bates in *Emma* immediately spring to mind. Austen did not spare male garrulity either, of course, nor did she commend the silent woman as highly as some of her contemporaries: Elizabeth Bennet stands out from the crowd as much for her intelligent conversation as her 'lively eye'. What does come through Jane Austen's novels, however, is the message that words are powerful and must be used carefully. Her female characters, even her heroines, frequently do not choose or use them with due care. Emily Brontë's narrator, Nelly Dean, is an interesting character in this respect: her words are a unifying element in the fragmenting world of and around Wuthering Heights, but Dean herself is portrayed as thoughtless and at times cruel; her propensity to talk reflects, and articulates, her lack of sensitivity to the unutterable suffering around her.

In real life as in literature, women have had the play of language withheld from them, through the persistent denigration of their words, spoken or written. In the public sphere, as in the private, women have encountered fierce objections and obstructions to their desire and ability to play with words. When Charlotte Brontë sent the Poet Laureate Robert Southey a collection of her poems in 1837, she was told in response, 'Literature cannot be the business of a woman's life and it ought not to be. The more she is engaged in her proper duties, the less leisure she will have for it. To those duties you have not yet been called. You will then not seek in imagination for excitement.'[22] Brontë eventually got her own back by writing *Jane Eyre*, but Southey's response deterred her from writing for several years. She and her sisters, like their contemporary, Mary Ann Evans, who chose to be known as George Eliot, circumvented male disapproval of female word-play by submitting and publishing their novels under male pseudonyms. Others, like

Fanny Burney, had previously published anonymously.

For every profession in which women have upheld their right to word-play, there has been a popular caricature that demeans their achievement and discourages others from following in their footsteps. Until very recently, the actress was virtually synonymous with the prostitute; certainly she was seen as a woman of lax morals and dubious sexual standards. The female politician and the female philosopher are frequently caricatured as ball-breakers, emasculating their male colleagues, lacking femininity themselves. The female comedian is still regularly stereotyped as a lesbian. When in 1994 the BBC discussion programme 'Question Time' made it official policy to increase its quota of female guests, the response was a media kerfuffle, the sub- and not-so-sub-text of which was that women guests would ruin the programme by being lightweight, boring and uninformed. One newspaper provided readers with a line-up of acceptable female participants, a selection of sassy journalists and politicians, and listed their various pros and cons. This was a somewhat double-edged exercise, for while on the one hand it was a direct challenge to the idea that women would ruin the programme, on the other hand, by offering up women who could hold their own in male-style discourse, it did nothing to challenge the basic premise that the kind of debate on 'Question Time' was rightfully a male arena. The rumpus was short-lived and inconsequential in the broader scheme of things, but it served to reflect the fault-line along which male and female talk is so often divided. It is acceptable (if not necessarily desirable) for women to talk about emotional matters, à la Oprah Winfrey, but intellectual talk still tends to be reserved for men.

Another area of word-play that is frequently 'reserved' for men is funny talk. Women are consistently under-represented on television and radio quiz shows, and particularly on programmes which rely on panellists being funny, for wit, above all, has long been considered a male preserve. Most women will have had the experience of laughing at a man's jokes and then finding their own fall flat. Yet, as Deborah Tannen observes, 'making others laugh gives you a fleeting power over them'. It is not just coincidence that men resist finding women funny. It is a way of saying to women: your experiences, your perspective on life, are irrelevant. Perhaps one reason why comedians like Dawn French and Jennifer Saunders have such a staunch female following is because they say precisely the opposite; they say, loud and clear, your experiences count – the piles you got from giving birth; the arguments you have before a period; the vomit your two-year-old deposited down your new M&S nightie. Your perspective on life, they say, is funny, it is sad, it is real, it is relevant.

Radio programmes like 'Just a Minute' or the 'News Quiz' routinely have all-male panels, which as listeners we take for granted. We barely register the imbalance because it is so normal, it mirrors what we hear and do all the time in our daily lives: make way for men's word-play, put off or keep hidden opportunities for our own. All-female programmes do periodically make an appearance, and they invariably provoke a good deal of attention, usually of the 'But who on earth will want to listen to this?' variety. When a spate of talk shows hosted by women was launched on British television in 1994, the *Guardian* newspaper could not resist sending up the whole lot of them. 'Prepare for an avalanche of confessions, revelations and wall-to-wall peek-a-boo as every national network and most of the regional channels get set to launch talk shows/discussion programmes powered by female-propelled *bonhomie*,' wrote journalist Jan Moir. She reserved a final dig for Germaine Greer, 'who can't be with us today because she's too busy being important but whose producer would like to point out that "The Last Word" is a serious discussion programme where powerful women will debate important topics of the day. (Germaine Kills People Who Don't Take Her Seriously).'[23] Sure, Jan Moir was being playful herself in this article. Print journalism is one area in which women are more able than most to be mistress of their words. Nevertheless, Moir's playfulness in this case should not obscure the fact that mocking women presenters and the programmes they present is an easy and entertaining journalistic gambit, one which effectively contributes to an entrenched bias in favour of men's talk.

Women are discouraged from holding the floor with their words (although they are allowed to do so with their bodies), and they are discouraged from drawing attention to themselves through words. A woman who talks at length and with confidence is often depicted as domineering, self-important, aggressive, or just plain boring. And yet, despite the stereotype of the loquacious woman, research shows that we do not talk as much as men, nor are we listened to as often.[24] Not in public, not in mixed groups, not even in our own families. When Deborah Tannen studied transcripts of taped conversations within families, she found that girls talked less and were listened to less than male family members. They were also interrupted more often. Most girls, it seems, learn to listen, not to be listened to. In meetings at work, women also tend to talk less and be interrupted more.[25]

By casting women's word-play negatively in these various ways, the significance of women's talk as a means of social cohesion, personal connections and psychological support, not to mention enjoyment, is frequently denied. Countering the traditional view of female talk as being frivolous, biological anthropologist Robin Dunbar has argued that gossip may well have been an essential evolutionary development, allowing humans to manage a large number of social relationships, and that women's talk may have taken the lead in this process.[26] Dunbar found that 70 per cent of conversation time in a university refectory was devoted to social relationships and personal experiences. Males tended to talk about their own relationships and experiences while females tended to talk mostly about other people's, 'suggesting that language evolved in the context of social bonding between females'.[27]

Language defines and confines, it demarcates and it restrains, it can be a prison or a route to freedom. Taking ourselves and each other seriously as talkers is therefore very important. Exchange of information, in any context, is about power. One of the most fundamental forms of punishment is to withhold or prohibit speech. Censorship is a devastating political weapon, solitary confinement a form of torture. Even as children, being 'sent to Coventry' is a potent form of battle, as is sulking in adults. The playground counter-taunt 'Sticks and stones may break my bones, but words will never hurt me' expresses a view that few children subscribe to in reality – as everyone knows, the cruel nickname, the relentless teasing, the razor-sharp put-down are words that can wound very deeply. Words are powerful; words that designate names especially so. Ancient Celts considered a person's name synonymous with their soul. Amongst certain tribal people in New South Wales, an individual's name is revealed by a father to his child at the moment of initiation, but known to few others. In Orthodox Judaism, God's name is both unpronounceable and not to be pronounced.[28]

Valuing women's talk is a way of valuing women's experience and perception of the world, for language is the means by which we make our thoughts, and thus ourselves, manifest.[29] The free play of words and thoughts strengthens our sense of reality; it is a way of owning our world.

Rewriting The Play-Script

Both the language of play and the play of language have been monopolised by men. Women's experiences of play have not adequately been accounted for in the words, images and activities associated with play, nor have they enjoyed equal access to language itself as a source of play. By frequently defining play according to a *male* perspective, and by permitting the word to be appropriated to describe predominantly *male* activities, we have created a far-reaching cultural bias that not only favours male play, but also, by extension, male power. In the deep-seated resistance that we have seen exists in relation to women's play in general, and women's word-play in particular, we can detect a resistance to female power. The very act of opposing the pleasure that women derive from the sharing and exchanging of words is implicitly a recognition of the power that resides in that pleasure.

According to French philosopher Luce Irigaray, women's pleasure is 'the greatest threat of all to masculine discourse', for it exists beyond the constraints of a man-made world.[30] Underlying the anxiety which women's play arouses, especially women playing in groups, whether they be playing through words or deeds, is the tacit understanding that play is empowering. To control talk, writes Dale Spender, is to control reality.[31] But to control *play* is to control not only reality, but also supra-reality, the realm of fantasy, imagination, possibility. Somewhere in the murky depths of our consciousness, male and female, is this knowledge.

The appropriation of play by one half of the population has significantly diminished its scope and its capabilities. A predominantly male perspective on play – what it consists of, where it takes place, who does it – is bound to fall short since it consistently fails to take adequate account of the *female* experience of play. Confronting the implications of this bias for women is of prime importance. By having their experiences of play linguistically denigrated, women have themselves been denigrated. It is not that women necessarily need to create an entirely new language, as some commentators would have it, but that we need to be aware of how the play-script has been written, and who has done the writing; we need to become conscious of how language can constrain us, and, equally, conscious of how we can use language to uphold our experiences, rather than deny them. We can object when other people call our talk 'gossip'; alternatively we can invest the word with positive connotations of our own. We can start to override the images of the player-as-male in our own heads and other people's, and tell ourselves that if we want to kick a ball in the park we can do so; we can start to create mental images of the player-as-female, attach positive words to those images, then act out those images for ourselves.

In the same way that we are only just beginning to recognise the need to rethink fundamentally the structure of the labour market and the conditions of employment in order to accommodate women's needs in the work-place, rather than force women to become pseudo men, so, in the realm of play, we need to resist the pressure to adapt ourselves to male models of play, and instead challenge the underlying assumptions about what play is and who is entitled to it. By having their definitions of play denied, women have been denied access to play itself. Conversely, by recognising their own definitions of play, women can start to uphold the value of their own *experiences* of play. By affirming play as they experience it, they can start to uphold the reality of female play. They can start to discover a playful self that is genuinely in line with their experiences and needs. They can start to resurrect a genuinely *female* playful self.

His Play, Her Play

What we need to do now is to recreate play in ways that take account of *women's* experiences. We need to step out of the arc-light of male-defined play into the shadowy realms where women's play is taking place. To do this, we should start by recognising that men's play and women's play are not necessarily the same.

A salient feature of man-made play is that it is inclined to be compartmentalised and regulated; it is often segregated from the other kinds of activity, and often occurs in particular places and particular ways. It is also likely to involve an element of competitiveness. Men's play frequently takes place in a pre-designated space according to pre-designated rules: a playing field, a squash court, a pub. Women's play, on the other hand, is less easily identifiable. It is altogether more informal, running through a woman's day as she sings to her baby, drives to the office, laughs with her friends, walks round the shops. This is how women find time and space for themselves, not in clearly defined chunks, but in a narrow thread shot through the fabric of daily life. We do not usually identify these things as play because of our tendency to subscribe to male definitions of play, but here, as in so many areas, we need to reclaim the validity of our own experiences. While we can derive great enjoyment from 'male' forms of play, the competitive games and battles of wit, will and strength, we also need to redefine play for ourselves, so that we can recognise and value the sources of pleasure that are more specifically 'female' in nature.

If we look for the compartment in our lives where play is meant to be, we may never find it, because women's lives so seldom divide neatly into separate compartments. I sit here at my desk, writing about play, but also thinking about what food there is for my daughter's lunch, about the plates I have to borrow for the party we are having on Sunday, about whether I have enough money to pay the childminder, about the clothes still languishing in the washing machine, about the girlfriend I have not spoken to for a fortnight. There are simply not enough gaps in a woman's day for her to enjoy segregated play on a regular basis. In recapturing the playful self, we need a two-fold approach: we need both to stand up for our need for real time off, for those chunks of time to ourselves, but we need also to cultivate a playful attitude that will enable us to find room for the playful self right in the thick of our daily lives.

Most of us today – men and women – are under pressure to compartmentalise, rationalise, schematise, yet the failure of contemporary society to make this a sustainable way of organising our time has led to more and more of us living with a sense of chaos, stress and pressure as we struggle to keep control. Let us turn our backs on this western, industrial nonsense, and go instead for fusion, unity, coherence. We want balance, let us go for balance; we want to live rounded lives, let us bring play right back into the circle. Instead of accepting man-made play (and feeling dissatisfied because we cannot get enough of it, and when we do, we do not necessarily enjoy it that much), we need to reclaim the significance and importance of *female* play; we need to establish a *woman*-made play. We are in danger of becoming like the foolish father in the fairy tale who spurned his daughter for saying she loved him as much as she loved salt, and only later realised that an ingredient he had barely noticed was the substance that gave flavour to his life. So we need to start noticing and valuing the myriad opportunities for play in our lives – and relishing them!

Playing Against The Odds

Language – male language – has shaped a notion of play that may not adequately take account of women's experiences of play, but that has not completely prevented women from playing. One of the positive effects of the marginalisation of formal opportunities for play in women's lives has been that our innate playfulness has had to come out in other ways. It has, to some extent, thrived on neglect. Even in the most misogynistic societies and during the most repressive periods of history, there are tell-tale signs of women at play: in Akko in Israel, you will see Palestinian women paddling in full purdah on the shores of the Mediterranean. In the west, intrepid women travellers for centuries have been tightening their bonnets, hitching up their skirts and heading off in search of adventure. Asked why she persisted in exposing herself to the dangers of foreign travel, Lady Richmond Brown, writing in the early twentieth century, touched the play-nerve of travel's appeal in her reply: 'The horizon of my vision is broadened and an indefinable something impels me to continue. Some gamble at the tables, others on the race-course, but the greatest of all gambles is with life.'[32] This is the visionary potential of play: it breaks down boundaries, it circumvents barriers, it makes the impossible a possibility.

Where women have been unable to go out to play, they have found ways to do so whilst staying in. Tied to their tapestries, women have encoded their playfulness through the subversive stitch.[33] In Turkey, the Grand Seraglio in Topkapi Palace was, for four hundred years, a gilded cage in which thousands of women were forcibly imprisoned in the Sultan's harem, watched over by eunuch guards, hapless pawns in the schemes and whims of the *valide sultana* (mother of the sultan – a powerful figure in the harem) and the *kizlar agasi* (the chief black eunuch). Yet behind the high walls and locked doors, these hopelessly imprisoned women still found opportunities to play: they swam in the palace pools, played games in the palace gardens, enjoyed massages in the hammam, made love with each other and, where possible, the male guards. Singing and dancing were not just public duties, but precious forms of private pleasure and enjoyment. In the Arab world today, dancing is still a treasured form of self-expression and entertainment, performed by women and for women in the privacy of their homes.[34]

In the western world today, too, women find ways of playing against the odds. Some play rugby; some do ballroom dancing; some paint or draw; some write or sing; others go camping; others still take up paragliding or surfing. For some, it is simply a case of setting aside time to be with friends, and making sure that time is spent enjoyably. Jeanette, 42, has been meeting with a group of friends every Tuesday evening since they first met at ante-natal classes, fifteen years ago. Usually they go to the pub; sometimes they arrange an outing to London or Cheltenham. Jeanette and her friends are aware of the constraints on their play, but have devised ways of circumventing them. 'We do things that the men won't mind or worry about, not clubs or anything, and that way we don't get hassle from them. And we always have fifteen minutes at the start of the evening, when we're allowed a moan about all our problems with our children and our husbands and our health. We call it "surgery time". But that fifteen minutes is *all* we're allowed. After that we've got to get on with enjoying ourselves!'

Wherever women do manage to find time and space for their playful self, the evidence suggests that they benefit from doing so.

The Power Of Word-Play

Nowhere is the infrangibility of women's play more apparent than in the use of language itself. Women may have been discouraged and prevented from playing with language in the public sphere, but in private they have always been closely acquainted with the playfulness of words, and the power associated with word-play.

Women themselves *know* the profound sustenance to be found in talking, whether it involves debating world politics, exchanging information about children, reminiscing about the past, discussing problems at work, or joking about their sex lives. Many women go to great lengths to talk to friends; as well as great pleasure, they derive self-confidence, encouragement and support from their word-play. As 24-year-old Joanna puts it, 'Nothing beats an evening with a group of friends, just chatting about everything under the sun. You go home afterwards feeling great, all warm and buoyed up inside.'

Through their traditional proximity to children, women have always been privy and party to the delight that children instinctively derive from words: discovering them; inventing them; exploring their possibilities. Many of the women on the Play Day recalled with delight the word-play of their childhoods: making pretend magazines, writing stories, inventing clues for treasure trails, putting on plays for their parents. From my own childhood, I remember how the playground rang with the incantation of special words and rhymes, essential to the skipping and clapping games that we all tirelessly played. At home I would annoy my brothers by chatting with my sister in our private language, 'googely', an entirely made up affair, which neither she nor I could understand any better than they. And then there was my extensive stable of imaginary horses, hundreds of them, created chiefly for the pleasure I derived from naming them, each name a carefully selected piece in some complex and enchanting picture in my mind. 'There is no better play material in the world than words,' writes Lucy Sprague Mitchell in her introduction to the *Here and Now Story Book*. 'They surround us, go with us through our work-a-day tasks, their sound is always in our ears, their rhythms on our tongue. Why do we leave it to special occasions and to special people to use these common things as precious play material? Because we are grown-ups and have closed our ears and our eyes that we may not be distracted from our plodding ways!'[35]

Women have never entirely closed their ears to the play of

language. As mothers, grandmothers, nurses and nannies, they have always woven magical worlds from words. Generations of children have been nourished by the wealth of women's word-play in the form of fairy stories and nursery rhymes. The best-known authors of fairy stories in their written form have been men – Charles Perrault (known for one of the earliest collections of fairy stories, *Contes de ma Mère l'Oye* or *Mother Goose Tales*, published in 1697); the Brothers Grimm; Hans Christian Andersen; Oscar Wilde – but a great many of their sources were women. Perrault was influenced by the fashionable ladies of seventeenth-century Paris, several of whom were themselves authors of fairy tales, notably Marie-Jeanne L'Heritier and Marie-Catherine D'Aulnoy. The Brothers Grimm got a great many of their stories from female friends and close relations. One of their key sources was Dorothea Viehmann, an innkeeper's daughter. Oscar Wilde's stories were influenced by the tales which his father, a doctor, took as payment from his poorer patients, and which his mother, Speranza Wilde, then collected. In her extensive study of fairy tales, *From the Beast to the Blonde*, Marina Warner reveals the extent of women's contribution to fairy stories, pointing out that 'although male writers and collectors have dominated the production and dissemination of popular wonder tales, they often pass on women's stories from intimate or domestic milieux'.[36] Even when the stories are written down by men, they are very often narrated by a female story teller, from Scheherazade in the *Arabian Nights*, or the spirited young women who narrate half of the stories in Boccacio's *Decameron*, to Old Mother Goose herself sitting spinning by her fire.[37]

Through fairy stories and nursery rhymes, women have held on to the pleasure of word-play, passing wisdom and warnings down the generations. In many cases, the content of those stories and rhymes celebrates the power that resides in the words of girls and women. Little Red Riding Hood keeps the wolf at bay by repeatedly commenting on his appearance. Even after he has gobbled her up, some versions of the story have the sound of her voice coming out of the wolf's belly alerting a passing huntsman to her whereabouts, upon which he kills the wolf and sets her free. (In an English version of 1840, Red Riding Hood's shrieks bring her father and some other woodcutters to the house before the wolf has managed to eat her.) In the story of *Rumpelstiltskin*, the queen breaks the evil spell by discovering and uttering the dwarf's name. In *Hansel and Gretel*, it is Gretel who outwits the witch with her clever words. In *Blue Beard*, the wife escapes death by getting her sister to call from the castle tower to her brothers, who arrive in the nick of time to save her. In *Beauty and the Beast*, the spell of disfigurement is broken and the Beast's life is saved when Beauty utters her heartfelt words of love.

Marina Warner has observed that 'Fairy tales give women a place from which to speak, but they sometimes speak of speechlessness as a weapon of last resort.'[38] Yet even where the heroine is silent or silenced, the framing of fairy tales as stories told by women allows the tales to enact the power of female word-play. Even when it is men's actions within the tales that bring about the happy ending – the prince's kiss; the brother's sword; the woodman's axe – it is women's words that beget the happy ending, that ensure the princess gets the prince, that the wicked stepmother is exposed, the evil dwarf vanquished. Through the act of speaking, of telling stories, of creating imaginary worlds, of shaping events through narrative, women have laid claim to life. If their stories have tended to reflect reality rather than challenge it, that is because women's experience has more often been of endurance than insurgence.[39] The stories, though not always politically correct, nevertheless reflect and articulate women's experiences. The stock opening and ending of the fairy story – 'once upon a time' and 'happily ever after' – signal to the listener or reader that this is an imaginary world, in which all things are possible, in which impossible things happen.[40] The symbolic act of creating these worlds is more significant than the actual events that occur within them.

Women have found solace and delight in playing with words, not only by telling stories to children, but also by telling stories to each other. Egyptian women living in and around the tombs of the vast, ancient cemetery in central Cairo known as the City of the Dead, gather almost every evening to exchange news and views and to tell stories. The gatherings happen spontaneously towards evening time, when the day's chores are done, but before the men return for their supper. The gatherings can be interrupted and halted by outside happenings at any moment, but whenever time permits it, the dark, crowded room in which they meet becomes a playground for the most extraordinary verbal games. Anthropologist Helen Watson spent a year living with these women, sitting in on their gatherings, recording their stories and interviewing them about their lives. The findings are collected in her remarkable book, *Women of the City of the Dead*. The gatherings are lively occasions:

> The atmosphere is warm and intimate . . . High spirits and revelry have a cumulative, infectious affect on most occasions

> . . . The women swap news and gossip much as they do whenever and wherever they meet, but, unlike doorstep encounters and communal laundry sessions at the water-pump, conversation among women in the curtained-off room is much more informal, unbridled and candid . . . While local news and views form an important and highly significant part of the social content of gatherings, story telling is regarded as the highlight of an evening together. Women often explained that a tale was the perfect end to an entertaining evening . . . As soon as a story teller identifies herself the level of noise in the room falls sharply and everyone gives the speaker full attention. Although the background chatter ceases when a tale begins, there is nothing akin to respectful silence while it is being told. On the contrary, audience participation is expected and delivered with gusto. The women sigh, gasp, exclaim, roar with laughter and make ironical or witty responses to rhetorical questions.[41]

As Helen Watson became more familiar with the community, she began to realise that the stories she was hearing at the evening gatherings were not fictional in the strict sense of the word; the narratives were woven through with details from the lives of real women in the community, so much so that individual women could often be 'matched' to a particular tale. The story tellers, usually the older women, dramatised and universalised everyday experiences, the joys and sorrows, the foibles and virtues of the women themselves. One woman who was unable to have children inspired a story about an empty pot. Another, whose habitual pessimism was a source of great irritation for everyone else, was treated to a story about a foolish beetle who spent all day running round in circles complaining about its lot, not appreciating that life was really quite nice: 'The beetle would shake its head slowly from side to side, "Poor me, poor little me," it would say in its most sympathetic tones. The beetle kept these sweet words of sympathy all for itself, none of the other creatures had heard the beetle address them in this way although many had greater need of kindness and pity.' These stories are both given by and given to the women whose real life stories lie behind them.[42]

The women in the City of the Dead quite literally tell tales about one another, drawing on their intimate knowledge of one another's lives, moving beyond the rules of ordinary discourse that forbid revelation and scrutiny of such knowledge, crafting and shaping the ordinary into the extraordinary, the personal into the universal. The stories celebrate the connection between the specific and the general, the individual and the communal; since forging and maintaining this connection is at the heart of women's everyday work, the stories are a way of celebrating the women themselves. By lifting the everyday into the realm of the eternal, the stories reveal the power of play, and of word-play in particular, to release the individual, to transform her, and to validate her.

Although the lives of these women may appear desperately restricted and arduous to western eyes, they have nevertheless kept alive the liberty that resides, though word-play, in freedom of imagination. 'Customary modesty and demure attitudes get lost in the telling of tales,' Watson writes. 'Bawdy, gaudy images spice each story as a matter of course. Among themselves, behind closed shutters, women can say what they want.'[43] Story telling is recognised as a high form of entertainment, an important and skilful art form, in which real life and imagination become the sources of a joyful interplay – words, ideas and images weave, climb, lure, seduce, provoke and amuse by turn. This is linguistic and creative play at its most sophisticated and most effective.[44]

Although the men in the community routinely interrupt the gatherings and regard them as a waste of time, the women's gatherings play a vital part in sustaining a fragile community; their words and word-play not only boost the confidence and morale of the women themselves, whose lives are often hard and unrewarding, but also weave a fabric of social and personal connections. The gatherings effectively create a community and monitor its progress. It is as if, with their words, these women are weaving a blanket from the pieces of their own lives, which blanket, once woven, they then mend, amend and enlarge.

As novelists, poets, letter writers and diarists, women have clung tenaciously to the freedom that comes through word-play. Julian of Norwich, the medieval mystic, asserted a female experience of Christian faith long before feminist theology appeared on the scene; the poet and historian, Christine de Pisan, who died in 1430, challenged the way women were portrayed in literature through her own writing; Emily Brontë wrote herself out of the restrictions of the nineteenth century (the sense of anarchy that permeates *Wuthering Heights* is still astounding readers at the end of the twentieth); Angela Carter in the 1970s and eighties enshrined female experience in her experimental and innovative prose style; in the nineties, French novelists like Monique Wittig, Hélène Cixous and Michèle Ramond strive to create an *'écriture féminine'* in which the conventions of (male) narrative are resisted and overturned.[45] Above all, as *readers* of other women's words, women have taken delight and refuge in the world of words, whether in the 'right-on' imprints of Virago and the Women's Press, the romantic fiction of Anita Burgh or Celia Brayfield, or the formulaic novelettes offered by Mills and Boon.

Despite the negative images, the belittling comments, the risk of censure, women do play with words. In private, women have always got together to talk, laugh, commiserate. In public, they are an increasing presence as politicians, actors, singers, comedians, chat-show hosts, despite the conventions they have to challenge in order to be so. Women are reclaiming their right to play with words, in earnest and for fun. The number of funny women in public life has grown fast in the last ten years. The lone stars of Mae West ('Is that a gun in your pocket or are you just pleased to see me?'), Marie Lloyd, Lucille Ball and Joyce Grenfell have been succeeded by the veritable constellation of Dawn French, Jennifer Saunders, Joan Rivers, Roseanne Barr, Victoria Wood, Ruby Wax, Vanessa Feltz, Angie Le Mar. Laughing, joking, punning, teasing, quizzing and riddling, are all creative, exhilarating, liberating forms of word-play, ways of expanding, testing and pushing back boundaries. Instead of being tied to how things are, word-play allows one to experiment, to suggest how things *could* be. To live always with certainties is as crippling as to live always with uncertainty. To move between the two, through play, is to experience life as graspable, malleable, a play thing, rather than a yoke. Through words we invent the world; through word-play we reinvent it and ourselves.

Who Plays, Wins

Man-made play is a consequence of the way in which reality has tended to be shaped and upheld through man-made language. A male perspective of reality is taken as the norm, set against which is the other, female, perspective. Where women's experiences differ from the norm, they are seen as deviant, wrong. The norm of female behaviour from the male perspective is for women to be engaged usefully (i.e. to be useful to others) and selflessly. Female play is not the norm according to male reality. It can never have equal status with male play, even where the form of play is identical. By invalidating what women do, man-made language ensures that women themselves are invalidated: their activities have no intrinsic worth, they are of value only to the extent that they serve male reality. This is why it is so vitally important for women to stand up for the validity of their own reality, to take it seriously, to resist invalidation, not to channel all their energy into succeeding within the framework of a male reality.

Play is not just a way of finding relief from oppression, it is a way of subverting it. Dance for the women in Arab cultures is a way of turning the restrictions on their public and physical actions into an opportunity to assert and celebrate their power and physicality behind closed doors. They do so with a confidence and abandon that western women, with all their apparent freedom, do not possess. Through play, women can, and do, challenge and resist male 'truth'. Though the son thinks belly dancing is worthless, the mother knows differently. Though the husband calls her talk gossip, the wife knows otherwise. Though the men say our jokes are not funny, we know they are. Through play, women uphold and exult in their own reality.

Reclaiming the play of language is to use words to account for reality as we experience it, not as we have been led to believe we should experience it. It is to resist thinking of talking as frivolous, and believe what deep down we know, that women's word-play holds the world together. Reclaiming the language of play is to recognise that play speaks, and to let ourselves listen to what it tells us and says about us. 'I can play! I have played!' declared Caitlin, jubilantly, at the end of the Play Day. To recognise that one has played and one can play, as Caitlin did, is to recognise one's ability to rewrite the play-script, to recognise a realm of pleasurable experience that, in the most fundamental way, declares one's right to exist, the validity of one's presence. It is to proclaim: 'I am alive.'

PART THREE

9

Child's Play

'At evening, when the lamp is lit,
Around the fire my parents sit;
They sit at home and talk and sing,
And do not play at anything.'
(R. L. Stevenson, *The Land of Story-books*)

If there are real obstacles to play in the lives of many women today, there are also real ways of challenging, overcoming and circumventing those obstacles. If, as we get older, a combination of internal and external pressures wage war on our play-instinct and severely restrict the opportunities for play, then there are also real incentives to fight back and resist these pressures. Lack of play is a real problem in our lives, but there are also real solutions to this problem. First of all, it is crucial that we remember that almost all of us, at some time in our lives, *have* had experience of play. On the Play Day, Alison spoke for many when she said, 'I used to play all the time as a child – whatever happened to all that playfulness?' For most of us, the playful self will not always have been so marginalised. In childhood, our play may have been directed in gender-appropriate ways, but the full-scale assault on the playful self occurred gradually, gathering pace, as we have seen, in adolescence. It is highly likely, therefore, that all of us have enjoyed some moments of genuine playfulness at some time in our past. Rediscovering this past self who played is a vital first step towards reincorporating a self who plays into our adult lives.

We use the expression 'child's play' to mean that something is easy, that it requires no effort, that it comes as easily as play to a child. Ah! If only we *could* play as effortlessly as children do! As we start putting play back into our lives, the first thing we need to do is to remind ourselves of the untrammelled instinct for play that we possessed as children.

Back To The Future

On the Play Day, many of the exercises were intended as memory joggers, designed to help people to remember and experience once again the wealth of their childhood play. The workshop started with an exercise which Elinor called 'The Photograph'. At first it was hard to see what it had to do with play. All the participants had been asked in advance to bring along a photograph of themselves as very young children, preferably as babies, and the day began with people getting into small groups of two or three and spending ten minutes chatting about the photos they had brought, explaining the background to the picture and talking about the child in the picture. Deceptively simple, this exercise proved an extraordinarily powerful way of giving people access to the world of play with which they had previously been so familiar. This is what some of the women said:

> Alison: 'I found a picture of myself aged about one, with my hands on my head, playing pat-a-cake, pat-a-cake. Looking at and talking about the photo, I had a sense of all the different selves that were in me still, including the me playing aged one. It put me in touch with a side of myself I wouldn't normally feel connected to. It reminded me of a time before stress and responsibility and always worrying about how you look.'

> Beth: 'I've always been told that I was rather withdrawn as a small child, but I found a photograph of myself aged about five months and, when I really looked at it, I found a little spark in my eye. Looking at that photo, there was no doubt in my mind that I knew how to play then, I looked quite a chirpy little baby.'

> Ella: 'When I was in my teens, my mother had a nervous breakdown and destroyed all the photographs of the past, so I've had no visual record of my childhood, but I recently found a suitcase stuffed full of negatives, over 600 of them, and I had the whole lot developed. Amongst them, I found three photographs of me as a young girl. Talking to the others in the group about these photos brought back very powerful memories of that time that I'd completely forgotten. I was quite a tomboy and spent most of the time scampering about building tree-houses and playing Red Indians. When I look back on my childhood, I tend to remember the sad things, the loneliness, my mother's illness, but talking about the photo made it possible for me to focus on the happy memories, it brought alive a period of my life that I'd had no real sense of before.'

Elizabeth: 'I went through my desk drawers the night before and found a picture of myself aged about three, in a little white dress, taken in Scotland just before the war. Looking at the photo brought back a tremendous rush of memories. There was no television and it got dark early in winter, so in the evenings we'd all sit down and do embroidery or sewing, and my aunts, if there were no men around, would make sanitary towels with cotton and gauze. I used to spend a lot of time playing out in the garden on my own. I remembered making houses in the bushes, dressing up dolls. I can still see my house in the bushes! I used to sweep the floor clean, and I had all the empty jars, and I would make them into teapots and pans. I was totally in another world, making up for the things I didn't have, I suppose. I could get right away into a fantasy world of my own. I wasn't at all inhibited then. The photograph just brought it all flooding back.'

In another exercise, each person was given a basket full of miscellaneous objects, from which they had to select just three items. They then explained to a partner what the significance of their chosen objects was. Once again, an exercise with little apparent relevance to childhood play opened a door on to a forgotten world, in which the smallest, most ordinary thing could be the source of delight.

Caitlin: 'I chose a coaster with an apple on it, which reminded me of the miniature foods I'd had in my doll's house as a child. I also chose a glass marble, because I'd had one like it in my treasure box when I was little. I used to love the smoothness of the glass, and the way the light shone through it. I used to spend hours just looking in my box and ordering all the things in it.'

Ella: 'I've always liked natural things, and these were the things that sprang out at me from the basket: a stone, a piece of tortoiseshell, a pine cone. I really enjoyed feeling the different textures, the coolness of the stone and the roughness of the pine cone. I loved having time to look at the different colours and shapes. That's how I used to play as a child: completely absorbed, oblivious of time passing. It was wonderful to feel that way again.'

Alison: 'I loved doing this exercise. I chose a button, a little purse and a tiny doll. It reminded me of the child's delight in the miniature, which you gradually learn is sentimental and unacceptable. I used to love those little glass ornaments when I was a child, but I gradually learnt from my mother they were vulgar.

> The button reminded of a button box I'd had. I loved digging my hands in and feeling them all running through my fingers. There was a wonderful sensuality to childhood play that I'd quite forgotten.'

In a round-up session at the end of the morning, everyone gathered in a group and collectively brainstormed the games they had played as children. As each person called out a game, several others would exclaim 'Oh yes! I did that!' before pitching in with several games of her own. It was like opening a wonderful treasure chest, out of which more and more lovely things came tumbling. Memories triggered memories, and the list grew and grew. There was hopscotch, french skipping, hide-and-seek, grandmother's footsteps, kick-the-can, tig, marbles, conkers, skipping games and clapping games, dressing up, making dens, climbing trees, treasure hunts, snowball fights, tobogganing, cowboys-and-Indians, cops-and-robbers, making up stories, putting on plays and concerts, playing with imaginary friends, sewing, knitting, cooking, making jewellery, collecting things, card games, board-games, games with dolls, games with teddy bears . . . The list went on and on. Most of the women were staggered to recall the wealth and variety of their childhood play. They found the memory immensely exciting, though also tinged with sadness. 'Remembering all the games we used to play made me feel sad that it's so hard to play now,' was how Jane expressed it.

In Ian McEwan's novel, *The Child in Time*, the main character, Stephen Lewis, is violently catapulted from his contented existence when his small daughter is abducted while they are out shopping one morning. A desperate search ensues which takes Stephen through the streets and schools of London, but also through the emotional debris of his own life. At one point, he reflects how badly he needs his daughter: 'He needed her good influence, her lessons in celebrating the specific; how to fill the present and be filled by it to the point where identity faded to nothing.' This is the magic of play, a magic that the child teaches the adult, not the other way round. Soon afterwards, Stephen goes to see his old friend, Charles Darke, at his home in the country, where he finds that Darke has undergone a terrible transformation. No longer the suave, confident government minister, Darke has gone mad: dressed like a prep school boy, he is living in the woods, climbing trees, chewing liquorice and swigging home-made lemonade. He proudly turns out his pockets to show the horrified Stephen a penknife, a magnifying glass, marbles, a dried newt, a compass, a feather, a piece of rope. Charles is not just behaving like a ten-year-old, Stephen is appalled to realise, he has studiously become one. The only time he drops his child persona, he tells Stephen, 'It's a matter of letting go.' In McEwan's novel, the ability to play like a child is seen as desirable, but also pathological. Charles Darke's retreat into childhood expresses his refusal to live in the real world, his inability to reconcile conflicting aspects of his public and private self.

Attempting to live as if we were children may lead into the realm of psychosis, but retaining the ability to recollect our childhood play is anything but pathological. As the table below shows, for every kind of play that we enjoyed and benefited from as children, we can enjoy and benefit from an equivalent form of play in adulthood.[1]

child's play	***adult's play***
Using clay, dough, sand or water to express creativity; to resolve feelings of aggression, anger or fear; to be sociable in non-confrontational way.	*Pottery, woodwork, making bread, to release pent-up tensions from a day at work, perhaps with few chances to be creative; 'hand' play to counter the 'head' work of the day.*
Using puppets, telephones, mirrors, dressing-up, to overcome problems with language and help to develop verbal play.	*Amateur dramatics, singing, chatting on the phone, as forms of verbal play, and to overcome problems of shyness.*
Sorting – natural and man-made materials – to help children with perceptual difficulties and retention problems.	*Tidying drawers/cupboards, sorting sewing boxes and button tins, to give a sense of mastery, order and calm. (The absorption that comes with this kind of activity can be very playful.)*
Using picture books to help language development and group participation; to enable children with fears or anxieties to find support through stories.	*Reading, going to the theatre, museums, galleries, to provide escapes from ordinary life into art, a vision of alternatives, and the possibility of support.*
Using climbing frames, swings, walks, to help a child who is lethargic or overactive to find legitimate experiences of energy or tiredness.	*Physical exercise, sport or dancing, to counter the tiredness that comes from desk-bound or repetitive work.*

The text in the left-hand column of the table gives examples of forms of play that are used to help children with specific problems or difficulties they may have, while the text in the right-hand column provides suggestions for adult versions of these forms of play. For where there are problems or difficulties in our adult lives, we can be helped through play in just the same way as children with problems are helped.

Recalling and recreating ways of playing as we did in childhood puts us back in touch with aspects of ourselves that adulthood makes little space for: the ability to be totally absorbed, the ability to forget time, to be the curious, questing, uninhibited selves we once were. The strength of the impulse to play is evident in the many kinds of adult play that closely resemble childhood activities. Think of *Star Trek* Conventions, where people dress up as Captain Kirk or Mr Spock, murder-mystery parties, war games weekends, video games, board games, and the old failsafe, the children's train set. Some of these forms of adult play are pretty bizarre, admittedly; some may actually be morally dubious, but they testify to the longing which many adults feel for some respite from adulthood, for a return to the easy pleasures of childhood. My sister-in-law complains that her husband buys toys for their son so that he can play with them; she finds them sitting on the floor together, both equally engrossed in that week's purchase. One night after we'd got the baby off to sleep, my partner and I spent a marvellous hour playing with her building bricks, seeing who could build the highest tower, the widest one, the wackiest one. We felt far better for that one hour of reliving our childhood play than we would have done from a whole week of more grown-up forms of relaxation.

The Changing Face of Child's Play

The international charity UNICEF states play as one of the basic rights of childhood, and, however uncertain people may feel about play's place in adulthood, most would agree, in theory at least, that play in childhood is beneficial. An enormous industry has sprung up to cater for the play needs of children, to make sure that they are, at all times and at all ages, happily occupied. There are vast warehouses on the outskirts of every major town filled to the brim with children's toys; there are catalogues of toddlers' toys to peruse and select from; there are whole floors of bookshops devoted to children's books (and several shelves devoted to telling parents how to play with their children).

Yet the approval with which childhood play is currently greeted is a relatively recent phenomenon. Well into the twentieth century, parents were being actively discouraged from playing with their children. The mother of 1914 was told, 'The rule that parents should not play with the baby may seem hard, but it is without doubt a safe one.'[2] Childhood was seen as an accelerated evolution, in which the child romped through the evolutionary stages that led from ape to man. Likened to small animals, children needed to be trained and restrained; play was a bad idea since it made space for impulses that needed to be stamped out, not encouraged. The prevailing attitude, of the professionals at least, was one of caution and prudery. In 1928, when John Watson published his influential guide to childcare, *Psychological Care of the Infant and Child*, he wrote: 'Let your behaviour always be objective and kindly firm. Never hug and kiss them. Never let them sit in your lap. If you must, kiss them once on the forehead when they say goodnight. Shake hands with them in the morning.'[3]

Changing ideologies of childcare are interesting because they often embody predominating attitudes to less tangible aspects of human behaviour, such as impulse and restraint, seriousness and levity. They can also be read as a cipher for the changing place of play in a society, which is why they are of particular relevance to our current concerns about the marginalisation of play in adulthood.

Between the First and Second World Wars, the child was increasingly regarded as an adult-in-the-making. It was to be controlled by its mother, subjugated to her will and law, and taught proper self-control. The emphasis was on training children to become worthy, polite and obedient citizens. A robust pragmatism underlined attitudes towards child-rearing and child-play. The child's impulses were seen as exploratory, inventive and benign, rather than wicked and wilful (although it still had to be trained 'not to use its body as a play-thing'), and the loving parent's task was to educate children to master those impulses.

Childcare experts after the Second World War began actively encouraging mothers to play with their children, and by the middle of the century, playing with your child had become a duty, not just permissible, but obligatory.[4] The United States Department of Labour Children's Bureau was making no bones about it: 'If you feel hurried, bath time won't be the fun for either of you that it should,' it declared ominously in its 1951 directive to parents.[5] From the mid-1940s on, a baby's emotional and psychological needs were seen as just as important as its physical and intellectual requirements, and parents were suddenly given the awesome responsibility of making sure their offspring were protected from all possible forms of psychological distress. From the fifties on, John Bowlby's hugely influential theory of maternal attachment put considerable pressure on mothers to be constantly available to their children, and it was considered a serious dereliction of maternal duty to leave your child in anyone else's care before the age of three at the very earliest. Intellectual development also became an increasingly important aspect of child-rearing from the sixties onwards, and play was seen as a crucial means to that end. According to Christina Hardyment, in her study of changing fashions in baby-care, *Perfect Parents*, the way in which the work of Jean Piaget was interpreted for the general public turned parents into 'handmaids to intellect', with every child a potential Einstein, and every parent responsible for releasing their child's full intellectual abilities.[6]

It is highly significant that current childcare directives emphasise again and again the *usefulness* of children's play, which it is the parents' *job* to maximise. In her best-selling *Baby and Child*, Penelope Leach is quite explicit about this, setting out the exacting 'conditions of service' that parents must expect. Hugh Jolly, another childcare guru of the late eighties, tells parents to '[regard] his care as your present job'. For both children and parents, play becomes a form of *work*. Toys must be educational; books must develop visual and verbal skills; nurseries display lists of the day's play 'tasks' and issue children with 'work books'; parents want to know what their child has been learning, ever fearful that they may have been wasting time. Judith Schwartz, author of *The Mother Puzzle*, points out, 'Play is not just play anymore . . . Toys for young tots derive not from whimsy but from scientific research on infant development. Just as packaged foods must list their ingredients, today's toys spell out their "developmental value".'[7] The guilt that many modern mothers feel if their children do not have 'enough' toys is testimony to the pressure they are under. Play is now part of the maternal package of responsibilities, not time off from those responsibilities. Today's toys are not just for fun, they 'develop hand-eye co-ordination', or 'teach colour awareness', or 'stimulate motor skills'. As Schwartz remarks, 'Companies that sell toys and educational material for infants and young children sport names like "Right Start" and "One Step Ahead", giving the impression that childhood is not a stage so much as a race.'[8] Nursery schools are as busy sprinting to the finishing line as everyone else: a mother recently complained to me that her daughter's nursery was starting to teach the children to read. 'She's only two! What's the hurry? Can't she just be a baby for a while longer?' Many middle-class children today spend their 'free' time speeding from ballet classes to music lessons to tennis camp to the riding school. Their experiences take little account of evidence from research that 'Unstructured time for fantasy and play is ultimately more important for the child's well-being than an added skill, no matter how pertinent or impressive.'[9]

The multi-million-pound toy industry relies on parental anxiety about their child's developmental progress, but contemporary toys constitute a form of experiment, with today's children as the guinea-pigs: for who is to say that mass-produced, skill-oriented toys do not actually stunt development in some ways, encouraging rigid, schematised thinking, anathema to real creativity and learning? There is little research done on this as yet, but some professionals are beginning to express concerns. In the view of Professor Elizabeth Newson, head of the child psychology unit at Nottingham University, children are being deprived of 'a sense of wonder'. According to Newson, 'Something has been lost and I don't know how you make up for it.'[10] Professor Jeffrey Goldstein, a psychologist at the University of Utrecht who specialises in children's play, thinks that children are bound to be influenced in their play by what is around them. 'When I was a kid it was daring: walking on a wall or climbing a tree. Now kids do it by having a high score on a video game or something with technology because that's what we've given them. For better or worse, we breed children like us.'[11]

We are light-years away from the world of childhood play enjoyed by writer Alison Uttley:

> The fields were our toyshops and sweetshops, our market and our storehouses. We made our toys from things we found in the pastures. We ate sweet and sour food of the wild. We hunted from hedge to hedge as in a market, to find the best provisions, and we had our wild shops in corners of fields, or among the trees. The flowering spikes of plantain were picked for the game of 'Soldiers'. With a bunch of the green flower-heads we chose out the likely warriors and challenged another soldier flower to combat. When his head flew off a fresh one from the bunch took his place, and fought on . . . The green rushes made whips, plaited for the lash and tightly bound for the handle. They made bracelets with brown flowers for clasps. They were girdles and shoelaces, and necklaces with flowers as beads. They were woven into round baskets to hold a couple of hen's eggs, into rattles for a baby, into mats and frames for tiny pictures, and

> many a small conceit and game . . . We gathered burs from the giant burdock and pressed them together to form baskets and nests. There were games with flowers too, when we popped the seed of the great balsam, which went off like a fairy's gun, and we listened to the broom shooting its own ammunition in the fields. We made peepshows out of the smallest, prettiest flowers, or dolls from the garden poppies, or a set of glove fingers from foxgloves. Cowslip-balls and daisy-chains – there was no end to the toys we found . . . Down by the river grew willows, but we never played by the wild waters of the stream, which galloped along faster than the horses on the road alongside. Death lurked there, pot-holes and currents, and crumbling falling banks. We kept to our own hillside, to the small kingdom that was our country, and there we found enough to amuse and entertain us during the long years of childhood.[12]

In part, the current, frenzied emphasis on structured, directed play can be seen as a backlash to the liberal approach to education advocated in the sixties, when it was fashionable to think that, if only teachers and parents could stop repressing the child's innate creativity, the child would be able to realise its own unique talent in its own unique way. The wheel has come full circle with the introduction of a National Curriculum and a renewed emphasis on structured teaching, targeted learning and standardised testing.

Today, the years of childhood are likely to pass in a hectic rush. The sense of urgency and anxiety which is so pervasive a characteristic of adulthood in contemporary western culture seems to have seeped into our children's lives too. The new parent, confronted with the bewildering array of toys on offer, feels an awesome burden of expectation. It is hard to remember that a small baby is perfectly content with a loo roll holder, when the voices of a million copywriters are demanding to know what you are teaching your baby, whether she is learning some new skill from her play, whether you are enabling her to maximise her intellectual potential. This is in stark contrast to the mother of a hundred years ago, who was instructed not to play with her baby at all until it was at least six months old because stimulation was considered harmful to the baby's nerves.

The subtext of current trends in child-rearing is a disturbing one: in a culture which values work above play, childhood has become infected with the same spirit of industriousness that poisons adulthood. Far from following Plato's dictum and living life as play, we have become wedded to the idea of living life as work. In doing so we have not only seriously reduced the quality of life in adulthood, but have inculcated the concept of busy-ness into children's play. We have succeeded in transforming childhood play into a kind of employment. As a leading childcare expert ruefully commented recently. 'One problem for nursery and infants teachers and playgroup leaders has been to convince parents that their child is well occupied "just playing".'[13]

Instead of learning from children how far wrong we have gone in our adult lives, we are busily moulding childhood to the unseemly and unceasing haste of adulthood. Increasingly, children's lives resemble those of little adults, and, perhaps not surprisingly, there is some evidence to suggest that children are beginning to exhibit many of the stress symptoms commonly associated with adulthood, such as headaches, stomach aches and lack of motivation.[14] The tragedy of this state of affairs is that play in childhood is not only enjoyable and beneficial for children, it also greatly increases their chances of maturing into well-balanced adults able to cope with the pressures and demands of adult life. It does not require much mental effort to realise that, as well as doing our children a profound disservice when we impose our values on their play, we are also effectively undermining the long-term well-being of society by creating a future generation of adults whose ability to play may well be chronically undeveloped. Thus, a downward spiral is quickly established: if as adults we are unsure how to play, how can we begin to play properly with our children? If as children our capacity to play is not nurtured, how as adults can we hope to maintain play as a valuable part of our lives?

Play Through The Ages

Play in childhood may not be impervious to social change, but childhood nevertheless remains the time that we most readily associate with play. Childhood play may be under threat from the work-obsessed world of adulthood. It may also, for girls particularly, as we have seen, be hampered by gender stereotypes about what is appropriate play for a girl and a boy, but childhood play still has much to teach adults about the playful self. Childhood is still the time in our lives when our ability to play is least restricted and the range of our play is at its most diverse.

Rousseau wrote of the child, 'Whether he is at work or at play, both are alike to him; his games are his business, he knows no distinction.' To a small baby, everything is of interest; the fundamental attitude is a playful one. When I had my daughter, I was amazed to discover how innate playfulness is in human beings, how quickly a baby begins to reveal a sense of humour. Even a tiny, helpless infant, who cannot walk or talk or feed herself, is nevertheless capable of having fun. From the age of just three or four months, my daughter was able to show her appreciation of a game of peek-a-boo by smiling, laughing, waggling her arms and legs; by the age of eight months, she was able to instigate the game herself by pulling a tea-towel up and down in front of her face; by ten months, she would tempt us into a game of chase by crawling a little way off, pausing and looking over her shoulder with an expectant look, until she caught our eye, when she would burst into giggles and crawl off again at top speed.

The imaginative diversity in the play of even a very small child is extraordinary to watch. From the age of just a few months, a baby will become deeply absorbed in exploring objects that attract her. It may be a toy or a jar lid or a pine cone or a boot strap: she will look at it from every angle, pass it from hand to hand, turn it this way and that, bring it to her mouth to taste.[15] As she plays, the baby engages with the physical world with the whole of her own small physical being, not just her eyes, ears, hands and mouth, but often her feet and toes as well. The body of the person caring for her is a rich source of play: her mother's hair, her father's ears – interesting things happen when you tweak and tug. The changing expressions, the familiar smells, the different tones of voice, all are intensely intriguing.[16]

Yet even in childhood, play is multi-faceted, and the type of play adopted by children varies markedly according to age. For young children, play is primarily centred around intent exploration of one kind or another. Exploration and play, one researcher concluded, are indistinguishable in infancy since they tend to occur simultaneously.[17] You can see this same intent exploration in slightly older children. Given an unfamiliar object, children aged between three and five years will set about investigating its shape, weight and texture, learning about its strength and pliability, and testing its applicability to a variety of tasks. The tireless curiosity of young children's play is not only enjoyable in its own right, but serves an important purpose in familiarising them with the physical world which is their primary defining context. Without this familiarity, they would be at considerable risk – as indeed they initially are – from phenomena as commonplace as knives and stairs, heat and water. Exploratory play is thus directly linked to the instinct for survival. But it is also connected to a seemingly innate desire for mastery: even in infancy, play is fused with a powerful drive to understand, to know, to conquer.

Older children use play to explore their social and moral world, as well as their physical one. Fantasy play is a central ingredient of pre-adolescent play from the age of three or four onwards. Pretend worlds and imaginary friends are paramount; a broomstick is a horse, a curtain is a queen's cloak. The child's capacity for invention is given its fullest rein by fantasy and make-believe; here, the rules are entirely of her own making. Make-believe play allows the child to bend reality to her intellectual and emotional requirements, thus helping her to assimilate experiences, rather than be overwhelmed by them.[18] As a little girl, my sister was accompanied at all times by a large imaginary ostrich, her greatest friend and a creature possessed of wicked wit and dastardly intentions. It was Ostrich who incited my three-year-old sister to swallow my mother's contact lenses one afternoon; and Ostrich who was behind the scheme to hide all the family's shoes in the freezer. It was Ostrich, too, who was to blame for the troubling physical differences that my little sister had noticed between her parents, for she announced one evening, 'Ostrich fly away with my penis to Huddersfield.'

Between the ages of seven and eleven, games with rules become increasingly important. Skipping games, clapping games, hopscotch, french skipping, conkers and marbles, all come with complex codes of conduct. The zeal for establishing the rules of a game can itself become a game, with a whole set of rules of its own, and there are numerous rhymes with which children collect players for a game and then select which of them is to be 'it'. The rites and rituals of childhood play at this age are highly developed, but they are also ceaselessly evolving in the hands of the players. Children are not only learning through play how to adapt themselves to a given set of rules, but they are also exploring how far those rules can be adjusted, modified and even improved. Adhering to and experimenting with the rules of a game are both permissible, for both form an essential part of the play.

All these forms of group play, whether the group consists of two or of twenty, reflect the child's growing awareness of her social self, and the increasing need to develop the necessary skills to interact in this complex social world of which she is inextricably a part.[19] Key friendships emerge in these middle years of childhood, and lead in turn to a number of play off-shoots, such as dens, codes, clubs and gangs. I can still clearly recall from my own childhood the misery of not being in *either* of the two gangs that dissected playground society in my junior school. I longed to be party to their pass-words and whispered secrets, but was forced instead to watch their machiavellian intrigues from the tarmac sidelines. I can also recall the intense joy of acquiring my first best friend, at the age of about seven – an experience easily comparable, if not actually preferable, to the acquisition of my first boyfriend some years later.

It is in adolescence that play begins to get difficult for women. As the previous chapter showed, it is around this time that play becomes an ambiguous experience for girls, riddled with contradictory impulses and meanings. Much childhood play continues in new guises in adolescence, but the stakes are higher: looking back on my own childhood and adolescence, I recall how play changed around my twelfth birthday: my parents let me have a party with pop music and punch and coloured light bulbs. It was a mixed party. Sex was on the play-agenda. Flirting with the boys; experimenting with clothes and make-up; fantasising about pop stars: all were ways of testing and exploring social and sexual boundaries, just as we had done when we were seven or eight, but in adolescence it was much more important that we got it right. Chock-a-block with sexual stirrings, we could not risk exploring them without 'getting a bad name'; we wanted to go out in that little black skirt, but were not sure how to handle the attention it might bring; we were full of physical energy, but wanted to look demure and sophisticated; we were ready to take on the world, but the lyrics we memorised were all about falling in love and having our hearts broken.

Through play, teenagers retain their links with their childhood selves, but they are also, tentatively or recklessly, exploring their fledgling adult personae, 'the implications, opportunities, demands and constraints that fundamental social demarcations have for them, their social behaviour and their futures'.[20] Adolescence pulsates with hormones, and sex-orientated play takes on a leading role as teenagers explore and adjust to the upheaval of physiological and emotional change. Sport becomes an important 'container' of energies and abilities that as yet have no formal outlet in the adult world. It is not purely chance that at precisely the age when physical strength is often far more developed than emotional control, organised sport becomes a predominant form of play, particularly for young men. Sport provides an outlet for physical energy, but also a channel for 'anti-social' feelings of aggression, frustration, rivalry and hostility. This applies equally to girls too. Wielding a hockey stick and chasing round a netball court contain and channel emotions and energies that have no other legitimate outlets in just the same way that rugby and cricket do. It is a genuine cause for concern, then, that so many girls drop out of organised games and sports around this time. 'In my school,' one woman told me, 'you only did sport in the sixth form if you were seriously good at it, or else a bit soft in the head. But at the boys' school up the road, you took on hero status if you played sport.'

Since the invention of the teenager in the 1950s, adolescent culture has in each generation found new ways of celebrating its independence, autonomy and uniqueness: the Rockers, the Teddy Boys, the Mods, the Hippies and the Punks all carved out their own particular ways of playing. But whether these teenagers are riding mopeds or motorbikes, whether they're driving Chevrolets or Beetles, it is invariably the boys at the wheel, while the girls are riding pillion or in the back seat. They are there to acknowledge, admire, applaud; they are there primarily as members of the audience.[21] Old footage of Beatles' or Stones' concerts shows row upon row of helplessly screaming girls, lost to their overwhelming emotions, but all the time worked upon by those four guys up on the stage. Ten years later as we struggled into skin-tight jeans and rushed out to head-bang the night away to Led Zeppelin, Free and The Who, we were still caught in a trap of compliant defiance: strutting our stuff in clothes that made our mothers squirm, but conforming utterly to the dictates of fashion and our boyfriends' preferences. In the nineties, teenage girls go clubbing, listen to records (over and over and over again), see films, hang out in town, go skating, riding, shopping, try out new hair-cuts, experiment with make-up, flirt with the boys and with their own incipient womanliness. But it is still a rollercoaster ride, and play in adolescence faithfully mirrors all the highs and lows. You feel powerful and powerless. Everything is possible, and nothing. One moment, the world is your oyster, the next it is a prison. Friends are angels one day, demons the next. Yesterday's fun is boring this morning; tomorrow's escapade is unthinkable today. You are fifteen one day, eight the next, twenty-five the day after. It's exciting, perplexing and exhausting.

Play gets confusing in adolescence: it becomes intense, risky, double-edged. And it is the confusion of our adolescent play that we tend to take with us into adulthood, rather than the ease of our childhood play. It is the legacy of our teenage selves that tends to colour our attitude to play in adulthood: the anxieties about entitlement to play, the agonies of self-consciousness, the conflicting needs, the problem of accommodating others without abnegating ourselves.

In theory, adult play should be particularly varied and enriching, synthesising all the different types of play which we learnt and enjoyed as children: a way of exploring, testing and developing physical, emotional or intellectual abilities; a form of escape from the responsibilities of everyday life. It should be imaginative, sexual, sensual, physical or social – whatever we *want* it to be. Play in adulthood is potentially a richer source of pleasure than at any other time in our lives, for in adulthood we have many more ways of playing at our disposal, if only we chose to use them. To do so, however, we need to take a step back from the confusing din of adolescence to a time before play got complicated. If we want to listen to the straightforward music of our childhood play, we need to shut out all the background noise that deafens us to the play-impulse in adulthood. Play in childhood has its dark sides too; it can be aggressive, jealous, destructive but, whatever else it may be, it is rarely complicated by issues of entitlement and conflicting demands. Whatever the adults around may think, children know instinctively that it is right to play and, left to their own devices, they will get on and do so.

If we are to put play back into our adult lives, we must return to our childhood to discover what we learnt there through play, both about ourselves and about play itself.

Films like *Vice Versa* and *Big* prey on our adult yearnings for childhood by presenting us with adults who are in fact children. In *Big* Tom Hanks plays a young boy whose wish to grow up is magically granted. The problem is that while he now looks grown up and is treated like a grown-up, he is actually still a child inside, a situation which quickly gets him into difficulties. Things take a turn for the better, however, when he is employed as a consultant to a toy company. With his finger right on the pulse of what children want, his ideas for toys are a runaway success. One of the messages of *Big*, like Spielberg's *Hook*, is that adults have not really got a clue about playing, and they need children to show them the way. Like the grown-up Peter Pan, we must do this by returning to our childhoods and becoming re-acquainted with our child selves who were so able to play, whose lives were so rich in play.

From the very beginning, human play serves both our practical needs for survival *and* our metaphysical yearnings. Through play we are in the magnificent process of creating our selves, not only our eating, sleeping, walking selves, but also our thinking, being, shaking and moving selves. As Arthur Koestler asserted, 'The act of creation is embedded in the act of play.'[22] For women whose adult lives are often so strikingly unplayful, whose expression of creativity is so often limited to the realm of physical reproduction, the experience of rediscovering the wealth of childhood play can be intensely exciting and profoundly liberating, for it is a vital way to reproduce their playful self, to retrieve it from the past to which it is so frequently relegated. Women want to play and they need to play; if we can only legitimate that desire in our own minds, we will have made enormous progress in healing the breach between our past and our present, between a self that felt entitled to play and a self that so often feels unentitled to do so.

10

Time for Play

'It is not a question of stopping the movement of life; it is a question of fulfilling it.'
(Simone de Beauvoir, *The Ethics of Ambiguity*)

Getting back in touch with our childhood selves, and with the sense of having played, of having been entitled to play, is a major step towards finding space for our playful self in adulthood. But if we are to build on this reawakening, we also need to legitimise play *time* in our adult lives. In our increasingly work-obsessed, time-bound culture, many of us experience enormous difficulty permitting ourselves this play time. In so many women's lives, the constant battle against the clock makes it hard to be genuinely playful, makes it hard to let go sufficiently to be playful. The pressure of time is acute and relentless, while the juggling of different roles requires a degree of organisation that would not be amiss in a military campaign. As one senior journalist and mother of three put it to me, 'If I'm to get the children fed, dressed and off to school, and make it to the office in time, I have to plan every second: there's simply no room for slack.' Time *is* problematic for women. It *is* hard for us to take time for ourselves when there are so many other pressures and obligations, and never enough hours in the day. On the Play Day this was the single most commonly voiced complaint. As soon as we started to explore ways in which play *could* be made a part of everyday life, nearly every woman in the room raised, in some form or another, the same objection: 'When on earth am I supposed to find *time* for play?'

The paradoxical answer to this question is: *by playing.*

Adult life is overwhelmingly constrained by time, but play itself is intrinsically forgetful of time constraints. Few mothers will not know the frustration of trying to catch a bus or train with a toddler in tow who has decided the moment is right to play with a fascinating pebble she has just spotted by the roadside. For the parent on a tight schedule between the childminder, the office and the supermarket, a child's impulse to play is not always an easy one to respect or respond to. Nevertheless, for both children and adults, play offers a way of transcending the inevitable limitations of time, and, in this respect alone, it is one of the most valuable skills at our disposal. Unlike so many of the things we do, play is not defined by time, and for that reason it is a particularly effective means of overcoming the problems caused by the tyranny of time in our lives. Play offers freedom both from the relentlessness of clock time, and from the restrictive time continuum of past-present-future. There *is* time for play in our lives, but it is only *by* playing that we find that time; it is only *by* playing, that we find that the time for play is now.

Playing For Time

The majority of the women who came on the Play Day began the workshop knowing they wanted to explore the idea of play, but uncertain what place it should have in their daily lives, and, more important still, how they were to make time for play when there was so little time to begin with. 'Isn't this just one more thing to worry about?' asked one woman. By the end of the workshop, these uncertainties had vanished: the women left with few doubts about the importance of play in ordinary day-to-day living. Those women I was able to interview a few weeks after the Play Day all said they had been more conscious of putting, or finding, play in their lives since the workshop. Having time for play no longer seemed to be such an issue either.

> Penny: 'I left the workshop feeling that there was definitely room for more play in my life, and wanting to make more time for doing creative things, companionable things. I've been reading more, getting out my paints, writing for pleasure rather than out of desperate need! I've even been thinking about taking up the clarinet again.'
>
> Maddie: 'I've been putting play into my life in a number of small ways: taking time over washing and doing my face, enjoying the rows of coloured beads in the earring shop, feeling mischievous.'
>
> Caitlin: 'Talking about play opened so many doors. It brought a rush of remembering. I've realised that there *are* opportunities for play in my life, but I don't make use of them. I find reasons not to play. I think, "Oh, I'm too tired." But since the Play Day I've been getting more pleasure from my life: looking at the silks

in Liberty's, or the chocolates in the Belgian Chocolate Shop near where I live. I've thought about play a lot more, about what I'd like to do, fantasising and day-dreaming. I consider that a kind of play, too.'

Ella: 'The Play Day made me aware of how much time I do spend playing. I was surprised and pleased when I realised that. I think I find it quite easy to play, and I play in a number of different ways: writing, drawing, photography, day-dreaming. I often play word games with my partner. We take a poetry book and pick lines from different poems, jumble them up and then try to guess where the lines come from. We play charades and card games too. Being playful, I've realised, is a state of mind more than anything.'

Alison: 'I've been saying to myself for a long time, "You must play more, you must have more fun," and since the Play Day I've been aware of unlocking doors in my mind, and already I feel more receptive. It's marvellous. I've been reading books from my childhood, and looking at children's games, and remembering that readiness to learn. I used to love collecting things, all sorts of things – old coins, sugar papers, car numbers – and I'm going to start again, I'm going to make a button jar, and maybe I'll collect silk purses.'

Emma: 'The night after the workshop I went out for supper and, because it was still very much on my mind, I asked everyone about their childhood play. At first the men went on about their games of physical prowess, but gradually we got talking about our memories, and we ended up getting to know each other in a way we wouldn't normally have done. We all have a playful child in us still, and we shared that and showed that aspect of ourselves. It was tremendously liberating.'

Elizabeth: 'I was playing right from the beginning of the Play Day, just by being there, just by giving myself the whole day. Since the Play Day I've had a strong sense of freedom that I don't think I had before, a sense that I have the right to do things. I've been seeing things that I already do as play, and getting more out of them as a result. Like swimming: I love swimming, but I usually have to feel that I've deserved the hour it will take. I don't feel like that any more. I'm very keen on massages and facials, too, and I've stopped feeling guilty about the cost and the time. I feel freer to do what I want to do.'

Time Permitting

Play, as one of the women on the Play Day said, stems above all from a certain state of mind. Although it often feels as if there is no time for play in our lives, play is something that becomes possible the moment we make time for it, the moment we give ourselves permission to play. If we wait for the moment in our lives when there is nothing else to do, we may find the time for play never arrives, for as Simone de Beauvoir wrote, 'It is contradictory to want to save up existence, which, the fact is, exists only by being spent . . . it is not a question of stopping the movement of life; it is a question of fulfilling it.'[1] Play does not have to be set apart from all the other things we do in a day. While it may have the effect of taking us out of the everyday realm, approached in that way it *will* become 'just one more thing to worry about'. Instead, play becomes possible once we start to approach the everyday things in our lives with a playful attitude.

Of all the women who have spoken to me about the meaning of play in their lives, few have impressed me more than 38-year-old Beth with the sheer playfulness of her entire attitude to life. Beth is a real play *aficionado.* Unlike most people, she has always regarded adulthood as a time for play, not a time to relinquish it, and she has lived her adult life in such a way as to maximise her chances of playing. She explained how this came about.

> I remember when I was seven lying on the grass looking at the sky and saying to myself, 'I can't wait to grow up. This is so boring!' My sister lying beside me was saying, 'I never want to grow up,' but I always thought being grown up would bring more opportunities for play. There'd be no one to call me to supper. In my teenage years, the situation at home was difficult and I was very unhappy at school too. I was very anxious about my future and what would happen to me. In my twenties I gave up a lot of things I'd enjoyed doing as a child, like singing, dressing up, going camping. In my thirties, I decided to do those things again. As I've got older and got to know myself better, it's got easier to do the things I enjoy, because I know what I enjoy, and I allow myself to do it. When I was working full-time I didn't know what to spend my money or my free time on, and I never enjoyed my holidays. I work part-time now and, even though I'm poorly paid, I so resented working full-time that I decided to make do with less money and have more time. I have to find cheap ways to play, but I find that quite challenging and creative. I get so much enjoyment from my time that it's worth it.

> Play is about taking risks. You have to have faith that you can do it, not be frightened of failing. And you have to give yourself opportunities to play. I find opportunities all the time. Doing things in an attitude of playfulness makes the most tedious things exciting. It allows for unexpected things to happen. A lot of it is bound up with how you view time. The other day I had to go all the way to Rotherhithe to deliver a film for processing, and I made a decision beforehand to do it in a relaxed manner, not to get hassled by it. On the tube into work, I play little games with myself, like trying to get a seat within one stop, or I make up stories about the other people in the carriage.

The constraints on women's play are many, varied and *real.* As previous chapters have shown, a combination of social, economic and psychological pressures constrain both women's opportunity and their inclination to play. Prevailing cultural attitudes towards both work and leisure further restrict the possibilities for play in women's lives today. But the 'disappearing play' phenomenon cannot be explained by external factors alone. The lack of play in women's lives is also due to internalisation of constraining attitudes. We prevent ourselves from playing by our acceptance of, and collusion with, preconceived notions of what a woman should or should not do. There are real constraints on our play, but there are also real ways in which we can overcome these constraints and make the time for play that we both deserve and need.

Marion, 54, took early retirement from her job as headmistress of a girls' secondary school. Before she left work, she had been worried about how she would manage with so much time on her hands and so much less money – only a quarter of her previous earnings. 'I'd always really liked shopping and used to spend a lot of money on clothes and books and, I thought, how on earth am I going to manage? But now I go and look round the shops and I don't feel I need those things anymore. I come home perfectly happy without having bought anything. What I realise now is that shopping used to be a way of compensating for all the time I'd had to spend doing what I basically didn't want to do. I have less money now, but I do far more.'

Since retiring, the play element in Marion's life has increased enormously. 'I play all day every day now,' she says, 'and it's wonderful.' Her play takes a number of different forms: she does an art appreciation class, a life-drawing class, an American history course, and a music appreciation class; she goes for walks, gardens, and sees friends; she's also become involved with an art sponsorship scheme. As she sees it, the financial cost of her previous lifestyle reflected the emotional cost of her job. Though poorer now in material wealth, she feels far richer in terms of quality of life. Central to her enjoyment of life post-retirement – a time when quality of life often sharply declines for many people – is her ability to play, an ability which she maintains was always there, but which has flourished now that time permits.

In the biblical story of Mary and Martha, Mary drops what she is doing to sit at Jesus' feet and listen to what he is saying, while her sister Martha wants to join them, but is too busy with her domestic tasks. Martha is annoyed by her sister's selfish behaviour and bursts out, 'Lord, do you not care that my sister has left me to do all the work by myself? Tell her then to help me.' Jesus replies, 'Martha, Martha, you are worried and distracted by many things; there is need of only one thing. Mary has chosen the better part, which will not be taken away from her.'[2] One sister bows resentfully to the imperative of service, the other permits herself time for play. We can be like Martha or like Mary in our attitude to play: we can put off play until all the other pressing requirements of our lives are dealt with, whenever *that* may be, or we can decide that the time for play is *now*. Maybe that means allocating specific time to do something you enjoy; maybe it just means feeling playful as you wash your face in the morning, or making a game of finding the mislaid car keys; maybe it means noticing the signs of playfulness all round you: the cat chasing its tail in the next door garden; the punning name of the local hairdresser's; the turnip that bears a striking resemblance to your great-aunt; the miniature gargoyle someone's had put up on the front of their house; the gold fleurs-de-lis printed on the supermarket's new-look loo paper.

Of course it is hard to value for ourselves what our culture deems frivolous, indulgent, inferior. The woman who holds down a full-time job, whose house is clean, who cooks supper every night, whose clothes are always ironed, and who remembers to clean out the fish tank before it starts to smell, seems more acceptable than the woman who is out three nights a week, on the phone to friends the other two, who prefers to make love than do the final washing load. We belong to a society that is strikingly down on pleasure, and are more likely to respect the hard worker than the good player. But which of them is happier? Which of them has the better quality of life? We make life difficult for ourselves when we seek to be perfect, and then we wonder why all our strivings do not make us happier. Both the stress-ridden lives of the employed and the misery of the unemployed indicate that something is seriously amiss in these societal evaluations. Time, so frequently cited as the reason why we cannot play, is not the real culprit here, for time is what we make of it. Time becomes a tyrant when we allow it to eradicate opportunities for play. Time permits play when we permit ourselves time for play.

Time Out

Through play, we can move beyond time's tyranny and find much-needed respite from the 'petty pace'. One of the most enviable features of childhood, from the adult's perspective, is the ease with which clock time is forgotten. While the bored child will complain ceaselessly about time dragging, the child at play will happily pass hours without noticing hunger-pangs, rain or cold. Interruptions for mealtimes will be greeted more often than not with annoyance or indifference, for this is the unwelcome imposition of adult time and has little place in the time-free zone of children's play. The expression 'time flies when you're having fun' is palpably true. Many of the classic children's stories derive much of their power from the careful juxtapositioning of adult time and children's time. Magic wardrobes, carpets, amulets, mirrors: all symbolise the transition from an adult world in which time is measured by the clock to a world of children's time in which anything can happen, and usually does. In *Tom's Midnight Garden* by Phillipa Pearce, the striking clock represents the intrusion of unwanted adult reality into the timeless world of the midnight garden. At the end of *The Lion, the Witch, and the Wardrobe*, the children find that no time has passed in the 'real' world, while they have had myriad adventures in the land of Narnia. By suspending the rules and regulations of adult time, these authors are recreating in literary form the experience of play. They are creating space for the unexpected, the fantastic, as children themselves do when they are absorbed in play. For a while, at least, everything is possible.

Adults too can experience the liberation from clock time that comes through genuine play. We can continue to be ruled by time, or we can take a leaf out of our children's books and learn to use play to keep time in its place. We have more choice in the matter than we realise, and deny ourselves a great deal of easy pleasure by not recognising that the choice is there. The benefits of doing so are considerable, and the reasons for not doing so are less insurmountable than they may seem.

If we can only allow ourselves to step outside the relentless regime of our daily lives for a moment, there is no reason why we cannot also savour the hour that passes like a blissful eternity, or the five hours that pass as effortlessly as one. When we hurry the toddler out of her contented absorption, we are shattering something truly precious which we should instead have treated with great reverence and care. When it comes to time-management, it is unquestionably the child who has something to teach the adult.

Through play we can also thwart time in another way: by temporarily releasing ourselves from the restrictive linear progression from childhood to old age, which for the most part defines our experiences of ourself and others. It is an irony lost on few parents that children choose to spend so much of their play time mimicking the very activities that parents would choose not to be doing. Toy cookers, toy ironing boards and toy tool kits testify to the child's curiosity and enthusiasm for the adult world that lies ahead. And the phenomenon is thoroughly cross-cultural. Pygmy children mimic a whole range of adult activities in their play.[3] In rural Zimbabwe, children are judged by their parents according to how well they have mastered adult tasks in their play, including cooking, washing clothes, and ploughing fields. Through play, children take the first tentative steps towards the future. The practical value of this accessing the future has already been discussed: it provides children with a safe, pressure-free environment in which to learn skills needed for adulthood; similarly, it enables them to practise in advance some of the social and sexual roles that await them in adulthood.

Play also enables children to approach the *imagined* reality of the future. They cannot only 'try out' the roles that most probably await them, such as husband, wife, mother and father, they can also explore rather more colourful options: play allows them to step outside the limitations of their childhood reality and become, for a while, a surgeon, an astronaut, a princess or an opera singer. In her memoirs, Simone de Beauvoir vividly describes escaping from the confines of childhood reality through imaginative play:

> The games I was fondest of were those in which I assumed another character. At that evening hour when the stillness, the dark weight, and the tedium of our middle-class domesticity began to invade the hall, I would unleash my phantasms; we would make them materialise with great gestures and copious speeches, and sometimes, spellbound by our play, we succeeded in taking off from the earth and leaving it far behind until an imperious voice suddenly brought us back to reality . . . I often

> imagined that I was Mary Magdalene, and that I was drying Christ's feet with my long hair . . . At times I was a religious confined in a cell, confounding my jailer by singing hymns and psalms. I converted the passivity to which my sex had condemned me into active defiance.[4]

Play also enables children to escape the pressures of the present by returning to an earlier state. Toddlers presented with a younger sibling will often revert in their games to being babies themselves; likewise, eight- and nine-year-olds will sometimes play at being far younger than their age, talking in baby language, or wanting to be cradled and nursed like an infant. The beauty of play is that, while allowing children the freedom to move along the time continuum irrespective of where on it they are actually placed, when they tire of the exciting autonomy of the future or the comforting dependency of the past, they can simply return to the familiar world of the present.

This imaginative journey from the present to either the past or future is a precious and unique feature of play. Significantly, it is this ability to move between different states of being, drawing on remembered experiences of the past and imagined experiences of the future, that often underpins the creativity of the artist, musician or novelist. Mozart, like many creative geniuses, retained in adulthood a degree of playfulness which many of his contemporaries regarded as verging on lunacy. He delighted in double meanings and word games, playing on his own and other people's names, while his letters to his cousin, Anna Maria, are full of sexual innuendoes, scatological puns, riddles and irrepressibly bawdy playfulness, 'like a thesaurus gone mad or a pre-Joycean frenzy of free-associated fragments rendered alternately in low comedy and in elevated mock-rhetoric'.[5] The letters of John Keats, too, are full of puns and word play. Nobel-Prize-winning physicist Richard Feynman describes in his autobiography his singularly playful approach to physics: 'I used to play with it. I used to do whatever I felt like doing – it didn't have to do with whether it was important for the development of nuclear physics, but whether it was interesting and amusing for me to play with . . . I'd invent things and play with things for my own entertainment.'[6] Feynman describes how one day, during his time as a young professor at Cornell University in the 1940s, he was sitting in the cafeteria when another man started messing about, throwing a plate up in the air. Feynman watched the wobbling plate and 'for the fun of it' set about calculating equations of wobbles. 'It was effortless. It was easy to play with these things. It was like uncorking a bottle:

everything flowed out effortlessly . . . There was no importance to what I was doing, but ultimately there was. The diagrams and the whole business that I got the Nobel Prize for came from that piddling around with the wobbling plate.'[7]

The imaginative journey back and forth along the continuum of time is not only available to children and geniuses, though it is most often travelled by them. While few of us would wish to be quite so unbounded by behavioural convention as Mozart, whatever the artistic spin-offs, we could nevertheless benefit considerably in adulthood from making greater use of this particular gift of play; for if play is a doorway through which children can begin to have access to the adult world, it is equally one through which adults can have access once again to the world of childhood, with all its wonder, curiosity and delight. Equally, it can provide an escape from the vicissitudes of the present to a more rewarding future. As one advocate of play has put it, 'In play, there is a childlike (yet also adult) dissolution, reconstruction and reorganisation of memories, experiences and events.'[8] Through play, past and future come together in an all-absorbing present; reality is momentarily transcended. T. S. Eliot captured with exquisite grace and clarity the illusory nature of chronological time in the famous lines which begin the *Four Quartets*:

> *Time present and time past*
> *Are both perhaps present in time future,*
> *And time future contained in time past.*

This is our experience of time when we are at play.

The importance for adults of accessing the past and the future through play is not yet clearly understood as it has been very little researched or considered. One of the few ways in which it is officially sanctioned in our culture is when a person is in distress about some aspect of their lives and seeks help from a therapist. The psychoanalytic world, at least, has recognised the importance of achieving a balance between past experience, present situation and future expectation, but it is a sad comment on our culture that so many people today can only set about finding this balance by first becoming acutely unhappy; even sadder that what is rightfully theirs must be paid for, literally and metaphorically, and often at a high price. Adult play is, tragically, most permissible when it is a form of work, whether that be helping a child to learn, or healing some deep-seated psychic wound.

A person who denies all reality of past experience is likely to be dysfunctional to some degree. As philosopher George Santayana said, 'He who cannot recall the past, is condemned to repeat it.' No more healthy is a refusal or inability to engage imaginatively with the future. Setting up a dichotomy, as Freud did, between play on the one hand and reality on the other is profoundly unhelpful. Instead, we should recognise in play a doorway that opens between the simultaneous realities of past and present, or, if we so wish, one that can lead us to a place where time as we usually know it is, for a while, suspended altogether.

Play is available to us all, regardless of age, class or race. It is especially valuable in women's lives, for it can counter the many pressures and demands on a woman's time and offer respite from the many constraints on how she spends that time.

In his stunning poem, *Whale Nation*, Heathcote Williams captures the quality of effortless playfulness in whales that we too need to rediscover.

> *Whales play, in an amniotic paradise.*
> *Their light minds shaped by buoyancy, unrestricted by gravity,*
> *Somersaulting,*
> *Like angels, or birds;*
> *Like our own lives, in the womb.*
> *Whales play*
> *For three times as long as they spend searching for food:*
> *Delicate, involved games,*
> *With floating seabirds' feathers, blown high into the air,*
> *And logs of wood*
> *Flipped from the tops of their heads;*
> *Carried in their teeth*
> *For a game of tag, ranging across the entire Pacific.*
> *Play without goals.*
> . . .
> *And they do not work to eat.*
> *They play to eat.*

It is surely not just chance that two of the most intelligent mammals, dolphins and whales, not only display a well-developed sense of play, but also spend much of their time playing. Perhaps this is actually an indication of their intelligence, in contrast to us humans who have so denigrated play, arguably one of the clearest indications of our stupidity. Jung wrote that one of the tasks of life should be 'to reconcile the civilised and the primitive in us, to rediscover that lost intensity of living'. There can be no better way to do that task of reconciling and rediscovering than through play.

In many women's lives, the acute lack of time seems like a considerable barrier to reinstating the playful self in our lives, but it is not insuperable. In many instances, it is primarily our conditioning rather than our actual situation that makes us feel there is so little time to spare. A minute is an impossibly short time in which to get anything useful done, but it can be long enough to entertain a playful thought, or enjoy the sensation of a playful impulse. It is long enough to pull a silly face at the reflection in the mirror, long enough to hum a tune, long enough to do a little jig on the pavement. While we need to start carving out for ourselves discrete blocks of time in which to play, we also need to have ways of playing regardless of everyday time constraints. If our attitude is playful enough, we may well surprise ourselves and find that there is, after all, despite everything, time enough to be playful.

11

The Way to Play

'. . . All the world's a stage,
And all the men and women merely players:
They have their exits and their entrances;
And one man in his time plays many parts.'
(William Shakespeare, *As You Like It*)

Each of us has many different ways of playing within us. By recalling the wealth of our childhood play, we have seen how we can rediscover the playing child we once were; by nurturing a playful attitude, we have seen how we can find time for play even when time seems in impossibly short supply; by rekindling the impulse to play, this chapter argues, we can, in countless ways in our daily life, discover the playing woman we want to be. There can be no one kind of play, nor one route to playing; instead, there are many ways to play, and it is up to us as individuals to choose what suits, and to seize the opportunities for play however and whenever they arise.

By looking now in detail at four areas of our lives, we shall see how the very situations which so often seem to us inimical to play can provide us with ample ways to do so. The oral, the physical, the sexual and the mental arenas of our experience – all these, which together comprise such a large part of our daily world, offer opportunities for the playful self to find expression.

Roof-Raising And Rabble-Rousing

First of all, there is the realm of oral and aural experience. This is made complicated for women by the negative associations that so often accompany it, and have done for generations. As we saw in earlier chapters, silence or quietness in women is frequently extolled, while talkativeness, verbal assertion or argumentativeness are frequently condemned. In all sorts of ways, we are culturally conditioned to curtail our speech, not to make jokes, not to 'interrupt', not to 'hog' the conversation.

It is not only speech that is problematic for many women. Besides words, a whole array of *sounds* which can come from the mouth are frowned upon when the mouth in question is female. Many adult women allow themselves neither the noise of joy, nor the noise of sorrow, nor the noise of anger. Women's angry noises are dismissed as 'hysteria' and 'nagging'. Loud, uncontrolled weeping is often described as 'ugly' or 'inhuman'. A woman who makes too little noise in love-making is 'frigid', while she who makes too much is 'loose'. For many women, considerable anxiety surrounds the question of how much noise is acceptable, whether in conversation, argument, love-making or childbirth. One woman I spoke to attributed her descent into alcoholism to the constraints on female expression, angry expression in her case. 'It was only when I was drunk that I was able to shout and swear. It was the only time I could lose my temper. The rest of the time I felt gagged.' Another woman described how she'd spent many years of her life in an agony of self-consciousness because she felt she had a horrible laugh. Many of us dislike the way we look when we laugh. The vital face that moves and twists and grimaces is not, we learn, beautiful. We are secretly shocked to see photographs of ourselves that show a face in motion. The faces of the Botticelli beauties are serene, composed; the images of models that stare at us from the pages of our magazines are usually static, often serious, or slightly smiling; if caught in a laugh, then carefully arranged so.

The tragedy of this state of affairs is that noise can be a wonderful form of play, and, besides, is closely connected to the fundamental issue of how entitled we feel, or do not feel, to express ourselves in a range of different ways, play being one of them. Noise is exhilarating, aural proof of the living sensate self. Singing, moaning, humming, whistling, shouting: all demonstrably declare our presence and express how we feel in that particular moment. To release the voice is to realise the self. This premise is used with great imagination and effect in voice movement therapy. In *The Singing Cure*, voice therapist Paul Newham describes the case of a woman who was suffering from aphonia, or loss of voice, as a result of her stifling, loveless marriage in which there was no space for this woman to express herself. As Newham writes: 'Aphonia represents the ultimate silence, and it frequently contains the only form of protest available to those who can withstand no more oppression . . . to withdraw from using one's own voice is sometimes the only way one can continue to make a point in the face of such oppression.'[1] This is the silence of the Little Mermaid, of Cinderella, of Anna Karenina, of Madame

Bovary. Significantly, 90 per cent of those who suffer from psychosomatic aphonia are women.

In any culture where women are muted, you can hear, if you listen carefully, the muffled howl of the frustrated player. You can hear it in the flattened intonation of depressed housewives, in the litany of indeterminate ailments in the GP's surgery, in the half-joking sharing of grievances between friends, in the anguished outpourings in a thousand therapy rooms. Instead of confident, joyous self-expression, there is self-doubt, anxiety, uncertainty, confusion. In *Women Who Run With the Wolves*, Jungian analyst Clarissa Pinkola Estes envisages a different kind of howl. Not a howl of pain, but a voice that can connect us with our intuitive, powerful self, the archetypal wild woman, as she gathers up bones and sings 'from deep within the body, deep within the mind, deep within the soul'. Pinkola Estes draws on myth, fairy tale, poetry and psychology in her impassioned case for the psychic power of the Feminine, which she finds embodied in the archetype of the wild woman. Finding our voice, Pinkola Estes asserts, is part of the task of discovering that power: 'To sing [as the wild woman sings] means to use the soul voice. It means to say on the breath the truth of one's power and one's need, to breathe soul over the thing that is ailing or in need of restoration.' Pinkola Estes ends her book with ten 'General Wolf Rules For Life'. Rule Number Ten is 'Howl often'.[2]

Noise-making is a way of taking your own desire for space seriously; it is a way of expressing your need to be there and to be noticed. Pleasurable and satisfying in itself, noise is a vital form of self-expression, a very direct way of asserting one's self on the circumambient universe. The newborn baby's cry is its first assertion of its existence in the world. The drive to conquer language and so be able to communicate verbally is astonishingly powerful: even before a child has mastered real words, it will babble commandingly to anyone who will listen. To scream, shout, sing, laugh, yell – all these extend the self by throwing inward experience out into the world.

Caroline, who attended the Play Day, described how she had discovered a playful side to herself when she decided to learn Italian in her mid-twenties, and fell so in love with the language that she has since become a regular visitor to the country:

> I'm not a very out-going person normally, but something about the rhythms of the Italian language, and the fact that it's so naturally expressive, just had this amazing effect on me. I become like a different person: more confident, more vivacious,

> much more talkative! All those lovely rolling bouncing sounds somehow unlock something in me. Even my voice changes, it gets louder and stronger. I think the language itself is playful, and I certainly feel much more playful when I'm speaking it.

I, too, had an experience of discovering a playful side to myself through the voice, not through speaking in my case, but singing. As a child I used to sing all the time: folk songs, pop songs, classical arias, anything at all. I would memorise the words of songs so that I could sing them to myself. My stepsister and I put on little concerts for our parents, in which we would go through our entire repertoire. If anyone asked, I told them I wanted to be an opera singer when I grew up. Gradually, over the years, however, I stopped singing. It became embarrassing. In school assembly, no one wanted to be heard singing. We all just mouthed the words. The music teacher made people sing solo to humiliate them in front of the class; at that age, none of the boys could sing because their voices were breaking, and the girls who could sing kept quiet about it. I just gave up – I did not even sing to myself. And with disuse, my singing voice dried up, until I actually found it hard to sing because I could not cover the range of even simple songs. Then, a few years ago when I was expecting my first child, I joined an antenatal yoga class run by an inspiring woman called Kay Millar.

Kay – calm, elfin, impossibly flexible – used to end each session with a humming exercise, in which we all sat round the room with our eyes closed, our hands folded on our expanding bellies, and hummed on any note we wanted, to the sound of 'ahhh', then 'oooo', then 'mmm'. The idea was to deepen the breathing and release tension by extending the out-breath. At first we all felt rather self-conscious, and tried to hum as unobtrusively as possible, but slowly the hums would start to be pitched more loudly and widely, until the most amazing sounds filled the room: not the kind of sounds women usually make. These were low and earthy, high and ethereal, wild, contented, soothing, terrifying – and they all came together in an extraordinary symphony of voices.

The experience of humming in this way was, for me, very liberating. It felt wonderful to be expressing myself through noise again for the first time in so long, discovering a new kind of voice for myself. A month or so later my daughter was born, amidst extraordinary noises of another kind, and in the weeks that followed I found myself singing again: nursery rhymes, lullabies, made-up songs about purëed apple and mashed banana. Gradually, in a process which had begun with that humming exercise, my voice opened up again, and as it did so I discovered again the enormous pleasure to be had from expressing myself through sounds other than the spoken word.

Singing is a playful pleasure for sure, because what else is singing if not a way of playing with sounds themselves? Noise-making in general is linked to the ability to feel and to be playful by virtue of its direct connection to self-expression. Next time you are in the shower, try singing an ablution blues; next time you are stuck in a traffic jam, try turning down the window and loudly whistling a tune of your choice; next time you are picking other people's clothes up off the floor, try growling. If we only can shrug off some of the inhibitions and prohibitions that surround making noise, we can discover a very immediate way of bringing ourselves several steps closer to our playful selves.

Having Our Cake – And Eating It

Another way in which we are often orally restrained when we could be orally playful, is in our relationship with food and appetite. Food is one of the most basic and readily available sources of play, and yet, paradoxically, what could provide pleasure is instead, for a great many women, the cause of anxiety, dread and self-loathing. Anorexia and bulimia have been described as expressions of anger, sexual uncertainty, poor self-esteem and fear of adulthood. In explaining these illnesses, experts have focused on the individual's apprehension about her changing sexual and social identity. Perhaps it is not only the sexual haven of childhood that the teenage girl is reluctant to leave, but also the rich opportunities for play that accompany childhood. Peering into the play-abyss of womanhood, is it any wonder that she pulls back? Perhaps growing up is too high a price to pay.

For women, too, the idea of allowing oneself to enjoy food can often be profoundly threatening: it conjures images of abandonment and self-indulgence that have no place in the identity of the responsible, industrious woman. We are so conditioned to give out, that taking in has become problematic. If we allow ourselves that particular pleasure, what general mayhem will ensue? Yet eating can be one of life's most essential pleasures. Blissful moments at the breast are amongst our earliest and happiest experiences. The intense concentration of the toddler, squidging, squeezing, dipping, tearing and shaping her food, testifies to the fact that food can be one of the sensual delights of life.

Sharing food with others is a way of creating and sustaining our emotional connections with others. It is not coincidental that food plays so important a part in courtship, whether it involves sharing a packet of crisps in the pub or gazing at one another through a candle-lit dinner. All cultures throughout the world have complex and highly developed rituals for the preparation and consumption of food; they mirror and celebrate our connection with others.

Eating is also a way of expressing our sense of connection – or disconnection – with ourselves. The ability to feed ourselves properly is obviously a physical necessity, but it has symbolic importance too as a way of loving, valuing and caring for ourselves. To fear food, and to use food as a cause of pain and discomfort, is to express a fear of self and a sense of self as deserving of pain and punishment. Using food in that way further compounds the problem: it begins by expressing self-denial, becomes a cause for self-denial, and finally provides the means to self-denial. The dish of the day is deprivation.

When psychologist Jane Ogden interviewed women about the meaning of dieting and thinness, she found that many of her respondents viewed dieting as a route to happiness. When she asked what that happiness consisted of, a frequent response was 'More time to myself.'[3] The evidence, however, suggests that dieting seldom leads women to the attainment of their physical and emotional goals. Instead it lures them into a behavioural cycle in which they become increasingly trapped by their obsession with food, weight, calories, energy expenditure, water retention, the size of their hips, the notches on their belt. Not eating takes up as much of that wished-for 'time to myself' as eating previously did. As a route to happiness, dieting and weight loss are singularly unsuccessful. Meanwhile the multi-million-pound diet industry feeds hungrily on a cycle of dissatisfaction.[4] Even anti-dieting books, such as Orbach's *Fat Is a Feminist Issue* or Kim Chernin's *Woman Size*, can seem to offer the message that if you move beyond these troubling longings, you can break free from the bondage of food. The difficulty many women have in implementing the feminist approach to dieting is that it still casts appetite as a problem.

Appetite is not the problem. It is not our *hungering* that we should be fighting, it is our sense of *unentitlement* to that hunger. To deny one's appetite for food is to deny one's appetite for life. Food both expresses and meets the appetite for life. If we want to find more time for ourselves, we need to do it by allowing ourselves the things we want, not denying ourselves still further. The problematic relationship that so many women have with food is part of the general self-denial that so many of us seem to suffer from. If we could only allow ourselves to play more, we might well find ourselves less troubled by our appetites, by our hungering; food itself could become a source of play, rather than a way of expressing our lack of it.

Food crops up frequently in literature as a form of, or means to, play: feasting and fun go hand-in-hand through the works of both Chaucer and Shakespeare, while food-play is a recurring theme in scenes of courtship and seduction from Fielding's *Tom Jones* to Hardy's *Tess of the D'Urbervilles.* Nor have films missed out on the cinematic potential of food-play, from the melting ice-cubes in *Nine-and-a-Half Weeks* to the sizzling fried eggs in *Top Gun. Babette's Feast,* a film whose action centres entirely around eating, plays visually and sumptuously with food from beginning to end. The delightful Latin-American film *Like Water For Chocolate* played explicitly on the parallels between food-play and love-play, telling the story of a young woman who is forbidden all contact with the man she loves, and can communicate only through the food she cooks for him. As her longing grows, so the dishes she prepares for him become ever more exquisite, until eating her passion-laden food causes all who taste it to swoon with delight. There is enormous humour in these scenes: the potential for food to be a source of play is exploited to the full.

In life as in art, food is, could be, should be, central to our ability to play, whether we are buying it, cooking it or eating it. By a roadside in Cairo, I stopped to watch a boy selling limes, who was carefully, intently, piling his wares into rows of tiny pyramids, not for practical reasons, but for the sheer enjoyment of doing so. On holiday in France or Italy, market day is more than a shopping trip, it is a visual and sensual pleasure, a playful process of seeing, squeezing, smelling, pinching, selecting, bartering and, finally, buying. During my childhood, Pancake Day was always a wonderful occasion for play: my mother doing her best to fulfil our requests for pancake pictures, while we children vied with one another to think of the most ludicrous things possible: a horse leaping over a stile, a leprechaun with a crock of gold, a leopard losing its spots . . . With our golden creations in front of us, there was then the delight of filling them: sprinkling the sugar, dribbling the lemon juice, swirling on the maple syrup, rolling the whole thing up with increasingly sticky fingers. Years later, there were hot, giggly afternoons with friends, preparing complicated dishes for our first grown-up dinner parties, in which we were playing with food just as we were playing at hostess. And there was also, of course, the food-play of love: sharing popcorn in the gloom of the cinema on that first date, fingers bumping in the cardboard carton as the pin-ball wizard strutted his stuff up on the screen; flirting over champagne cocktails, some years later, in a smart London hotel I could not afford to be in; sipping cherries from a lover's mouth; orange juice and crumbling croissant in an hotel in Paris. Who has not, somewhere along the line, tasted the playfulness of food?

As a sensual experience, as a demonstration of appetite for life, as a source of pleasure, shared or solitary, as a precursor to love, as a spur to friendship, food offers us a fundamental way of being playful. If we can only allow ourselves to recognise the opportunity for playfulness that food provides, rather than fearing food or seeing it as a tedious routine, we might find in and through food enormous scope for play. If we can only allow ourselves our physical appetite, and delight in it, we can begin to relish the textures and flavours, colours and smells of different foods; we can begin to see the opportunities for playfulness that food and appetite bring with them. Children adore cooking, all the pouring and tipping and stirring and tasting and touching and moulding it involves – it is pure sensory heaven.

Nouvelle cuisine took a leaf out of children's cookbooks by making extravagant pictures with food for adults too. At Raymond Blanc's celebrated Oxfordshire restaurant, Le Manoir Aux Quat' Saisons, the gastronomic creations arriving at the tables are greeted with smiles and sighs of delight. Slices of courgettes and carrots are arranged on the plate to look like flowers. A sliver of sole is encased in an extravagant creation of golden pastry. Passion fruit come nestled in a cage of spun sugar. A white chocolate mousse is serving in a small coffee-cup, which is itself made of wafer-thin chocolate. This is the marriage of food and playfulness.

Even the nightly struggle of persuading our daughter to eat can be playful when we remember not to be exasperated by it: one evening I came into the kitchen to find my husband with the handle of a spoon in his mouth while my daughter, shrieking with joy, tried to 'catch' the other end in hers. When we go to such lengths to make food fun for children, why do we so often forget the pleasure it can hold for adults too? Beans on toast is not exactly inspirational, but even that can be fun, if we choose to make it so. A friend tells me that she and her partner have recently started to make a joke out of the lack of romance in their lives these days by eating by candle-light, even when it is just beans on toast they are eating – the incompatibility of beans and candles adds to their enjoyment.

Shaking And Moving

As important as finding ways of playing orally, whether by what we take in or what we give out, is finding ways to play through forms of *physical* expression. One form of physical expression that tends to get written out of our lives as we get older is dance. Though denounced by the seventeenth-century Puritans as 'the very bellowes of luste and uncleannesse',[5] dance is, at its best, a form of physical play that combines the joy of making noise with the profound pleasure of uninhibited self-expression. The word 'dance' comes from the Sanskrit, *tanha*, meaning 'joy of life', while the Arabic word for dance, *raks*, and the Turkish, *rakkase*, both come from an Assyrian word, *radadu*, meaning 'to celebrate'.[6] Many religions, ancient and modern, have enshrined dancing as an essential part of worship, and in Jewish eschatology God as the majestic player will celebrate the coming of the kingdom of heaven by leading his people in a triumphant dance.[7] Dance teacher Wendy Buonaventura argues that 'All dance comes from life, and in particular from our need to express ourselves and make sense of our existence. By its very nature it is one of the most powerful means of auto-intoxication we have, developing energy in the body and then releasing it.'[8]

At its worst, however, dance can be a way of denying both body and voice. The growth of cabarets and clubs have eroticised dance in such a way that it is more likely to degrade and exploit the female body than to celebrate it. It is not the erotic element in dance that is of concern, but the way in which this element is singled out and exaggerated. When this happens, dance is no longer about the whole woman, but only about her sexuality. As Buonaventura says, 'Eroticising dance universalises its appeal, but ignores the humour, playfulness, pathos and sometimes sadness that is present too.'

Classical ballet in many ways epitomises the stultifying requisites of grace and control that are considered desirable and appropriate in women. When Deborah Bull, principal dancer of the Royal Ballet in 1992, first joined the company, she was described by a fellow dancer as 'a typical English girl with quite big hips and thighs'. She spent the next ten years reshaping herself, stretching and lengthening the muscles in her legs to slim her hips and thighs, reducing her weight to just seven-and-a-half stone, turning herself into the 'beautiful, streamlined creature' her profession required.[9] Ballet not only demands a female figure so slender that it defies physics to achieve the feats of strength this form of dance requires, it is above all a silent dance: the dancer must leap into the air and land noiselessly. Inherently contradictory, classical ballet embodies the body's escape from itself.

Dance can be, and often is, both expressive and liberating. According to Wendy Buonaventura:

> Women in the Arab world have a sensual ease and bodily awareness lacking in the west. Less hemmed in by external restrictions than in Arab countries, European and American women have, in a sense, created their own restrictions. These are manifested in a denial of the body and sensuality, as well as a physical stiffness and self-dislike from which Arab women in general do not suffer . . . One of the most rewarding sights at Arabic dance classes in the west is to see the enjoyment of big-hipped curvaceous women who have at last found a dance which allows them to take pride in their body . . . Many women who would love to dance have been discouraged by the demands of western dance forms such as ballet . . . The Arabic dance tradition, with its acceptance of the body, whatever its shape, and its affirmation of a woman's sensuality, whatever her age, offers her the chance to reassess her own, sometimes negative self-image in an atmosphere of support rather than competition.[10]

Dancing heightens the senses and lowers the inhibitions. This is what we thrill to as we watch, or try for ourselves, the clicking, clapping and stamping of flamenco, or the whooping, puffing and leaping of African dance. Instead of the fleshless bodies of ballerinas, there are bouncing breasts and quivering thighs, all part of the dance's celebration of life, of femaleness. On feast days in rural Ethiopia, men and women dance together in a powerfully erotic and playful dance. They come together and draw apart, hands on hips, swaying and thrusting their pelvises, dipping and leaping and soaring, jiggling their shoulders, casting provocative sidelong glances, and letting out rhythmic, quasi-orgasmic gasps; the women ululate, and give the men their shawls to tie around their waists and emphasise the movements of their hips, while they wear something of the men's around their heads. As the drums beat faster and louder, the whole dance builds to an intoxicating crescendo.

At the Douglas Bader Centre in Oxford, Debbie Macklin's New Dance Company teaches aerobics with a difference. Instead of the usual emphasis on controlling and constraining the body in a series of tight, rigid, mechanical movements, and where the only sound is the dum-di-dum of the music, Macklin's classes are splendidly noisy. The mood is of a tribal dance: energetic, pulsating, ferocious; the movements are expansive, the women fill the space. The classes are exciting to watch, exhilarating to take part in. They are not about constraining the body, but about demonstrating and exploring its power. From country-dancing and tea-dancing to rock-and-roll and Salsa, dance may be about sex and courtship, but it is also about dressing up, getting together with friends, having fun, and letting go.[11] It is, in short, a superb form of physical play, one that women of all ages can enjoy, one where a high level of skill is not necessary for a high level of pleasure, one in which the only real requirement is that the individual gives herself permission to have a go.

Sport is another form of physical play that many men enjoy throughout their lives, but which the majority of women abandon even before they leave school.[12] While little compares with the remembered horror of games for those who detested it, many women have fond memories of hockey, netball, tennis, gymnastics and athletics, and express regret that getting older has somehow also entailed dropping these activities from their lives. Veronica Jay, a 55-year-old teacher, recalls: 'I used to play netball all the time when I was younger. But after I got married there was somehow never time, you know, housework and decorating gradually took over.'[13]

Women who do continue to do sport of some kind are often eager to describe the immense pleasure it brings them. Sarah Girling, a barrister in her mid-thirties, was a keen rower as a student at Cambridge University. She rowed for the second University crew, and insists that her enjoyment was not linked to competitiveness.

> Rowing, for me, had very little to do with ambition. I wasn't very interested in succeeding or winning or coming first. But I loved the feeling of the boat moving through the water, and of the team working exactly in time together down to the billionth of a second. It wasn't the sense of individual achievement or power or co-ordination; it was the total immersion in the rhythm of the team, almost as if you were no longer there: you stopped thinking and acting as an individual, you became completely part of the group. That sense of oneness was amazing, incredibly exhilarating.

Sarah's description of the absorption, the loss of self-consciousness, the sensation of simultaneously losing the self and enlarging the self, points firmly to the large element of play that is present in sport. Many of the women interviewed by Gilda O'Neill for her book, *A Night Out With the Girls*, expressed the joy they derive from sport and physical activity in similar terms. One woman, an ardent player and supporter of football, says, 'It allows you to do things that women aren't traditionally allowed to do . . . I remember clearly enjoying this feeling of real physical release and realising that this was something that society had tried to stamp out of me. And suddenly here was this field – quite literally – where I could be. It was a fantastic, liberating feeling. I felt like I was flying.' Another of O'Neill's interviewees talks about her love of fishing, which she calls her 'hydro-therapy': 'Some days I never catch anything but fishing for me is far more than capturing a hard-fighting fish, thrilling though that may be. Aesthetically it is the freedom of the hills, the glint of a lochan, the darkening sky before a storm . . . that wonderful escape to the still, tranquil world of an isolated loch . . . I don't think I could function properly without fishing. It's probably the most complete form of relaxation in the open air that I know.'[14]

Despite its importance, socially, psychologically and physically, women of all ages take consistently less exercise than men. Running up and down stairs, lifting children and pushing prams may be exhausting, but they do not count in terms of physical exercise, still less in terms of play. With levels of physical fitness falling, obesity rising, and women at growing risk of coronary heart disease and strokes, sport is not only an enjoyable form of play, but an increasingly necessary one. Lack of physical exercise is a key factor in these illnesses, yet 88 per cent of women fail to meet government health guidelines on exercise. Only 12 per cent take enough exercise to counter cardiovascular disease. Twenty per cent of women in Britain currently have high levels in 3 out of 4 key risk factors for heart disease and strokes, compared with 18 per cent of men.[15] According to the Health Education Authority only 9 per cent of young women aged 16–24 take enough exercise to keep healthy, while 50 per cent of girls aged 1–16 do not even get the equivalent of a brisk ten-minute walk a week.[16] Insufficient exercise is significantly reducing the quality of life at the other end of the scale too: only 35 per cent of people aged 55–64 and 23 per cent of those aged 65–74 take enough exercise to be physically independent. In the 55–74 age group, according to one study, nearly *all* the women would have difficulty walking up a 1-in-20 slope at 3 miles an hour.[17]

Things may be changing. Between 1989 and 1991 there was a 50 per cent increase in female football players, and there are now around 9000 women footballers registered with the Women's Football Association. Nearly 60,000 women currently play netball, a figure increasing at the rate of 6 per cent a year, and there are around 90 women's rugby teams in the UK. The most popular sports for women are walking, swimming, cycling, keep-fit classes and yoga.[18] While physical exercise for women often becomes a form of self-punishment, a means to the depressing and usually elusive goal of burning off calories, toning the buttocks, or trimming the thighs (as if they were a kind of privet hedge), it need not be. Sport can be a wonderful form of play. It is a fulfilling experience in its own right, abounding in the 'pleasurable excitement' which 'is at the core of most play needs', according to sociologists Elias and Dunning.[19]

Proof physical of a woman's ability to stand up for her play rights, sport can also be profoundly satisfying on a symbolic level. It stands for autonomy, self-assertion and self-fulfilment. Playing through sport not only enables women to move beyond social and cultural constraints on female behaviour, it is also a way of overcoming cultural taboos on female aspirations; it can meet an otherwise unfulfilled need in women to take up space, to make large, forceful, assertive gestures, to celebrate one's strength, agility, power and determination. In the words of one woman, a badminton player, sport gave her the sense of 'pushing back frontiers'.[20]

In her study of 40 sportswomen aged 18–47, Margaret Talbot found that the physical sensation of moving freely in a large space was a source of great pleasure for many of the women. They also mentioned enjoying running fast in the open air, and wearing comfortable clothes and footwear. All are sensations often denied women by the dictates of fashion, domestic responsibilities and social expectation. Talbot's interviewees were top-level hockey players and non-club-member badminton players, all of whom played at least once a week, and some as many as three or four times a week. Their reasons for playing included fulfilment, fitness, sociability and time for themselves (i.e. away from home).[21]

We need to forget that sport was a weekly humiliation at school, and instead open our hearts and minds to the possibility of physical expression; our playful self, we need to say, might just enjoy this. We need to risk trying new sports, ones untainted with the horror of school hockey or, worse still, cross-country running. Roller-skating, juggling, hang-gliding, badminton, water-polo. Perhaps, if we allow ourselves to give it a try, we will find that physical play is not something to be banished to childhood memories, and instead that, as playful women, we are able to run and dance and jump and yell with the best of them.

The Agony Or The Ecstasy

Sex is possibly the area of our lives which can be the best playground of all, one of the few places we can both lose and find ourselves. However, although sex could be and should be, and sometimes *is*, the best playground of all, sex in general, and female sexuality in particular, has been so objectified that genuine playfulness can be as hard to attain here as elsewhere in our lives.

'Too bad if a girl doesn't know how to play,' wrote Ovid in his *Art of Love*, 'games often provide a quick lead-in to love.'[22] But Ovid was talking about what a girl needs to know in order to please her lover, rather than what will give her enjoyment. Similarly in John Cleland's *Memoirs of a Woman of Pleasure*: Cleland's novel caused a furore when it was first published in 1748, with its detailed account of how Fanny, a virginal serving girl at the outset, is transformed into an energetic and enthusiastic courtesan. On the one hand, Cleland's work can be seen as the portrait of a life of uninhibited sexual play, a celebration of female sexual desire; on the other, there is the fact that male gratification is the *sine qua non* of the heroine's existence, added to which the author was undoubtedly writing to titillate a male readership and pander to male sexual fantasies. Cleland's novel survives as a classic chiefly by the inventiveness of the writing and the ingenuity of the metaphors, but it is hard to ignore the fact that Fanny has a great deal in common with the stereotype of the innocent-but-eagerly-available housewife in contemporary pornographic literature.

The 1992 Louis Malle film, *Damage*, based on the novel by Josephine Hart, carried a more overtly hostile message about female sexuality. *Damage* tells the story of a respectable married man, whose contented, affluent life is entirely destroyed when he becomes infatuated with a beautiful young woman he meets at a cocktail party. It turns out that she is his son's girlfriend, but this fails to dampen his desire, and a passionate affair ensues. The film evokes another stereotype of female sexuality: the *femme fatale*, and shows all too clearly what happens to women who play sexually for their own purposes as opposed to others' pleasure: they wreak havoc, destroy marriages, kill happiness, murder sons. If the acting was anything to go by, they do not even seem to enjoy the sex that much.

Language too shapes our sexual experiences in ways that often take male sexuality and male sexual pleasure as the acceptable norm. American feminist Barbara Mehrhof has suggested that were female sexuality the norm, the word for coitus would be 'enclosure', not 'penetration'. Similarly, 'foreplay' is used to describe what happens before the sexual act proper begins, despite the fact that, from a female perspective, foreplay can be to the fore in importance as well as timing, and can lead quite satisfactorily to orgasm without any need of penetration/enclosure.

Our ability to be unselfconsciously, playfully sexual is directly diminished by the endless images that we encounter, in magazines, on television, in adverts, films and calendars. As Naomi Wolf has written, 'To live in a culture in which women are routinely naked where men aren't, is to learn inequality in little ways all day long.'[23] Media representations of women in an apparent state of sexual ecstasy act like pornography: they distance us from how we feel from the inside out, and instead focus our attention on how we look from the outside in. Whether these ecstatic women are being used to sell ice-cream, fast cars or chocolate bars, their celluloid sexuality becomes the visual barometer by which we try to measure ourselves.

When Haagen-Dazs brought out their recession-beating advertising campaign, they were exploiting a hunger that went beyond ice-cream. A scantily clad couple, limbs entwined, glistened with pre-orgasmic sweat. The woman pours ice-cream into the man's up-turned mouth in an inversion of penetration. The ice-cream is both breast and penis: the woman bearing this wondrous object is all-powerful. Yet she is also the object of his desire, sexy because he finds her so, powerful because he makes her so. The image captures a male fantasy of female sexuality, and shows women the fantasy they are meant to become. An advertisement for Flake released around the same time worked on a similar basis. Once again, the sexual metaphor is ludicrously emphasised. A woman lies in a bath tub, naked but for her face which is extravagantly made up, as if for an evening out. Her reddened lips open slowly to make space for the chocolate/phallus coming towards her. Her face bears an expression of sublime sexual arousal and bliss. As she bites into the Flake, water/sperm pours over her. She sinks back into the water in a post-coital swoon, and the over-full bath spills out on the floor unheeded. Again, the woman is both powerful and powerless, totally in the grip of her erotic ecstasy induced by the chocolate/phallus. Again, the image objectifies female sexual arousal: how it looks is synonymous with how it feels.

There is, of course, an element of playfulness in adverts such as these, which intentionally take their own messages to extremes and parody their own techniques. Advertisers want us to equate eating ice-cream with sensual pleasure, but they know as well as we that it is unlikely to bring us to orgasm. Audiences often respond to these self-parodying adverts with amusement, and I have been in cinemas where the whole room has erupted in laughter. However, set in the wider context of women's socialisation, the images of female sexual response that adverts present seem less benign, contributing as they do to the general self-consciousness that makes it so hard for many of us to experience our lives from the inside out. It is not hard to see how we all, men and women, begin to lose confidence in ourselves sexually, with questions buzzing round our heads: 'Do I look like that when I feel like that?'; 'Will I feel like that when I look like that?'; 'Do I look like I think I should look when I feel how I'm feeling?' Women's magazines sell copies on the basis of these anxieties, their covers emblazoned with tempting advice on how to 'Keep Your Love Life Sizzling', 'Learn To Love Oral Sex', 'Find Out What Turns Him On'. The articles themselves present sex as a world of reciprocal pleasuring, but they help to create a world in which mutual sexual fulfilment is primarily the woman's responsibility. We are told to be uninhibited, but the articles and books that tell us how to do so make it difficult to be so. Instead, with their injunctions to be sexy, to be natural, to be fun, they make us self-conscious in the extreme.

As women grapple with their own feelings about their sexuality, they have also to cope with the way in which their sexuality is being shaped by others. Sexual attractiveness in women has always been subject to the dictates of fashion, from the curved bellies of the Middle Ages, to the bulging bottoms of the Edwardians, to the flat chests of the Roaring Twenties and the slim hips of the 1960s. Great for those who match up to the current trend, a nightmare for all those who do not. In the 1990s, the messages about female sexuality are as confusing as ever: we must be in charge of our bodies (that is, use contraceptives), proud of our bodies (that is, keep them looking good for others), at ease in our bodies (that is, do not let on if we are dieting); we must be happy with our sexuality (that is, know where our clitoris is), and happy with other people's sexuality (that is, stop objecting to *his* sexual proclivities).

Despite the apparent 'coming out' of female sexuality in recent years, the proliferation of books, articles, manuals and guides to sex, mostly targeted at and bought by women, only adds to the process of dissociation between women and their sexual identity. Women's sexuality takes place 'out there' on the page, on the screen, in someone else's bedroom. It is taken away from us even as it appears to be given back to us. We are encouraged to identify with an external representation of female sexuality, which in many cases only distances us still further from our own individual, unique sexuality. We are given no more real guidance to fulfilling our own sexual feelings than we would by being shown a picture of food in order to satisfy a physical hunger. What should be internal, private, personal, is instead increasingly abstracted, public, external. Our sexuality in this way is a symbol and a symptom of the fractured male view through which we see and try to understand ourselves in general.

Sexual pleasure of all kinds would once have been described as 'play'. Milton's poem, *Paradise Lost*, written in the seventeenth century, uses the word in this way, when Adam says to Eve, 'Now let us play'.[24] This idea of sexual pleasure as a form of play survives in Sanskrit, where the word for copulation is *kridaratnam*, which translates as 'the jewel of games'. In Latin the word *lascivus* can mean 'free of restraint in sexual matters', but it can also mean simply 'playful, frolicsome'. In an ideal world there should not be a problem with the way these two meanings – 'free of sexual restraint' and 'frolicsome' – go together; in reality, however, there very often is. In the English language today, 'play' usually describes not sexual pleasure, but sexual conquest, as in 'playing around', 'playing the field', 'playing hard to get' and 'making a play for someone'. There is something very sad about this semantic evolution, indicative that physical love is no longer a playground, but a battlefield.

The date-rape case at King's College, London, in 1993, revealed the degree of censure that still awaits women who claim sexual and physical freedom. The case involved a male undergraduate accused by a contemporary of raping her after a party. What was interesting about the case was not so much whether the student had forced the young woman to have sexual intercourse (the court decided that he had not), but the way in which, as the case progressed, the media interpretation focused increasingly on the man as the victim of a predatory female. The tabloid press placed great emphasis on the young woman's sexual past, stressing that she had had several one-night stands. It seemed that we were to conclude from this information that she was therefore perfectly amenable to *any* sexual advance. What we can more reliably conclude is that the sexual double standard still thrives. A woman is still accountable for a man's sexual response, and a woman is still not free to express her sexuality as men have always expressed theirs, at least without running the risk of moral vilification.

Women seem increasingly to be reaching for uninhibited sexual playfulness in affairs. The figures for married women having extra-marital affairs vary from study to study, but the number has certainly risen from the 26 per cent arrived at by Kinsey in 1953, and may well now be in the region of 41 per cent, according to two separate American surveys.[25] In a 1992 survey of 1000 British women, over a third said that they had had or would have a one-night stand while in a relationship. Over 10 per cent had had or would contemplate having a long-term lover while in a relationship.[26] In response to the question 'How satisfied are you with your sex life?' over half were either 'quite satisfied' (41 per cent) or 'not very satisfied' (17 per cent); 7 per cent were 'not at all satisfied'. Less than half, in other words, were satisfied.

The appeal, conscious or unconscious, of the affair is that it provides a space that is free from the normal restrictions on a woman's sexuality; since she has already broken the rules, there is no point in now abiding by them.[27] In Dalma Heyn's study of women in extra-marital relationships, many of the women she interviewed mentioned the playfulness of sex in their affairs, both the playfulness they enjoyed in their partners *and* the playfulness they discovered in themselves. However, many of these women described a sense of a time limit on their sexual happiness, accepting that at some point they would have to endure the end of the relationship, whether triggered by their lover or themselves, and they would have to return to the 'real' world. For some of Heyn's interviewees, this meant embarking on a mission to incorporate a new degree of sexual expressiveness and playfulness into 'real' time and space. Some were successful, some were not.

Although the ending or the discovery by their partner of the affair caused enormous suffering and anguish, none of Dalma Heyn's interviewees regretted their affairs; instead, they all felt that it had shown them something about themselves, reminded them of something they had forgotten, which they were profoundly grateful to have remembered again, as one woman put it, 'something about pleasure, and the insistence on it and the effects of it even if it is not found in marriage'.

By modelling ourselves on men, adapting our sexual responses to meet their sexual needs and fantasies, we effectively shut out the possibility of sexual playfulness in the mainstream of our lives. The joy of sexual play, like any other kind of play, is that it takes us out of ourselves and at the same time gives us back to ourselves. Many women who have affairs seem to experience the transformation of themselves from workers into players.

Play is an embodying of self in activity, and sexual play can be one of the most pure experiences of this, for play both celebrates the self in all its uniqueness, and allows self and other to become merged. Play, and in particular, sexual play, upholds individuality and at the same time strengthens relatedness. Karl Groos saw the 'joy of being a cause' as a vital aspect of play, and this is as true in sexual play as any other. 'As an adult', said one woman on the Play Day, 'you have this whole new area of play, which is sex. I definitely regard sex as play, and talking about sex too! Playfulness in sex is very important, it's what stops you becoming a technical machine. Through sex, you can experience the absorption of play, absorption in yourself, but also the possibility for being absorbed with other people, which is wonderful.'

Through a healthy and hearty capacity for sexual playfulness we can experience the joy of being a cause of our own pleasure, and simultaneously the cause of another's pleasure. The circularity of sex at its best makes it not only fulfilling, but self-fulfilling. It is a way to play and a way of playing that we should permit ourselves and insist on if we want, as Dalma Heyn puts it, to prevent our 'expressive, creative, sexual selves from going underground'.[28]

It is easy to be sexually playful in an affair – there is no responsibility, no pre-charted territory, no washing up. Being playful in our sexual lives in the midst of the mundane routines of domesticity is rather more difficult. But not impossible. Once again, the key is permission. Until we give ourselves permission to be sexually playful, we can read manuals and magazine articles until the cows come home. Instead, we need to allow ourselves to step out of our own images of ourselves, to surprise ourselves, indulge ourselves, do something a bit different, say something a bit different, *think* something a bit different. Sex can be a pretty hilarious business, if we could just allow ourselves to stop taking it all so seriously.

Dreaming And Becoming

There is another way to play which is worth considering in some detail: the play of our imaginations. Of all the ways to play, this one goes to the heart of the theme of this book: how we can start to give ourselves permission to play. Underpinning all the obstacles thus far described is our fundamental lack of a sense of entitlement to be playful. However, through the play of the imagination, women can be, for a while, relieved of the shackles of responsibility for others, the requisite of emotional empathy and consideration for others. Through play, we can find reprieve from the taboos on thinking, imagining, contemplating, questioning.

Dreaming, fantasising, idolising are all forms of imaginative play, the vehicles by which as children we happily encounter the great shining IF of life, by which we transcend our troublesome brother or bullying father or distracted mother, our lack of friends, our difficulties with maths, our inability to hit the rounders ball. In the absence of female heroes to emulate, many girls choose male role models instead: Robin Hood, Dick Turpin, the Three Musketeers, Lancelot, Batman. We admire their daring, their strength, their resolve, their compassion, their integrity, their courage, and, through our fantasies, we momentarily possess these qualities for ourselves. But there comes a moment in the lives of most girls when we realise that we cannot grow up to be great men, and casting around for alternatives, for some great women to dream of, we are shocked to find a dearth of women to aspire to be, a want of female greats to embody our dreams. At this moment, the growing girl apprehends that in her particular prison house there are to be no fantasies of greatness, excepting, of course, the tired, asexual, trilogy: Boadicea, Joan of Arc, Florence Nightingale.

This crushing of fantasial exuberance, this clipping of the wings of desire, leaves us, inevitably, with ambivalent feelings about our femaleness, as well as mistrustful of our fantasies and, by extension, the whole realm of imaginative play. This is the genesis of the 'fear of flying', the self-imposed refusal to dream of greatness, to play with all the selves one could be if . . . Yet the ability to dream, to fantasise, to draw on our imaginations, is an essential resource throughout our lives. It is a fundamental prerequisite of play, and, in its own right, a wonderful form of play. Fantasising is the narcissistic act of being, of daring to shut out the world around one and fly into the world within one, blurring for a while the distinction between the two.

Playing through fantasy is what we do when we dress up, when we put on jewellery or make-up, when we give rein to our daydreams. Making one's external self beautiful can be a sign of enslavement to some cultural ideal, but it can equally be an expression of inner self-delight. The important difference between the two lies in the attitude of the adorner. In childhood the dressing-up box is a treasure trove; in adulthood its function is performed by countless dressing rooms in countless clothes shops up and down the country. 'Trying on clothes is a way of stepping out of reality,' says 32-year-old Caitlin. 'You look at yourself in the mirror and you imagine the lifestyle that goes with the clothes: a lifestyle of ease and luxury, where you never have to cook or clean, where there are no sticky fingers or squashed biscuits. A lot of clothes shopping is make-believe. You stand there in these wonderful clothes and you imagine yourself svelte, sexy, successful. Of course, once you buy the clothes the fantasy is over: you step back into reality the moment you leave the shop.'

Jewellery, a deliberate form of self-adornment, seems to be as ancient as human culture; there is evidence of jewellery dating back 20,000 years. In the caves at Lascaux, remains of jewellery have been found, made of fossils and shells, many of which would have been collected from beaches on the Atlantic and Mediterranean coasts and brought inland. Jewels have a special place in legend and myth: the secret cave always contains caskets overflowing with treasures; the brave prince's reward is always the princess *plus* a share of the King's treasure; villains in fairy stories go to great lengths to steal precious jewels. These myths endure to the present day: who can forget Fagin fawning over the jewels his boys have stolen for him, his dirty fingers lovingly caressing the sparkling trinkets, a crude anti-Semitic caricature certainly, but also a powerful evocation of the *gelt-lust* we are all capable of. Where would Aladdin be without his cave? What would the Tower of London be without the Crown Jewels? Bond films, romantic novels, Shakespearian tragedies and pantomime all testify to the importance we attach to jewels. No bride-to-be is complete without a sparkling engagement ring.

It is not the financial value of jewels and finery that enchants us so much as the intrinsic beauty. C. S. Lewis wrote that, 'We do not want merely to see beauty. We want something else which can hardly be put into words – to be united with the beauty we see, to pass into it, to receive it into ourselves, to bathe in it, to become part of it.' Our fascination throughout our lives, and throughout history, with jewellery and dressing up is in part an expression of the yearning to be united with the beautiful, to reach perfection through it, but it is also an expression of an innate human desire for *more*, part of the impetus to *know*, the aspiration to go *beyond*. As an expression of a universal and metaphysical acquisitiveness, transformation through adornment is quintessentially playful, an activity, or urge, that we need to rescue from the confines of societally imposed self-consciousness, and to value for its inherent, and liberating, playfulness. Huizinga wrote that, in the nineteenth century, 'all Europe donned the boiler suit', meaning it was at this point in history we assumed the trappings of industriousness, in our demeanour, our preoccupations and our conduct.[29] Dressing up – in fantasy or reality – enables us to cast off our boiler suits and our industriousness, and become, once again, the lead player in a marvellous drama of our own making.

Imaginative play can take many forms besides self-adornment – making music, painting, cooking, writing, story-telling, sewing, design. All start with an idea for turning something into something else: silence into sound, emptiness into an image, ingredients into a soup . . . If we can allow ourselves this mental space for play, the chance to play in our own minds with our thoughts, dreams, fantasies, ideas, then we have succeeded in finding the playful self. However the playful self may manifest itself in our lives, it originates in our own heads, as an attitude, a mindset, an openness, a receptivity. Imaginative play, then, is the germ of all play, it is the heart of the playful self.

Ludo, Ergo Sum

However we choose to play, whether through our bodies, our voices, our words, our thoughts or our dreams, play is a vital part of our repertoire. It has a key role to play in our social, psychological, emotional, physical and spiritual well-being. If, as Shakespeare put it, we play many parts in our time, then play itself plays many parts in our lives, sustaining us and healing us, relaxing and relieving us, encouraging us, protecting us, connecting us. Play, above all, is proof that we have a valid place in the world. It declares, affirms and celebrates the fact of our being alive. Play, truly, confirms existence.

Play celebrates one's right to exist, one's surety on living. Play takes place in the confidence of loving and being loved, of knowing one is and knowing one has an unassailable right to be. Play is the embrace of existence in which one is both the embrace and also the embraced. Play at its best is a celebration of wholeness and rightness, a state in which we feel so secure and assured of our existence that we can play with our place in that existence. To allow yourself to do that requires a belief in your own self, a commitment to your own experience of the world, both in reality and in fantasy, both inwardly and outwardly. That may be hard for women, who are so often discouraged from taking delight in the sensation of self, but it is not impossible. We need not dream of rescue by knights in white armour; we can and must dare to believe that it is possible to *be* the knight in our dreams, and still to be whole as women.

In this chapter we have seen how daily life offers us many ways to play, many ways to express the playful self. There is the oral play of making noise: singing, shouting, humming, whistling. There is the physical play of dancing, running, jumping, throwing. Food can be a way to play, providing pleasure for our senses and scope for our creativity. Enjoyment of our sexual appetite, too, provides us with a way to play, while bringing an appetite for play to sex makes sex all the more enjoyable; and then there is the play of the imagination, which finds expression through ideas, dreams, fantasies, and is at the very heart of the playful self, leading to and from all other kinds of play.

The odds against play in our lives are often great, but seldom insuperable. We have seen how play has been gradually marginalised and downgraded in western culture; we have seen why this is of consequence, what happens when people are deprived of play, and, more positively, what happens when they are encouraged to play. We have looked at the problems that women face in meeting their need for play, and at the many practical considerations that often prevent them from acting on that instinct. We have looked at the social, economic and psychological pressures that undermine women's ability and their inclination to play, and at the processes that so often direct women away from playfulness. But we have also explored and exposed the ways in which women *are* managing to play still, the ways in which their innate playfulness is finding expression, the ways in which they are successfully resisting the curbs on their capacity for play, and standing up for their right to play.

Play is not something meant only for a few; it is something that all women can benefit from profoundly. On a personal level, we can all revive our desire for play and reinstate it at the centre of our lives. We can start to do this by granting ourselves permission to play; we can start by fostering a playful attitude to life; we can start by reminding ourselves that one no sooner forgets how to play than one forgets how to ride a bicycle and that all of us, once upon a time, knew how to play; we can start by remembering that there is time for play, and that there are ways to play. By doing these things, by making these small beginnings towards cherishing the playful self, we can not only own our right to play, but thrive by it.

12

Play Rights

'No cause is left but the most ancient of all . . . the cause of freedom versus tyranny.'
(Hannah Arendt, *On Revolution*)

Of all the women I have interviewed in the last ten years in the course of writing this book, those who were coping best with their lives, getting the most out of their lives, were not those with the most money, but those with the most playful attitude, those who had determinedly nurtured opportunities to play. They had kept something alive in themselves that was missing in many of their contemporaries, who had allowed the seriousness of life to shut out time and space for play. Their lives were no easier in objective terms. They had the same trials and tragedies to contend with as everyone else, but they seemed to handle life's tribulations more easily than others, from the demands of small children or the stress of forced redundancy, to the death of parents or physical illness. Those coping best were always those for whom play and playfulness had remained meaningful concepts, whatever their age or stage of life.

In play, as in many areas of our lives, the personal is political. In this final chapter, it remains to look beyond the position of the individual woman and to locate her within a wider social context. For if a woman's need to play is to be upheld in private, it must also be valued in public. We need to stand up for our playful selves on a number of different levels: personal and political, public and private, individual and communal, social and economic, emotional and psychological, physical and spiritual. If play is to become a valued and valid part of our lives, we need to hone our play instincts, nurture our playfulness, and make time and space for playing. We must assert our right to play before others, with each other, by ourselves, with our words, with our bodies, with our thoughts. We must start to uphold our play rights as partners, as parents, as colleagues, as friends, and, above all, as individuals in our own right. Setting an agenda for play can help us to do this, an agenda which strives to remove the obstacles to our playfulness on the one hand, and to maximise opportunities for playfulness on the other.

An Agenda For Play

One of the biggest obstacles to women's play in practical terms, as we have seen, is the sheer volume of paid and unpaid work that they do, together with the low economic value attached to that work. The national work force is expected to grow by 900,000 in the next decade; 750,000 of them will be women. Most of those women will be working part-time, often on short-term contracts, doing shift-work or piece work, often without the benefits attached to full-time employment, such as holiday pay, sick pay, pension schemes or maternity leave. In addition, the number of women who are self-employed is growing all the time. Between 1979 and 1990, the number of self-employed women increased by 122 per cent, from 348,000 to 774,000. Self-employment may have the attraction of being flexible and therefore easier to fit around childcare responsibilities, but, like part-time and short-term employment, it comes with few financial advantages. Much of the paid work that women do is low status and low paid. Despite the Equal Pay Act of 1970, women still earn 30 per cent less than men on average. Only 6 per cent of women earn over £15,000, and 3 million women in Britain today earn less than £3 an hour. Hospital cleaners, the majority of whom are women, earn only £1.50 an hour; childminders, with daily charge of the children who will comprise tomorrow's society, command on average just £2 an hour.

The conditions of women's employment could easily be improved by the introduction of measures that would not only make working less demoralising, but would show a higher valuation of women's contribution to the economy. It is all very well for politicians, on left or right, to praise 'family values', but when are they going to implement policies that will help the people they expect to uphold those values? According to the 1988 Labour Force survey, 8 out of 10 women prefer to work part-time. This is not because they are work-shy or lack commitment to their job, but because the reality of women's lives makes part-time work the most practical solution, the best way to manage the double-shift that the majority of them face, the juggling of paid and unpaid work. Part-time work may not bring in much money, nor offer much in the way of promotion, benefits or security, but at least it leaves some time in the day for cleaning the house, doing the shopping, taking the children to school, collecting them again, washing clothes, ironing, tidying up, cooking supper and looking after elderly relations.

Improving the conditions and status of women's work should not be seen as a way for society to get more out of women, to make them work even harder than they do already, but as a way of enabling women to get more out of *life*, enabling them to assert their right to be playful as well as industrious. Introducing a statutory minimum wage; upholding the principal of equal pay for work of equal value; improving the conditions of employment for part-timers; improving pension provision for women – all these measures would raise the value of women's paid work in absolute terms, and remove many of the obstacles to women's play.

Another equally important area that needs addressing with some urgency is the burden of women's unpaid work. Measures designed to improve the status of women's paid work will only make it easier for a woman to play if accompanied by changes that also recognise the realities of the work for which she receives no payment. As well as addressing the existing inequalities in the status and conditions of women's employment, we need to put on our agenda for play a range of structural and fiscal changes aimed at lessening a woman's domestic load. Life could be made less exhausting and more rewarding by the introduction of a number of straightforward measures, many of which are already commonplace in other European countries. These include improved conditions of maternity leave; the introduction of statutory paternal and parental leave; guaranteed publicly funded childcare for all under-fives; the introduction of tax-relief schemes on childcare costs; improving childcare facilities in the work-place; introducing publicly funded or subsidised after-school care, and, most important of all, extending flexible working practices.

The acute lack of childcare provision is a major obstacle to play for a great many women, whether they're caring for their own children or their children's children. Woefully inadequate childcare provision adds considerably to the stress in a woman's life, and to that of her family as a whole. Freelance journalist Aine McCarthy, writing in the *Guardian* newspaper, complained bitterly that the lack of formal childcare provision forces women to rely on informal networks of family and friends. 'As well as letting the government off the hook, these networks help to keep men and their employers oblivious of the day-to-day challenges of caring for children,' McCarthy writes.[1] American feminist Gloria Steinem put it another way: 'I have yet to hear a man ask for advice on how to combine marriage and a career.'

Inadequate childcare provision places parents – and single parents in particular – under considerable strain. It takes huge chunks out of people's disposable income, traps them in positions of financial servitude, reduces their scope for challenging injustices and inequalities in the work-place, and severely restricts their opportunities for fulfilling leisure. Inadequate childcare provision also puts children at risk and is a major cause of child poverty.[2] The women who form 90 per cent of Britain's lone parents are not living it up on social security, but struggling in poverty to meet their children's needs.[3] Twenty-six-year-old Jackie, like many single mothers, has great difficulty combining work and family in the absence of good, affordable childcare. With three children under the age of ten, Jackie juggles her work as a cleaner to fit around school hours. During the holidays she is forced back on *ad hoc* childcare arrangements with friends and family. When these fall through, or one of the children is ill, Jackie has no choice but to forfeit her earnings. The lack of day care provision not only leaves women like Jackie vulnerable to the benefits trap by creating a major disincentive for single mothers to find paid work, it also diminishes their opportunities for study, involvement in public activities, and, last but not least, rewarding recreation.[4] Small wonder play has so negligible a part in so many women's lives.

Britain lags behind every other country in the European Union in terms of its provision for paternity leave, parental leave, tax-relief incentives and childcare facilities. Britain is now one of only three EU countries to make no provision for parental leave. According to Professor Susan McRae at Oxford Brookes University, Britain stands out from other countries in Europe by its refusal to see childcare as a joint parental responsibility. 'The policy debate in Britain is not about how families can reconcile work and family life, it is about how *women* can accommodate work and family life,' says McRae.[5] The exhaustive and exhausting task of juggling childcare, housework and a job outside the home directly impinges on women's inclination and opportunities for play. Until it becomes easier to combine and easier to share the dual demands of paid and unpaid work, the quality of life for the majority of women will not markedly improve. As long as responsibility for children and domestic work remains predominantly with women, so will the pervasiveness of work in women's lives.

This last point is crucial.

Employment structures are still organised around the outdated notion that employees are male and that women look after children. Changing the basic structures of our working lives is therefore a critical step towards reintroducing the play factor into our lives as a whole. The juggling act, required of the vast majority of women today, could be made infinitely less taxing in terms of time, finances, physical health and emotional well-being if employment structures were to take proper account of the reality of women's lives. Retainer schemes, re-entry schemes, term-time working, sabbatical schemes, career breaks and time account systems are all measures beginning to be introduced throughout Europe and the US, from which we could benefit in the UK too.

However, progressive measures such as these will do little to improve the quality of women's lives as long as they apply to women's work but not to men's. The National Westminster bank, for example, has successfully introduced a scheme of term-time working for female employees, who can now take time off, unpaid but protected, during the school holidays. Clearly this is a scheme that should apply to Nat West's male employees too. To date, much apparent progress in the work-place conspires to maintain rather than challenge the status quo. The fact is, most of the changes designed to help people combine paid work and children are aimed at women: how many men work flexi-time, do job-shares or take advantage of career breaks in order to look after small children? Even if they want to, and can afford to, they run the risk of being seen by colleagues and, more importantly, by employers as insufficiently committed to their job. For women, the problem is the opposite: how to convince employers of their continuing commitment to paid work in the face of the entrenched belief that a woman's only responsibility is to her children.

An American study in 1994 found that, irrespective of a family's relative wealth, children tend to be better educated and healthier in direct relation to the proportion of the household income that comes from the woman.[6] Other studies have linked unequal responsibility for children to poor mental health in the mother, and shown how children themselves benefit in a number of ways when their mothers are in some form of paid employment. Yet, despite these findings, attachment theory and its variants are thrown at women whenever they show signs of handing over even some of the responsibility for children. Equal parenting is still far more of an ideal than a reality, as is equal earning, and meanwhile women as individuals continue to take responsibility for what society as a whole is failing to provide. Until apparently family-friendly measures in the work-place are directed not only at women but extend equally to male employees, most women have little choice but to continue in their Sisyphean task of trying to combine two jobs: paid work and family. As long as men are perceived to be the ones who earn – irrespective of the reality – women are trapped into being the ones who juggle. As long as women juggle alone, they will find it extremely hard to play.

There is growing evidence that women are challenging, or at least beginning to baulk at, a status quo that largely erases their needs from the play agenda. A 1992 study by the National Council of Women found that many women today want *less* time with their children, *less* time with their partners, *less* time working, and *more* time for their hobbies and education.[7] Women are craving the time to invest in *themselves*. This is not selfishness, it is the way forward. So, in addition to removing some of the obstacles to women's play, an agenda for play must also set out ways to increase the *opportunities* for women to play. These could include:

- *Making play-space for women*

Women need places and spaces in which to play. Whether those play-spaces occur in the home, a sports hall, a nightclub, or a tranquil riverside walk, they need to be safe and affordable before women can make the most of them. Employers, councils and governments must begin to prioritise the creation of such spaces. But it is also incumbent on women themselves to claim play-space for themselves; to put aside the imperative of service and the straitjacket of self-consciousness, and become players in the spaces available.

One such space is the work-place itself. Companies routinely employ people to do their playful thinking for them. Those people are called advisers and consultants. It is no surprise that so few of them are women, because at work, as elsewhere, men have tended to colonise the play-space.

- *Protecting play time*

One in 10 women in Britain has been the victims of violence from their partners in the past twelve months.[8] Such figures explain why play is so difficult for many women. If you get beaten up for saying the wrong thing, being in the wrong place, being out at the wrong time, you are likely to comply not cavort. Domestic violence has only been logged as a crime by the police in Britain since 1987, yet tackling domestic violence is a key step towards ending some of the constraints on women which make it so hard to play. As well as space to play, we need time for play. Both require that women's time off is sanctioned and protected.

- *Investing in play*

Debating the subject of parents' responsibilities in the House of Lords in June 1992, Lord Beaumont insisted, 'An adequate basic income for all citizens is, quite frankly, the first *sine qua non* for rearing healthy families and securing responsible society. It is as important that a parent has some freedom as that he or she has a sense of responsibility. They need both freedom and a sense of responsibility.'[9] Women have responsibility in plenty; freedom to play and be playful they urgently require. This could be done in direct ways, such as putting more money into improving sports facilities for young women, improving crèche facilities for mothers, improving transport and access for the elderly. It could be done in indirect ways through improving pension provision and wage levels. A financial commitment should be made by employers, government and local authorities to start creating opportunities for women to play.

- *Sharing the caring*

The caring that many women do in their lives, whether it is looking after the children, ironing a husband's shirts, cooking and shopping for elderly relations, may have its own rewards, but it is also time-consuming and tiring. While most women would not want to relinquish altogether the role of carer, the quality of their lives could be greatly improved if they were more able to share the care – with partners, with employers, with the state. We need to stand up for our right to hand over at least some of the caring we do, so that we can take and enjoy opportunities in our lives for playing.

- *Valuing our play-needs*

To take the time, the space, the opportunity for play, we need to start placing a proper value on our play-needs. Much of the way in which society operates, both formally and informally, depends upon the deprioritising of women's play-needs (and of women's needs in general). Much of the smooth-running of society depends upon the fact that where there is a conflict of interests, the needs of everyone else will come before women's. Where women do not accept this pervasive devaluation of their needs, they often encounter outrage, hostility and even violence. But until we start valuing our play-needs, we cannot begin to stand up for those needs. Recognising the true worth of play in our lives is therefore a crucial step towards realising the potential of our playful selves. Once we know what we need, we can begin to find ways of getting it.

- *Honing our play-instincts*

The constraints on women's play in contemporary society, and in western culture generally, have not only restricted their opportunities for play, they have undermined women's ability to play, eroded their instinct for play. If we are out of touch with the instinct for play, we cannot take up even those opportunities for play which do exist. We need now to resurrect our ability to play and start to hone our play-instincts. We can do this by revisiting our experiences of childhood play; by setting aside time to think about play; by creating internal images of ourselves as players; by allowing ourselves to respond to our internal cues for playfulness, and by allowing ourselves to respond also to external cues. We need to stop seeing ourselves only as workers, always busy, always proving our worth, always serving others, and instead start to see ourselves also as players: curious, humorous, innovative, daring. Above all, play starts with the playful self.

The Playful Society

Setting an agenda for play is not only important for women, it is important for society as a whole. Women have particular problems in playing, as we have seen, and these need to be specifically addressed, but we are also part of a larger society that is itself suffering through the devaluation of play. As the historian Johan Huizinga put it, '[Play] adorns life, amplifies it, and is to that extent a necessity both for the individual . . . and for society.' At a most fundamental and profound level, play nourishes and upholds society by enhancing the lives of the individuals who make up that society.

Investment in women's well-being would lead to happier, healthier children, vital for our collective future well-being. Yet this is the very opposite of what actually happens: instead of looking after women as the first step to looking after families, and by extension, communities, and by further extension, society itself, we allow women's needs to slip to the bottom of the personal and political agenda. The results, as we can see from looking at our own lives and at those of the people around us, are not very satisfactory. Play is not selfish or frivolous; it is, as Lord Beaumont indicated, a form of social and collective responsibility. Fighting for women's play is not simply a women's issue, it is an issue for society as a whole.

For all women, young and old, rich and poor, married and single alike, play is about freedom. Removing play from a person's life is an effective way of limiting that individual's potential for free movement, be it physical, emotional, intellectual or spiritual. Play matters, and the absence of play matters too. One of the first rights to be confiscated from people whom others wish to be financially or socially dependent is their right to play. This may seem an extreme claim, but consider for a moment the effect of banning books in Ray Bradbury's futuristic nightmare, *Fahrenheit 451*, or the tight control of sexual pleasure in Aldous Huxley's *Brave New World* or Evgeny Zamyatin's *We*, in which people are allowed a 'personal hour' twice a week.[10] In all these books, controlling play is a subtle and powerful means of restricting individual freedom.

Turning from science-fiction to history, examples abound of dictatorships which have found it as necessary to curb people's play as to cut their wages. In communist China and Soviet Russia, the performing and visual arts were subject to extensive state control; censorship of all forms of writing was par for the course, a direct route to suppressing the free play of people's imaginations and creativity. Another way of curbing play is by regimenting leisure. Dazzling displays of organised sports were a characteristic feature of Germany in the late 1930s. Filmed and broadcast round the world, these displays not only demonstrated the might of the German fascist party, but were also a powerful symbol of the triumph of order over chaos. Under fascism, even the anarchy of play could be transformed into the neatness of leisure. One of the most sinister pieces of propaganda to emerge from Nazi Germany was the film made in the show-camp Theresienstadt, in which smiling Jewish prisoners were shown enjoying a game of football, cheered on by a happy audience of fellow inmates. The film was one of several used by the Nazis to convince the outside world that rumours of atrocities were unfounded, and that, on the contrary, German prison camps were models of humaneness. In reality, the light-hearted play was a set-up for the cameras, as false as with the tulips flown in specially from Holland to prettify the normally bleak surroundings. Theresienstadt in fact witnessed the degradation and slaughter of hundreds of thousands of Jewish and other prisoners. The chilling irony of the film is compounded by its macabre manipulation of play, symbol of freedom.

The suppression of play in an individual's life is always a powerful political weapon. Even in democratic states, freedom can be a dangerous entity, and most democratic governments have at some stage in some way sought to control people's play. Prohibition in the thirties in America is an obvious example; its counterpart in Britain at that time was a fierce moral crusade against sex before marriage. Fierce opposition to the Criminal Justice Bill in Britain in 1994 reflected a collective awareness that limiting opportunities for group activities, whether they be for the purpose of playing or demonstrating, comes dangerously close to an infringement of personal liberty. Campaigners and politicians alike realised that more was at stake than mere law and order. Whether their purpose is to play or to dissent, people gather of their own will in significant numbers to demonstrate their freedom and their power.

At its best, play will always involve or instill in the player a sense of freedom, whether it is the imaginative freedom that comes from writing a poem or telling a story, or the physical freedom that accompanies dancing or roller-skating.[11] A sense of freedom is an essential ingredient of play, as well as one of its most beneficial outcomes. Even games, which at first glance appear to be governed by a whole set of rules restricting what the individual may or may not do, create a ritual space in which the norms of behaviour are temporarily suspended. A game of hockey enables girls to display aggression and competitiveness, a game of football permits boys to embrace. By consistently failing to recognise the value of play, we have reached a situation in which our lives are dominated by work of one kind or another, while our leisure fails to compensate or fulfil, but simply becomes what the poet Louis MacNeice described as 'blinkers on the eyes of doubt'.[12] By relinquishing the freedom of play, we have become prey to the tyranny of work, against which all things are now measured.

We need to think now about establishing a different kind of employment – the 'full employment of the personality' that takes place through play. 'The alternative', warns one sociologist, 'is a further spread of nihilism, with people sinking more deeply into the despair of knowing they have lost their direction.'[13] As long as the world of play is seen as belonging to the world of childhood, while having little place in the responsible, serious world of adulthood, we will continue to be trapped by this polarisation of 'the work of adults' and 'the play of babes'.[14] By relegating play to the 'half-world' of the child and excising it from the 'real' world of adults, the worlds of both children and adults will continue to be diminished, not to say damaged. Separating work and play in this way divides individuals within themselves and between one another; it leads, for example, to incomprehension and tension between the world of the adult and the world of the young. This in turn makes for a two-way denial of reality: if the young person denies the reality of adult experience, it makes it possible to smash car windscreens for fun; the fun-haver will spare no thought for the time, money and energy that it will take to repair the windscreen, nor for the emotional upset, administrative bother or practical inconvenience that his or her 'fun' will cause.

Similarly, if the adult denies the reality of the young person's world, he or she will easily dismiss rising drug use as thoughtless stupidity, without pausing to consider what it communicates about the problems young people face in terms of unemployment, homelessness, debt, emotional and financial security, Aids, nuclear war. This two-way denial of co-existent realities has grave implications that should not be underestimated. It leads slowly but surely to the world of *A Clockwork Orange*, in which murder and rape are part of a young man's night out. It leads us to the real-life horror of two ten-year-old boys abducting, torturing and finally killing a helpless terrified toddler in a game that went appallingly wrong. As one letter to the *Guardian* in the wake of the James Bulger case put it: 'Children mirror the society that nurtures them, more accurately than anything else . . . If, as in this ghastly example, the mirror is a distorting one, the monsters we see in it are still ourselves.'[15]

Such horrific perversions of play become possible when there is an annihilation of the consciousness of alternative realities; they reflect the triumph of subjectivity in its worst guise. Here the true potential of play to enhance the individual's capacity for empathy, communality, connectedness and regard for others is horribly inverted. Play becomes a means of annihilating alternative realities, reducing experience to the sum total of one's own immediate reality. Seen in this light, virtual reality looks like the thin end of a devastating wedge: a way of playing that necessarily excludes others, while leading the individual into a solipsistic fantasy world.

On a large enough scale, this is the death of the individual, and by extension, the death of society. We are back at William Blake's vision of loss of innocence, the corruption of play, the silencing of the voices heard on the hill. In her analysis of Blake's *Songs*, Heather Glen argues that the poet was defending the crucial role of play in the healthy continuance of communal life.[16] In the *Songs of Experience*, individuals are isolated, 'destructively self-enclosed rather than creatively echoing and outward-pointing. [But in the] *Songs of Innocence* there is no isolated individual: no individual exists except in relationship.'[17] Language itself is used playfully by Blake in these poems to create the vision of 'an experience of self-realisation which is, simultaneously, an experience of recognition of and by the other.'[18]

Blake encapsulates in the magic of poetry what his German contemporary Schiller would shortly after set down logically in prose. Both men sought to celebrate a mode of human experience that was not a sentimental ideal, but an actuality. According to Glen, the *Songs of Innocence* 'is an attempt unparallelled in our literature to articulate what a modern psychoanalyst has called "the vital illusions by which we live" – the "illusions" that we are not at the blind mercy of fate, that we can actually construct the world which we inhabit, that desire may be undestructively fulfilled; that a non-instrumental mode of relating to one another is possible, that order can survive chaos, and love, aggression. These are the "illusions" which are necessary for any hopeful or creative sense of life, both for the individual and for society.'[19]

Once the vital role of play in the well-being of society as a whole is understood, it becomes clearer still why the right to play is as essential as any other human right, a cause worth thinking about and fighting for. This applies to all of us, male and female, adult and child.

The Unemployment Factor

It might seem ill-judged to be advocating the luxury of play when so many people today are suffering the hardships of enforced unemployment, but it is precisely in times of hardship that our need for play is greatest. How the unemployed cope in a culture that values employment inordinately highly is central to their subsequent and continuing well-being. Suicide rates are higher in times of high unemployment, as are crimes against property, drug abuse, homelessness and domestic violence. Journalist Donald Donnison writes:

> It is not only the unemployed who suffer when jobs become scarce. Unemployment hurts us all . . . We all pay a price of injustice and its most flagrant symbol – high unemployment. It is paid in anxiety about the safety of our children on the streets, higher insurance premiums, more elaborate burglar alarms, and in higher costs for hospitals, police and prisons. But the most grievous casualty is hope. In a hopeful society, every citizen wants to make the world a better place. What are your priorities? More equal opportunities for men and women of all races? More flexible retirement ages, enabling people to switch to part-time jobs and stop work when it suits them? More opportunities for students? More opportunities for people with handicaps? More opportunities for lone parents to earn a living? Every one of these reforms becomes much harder to achieve when there are lots of people out of work, and those in jobs feel compelled to defend them in any way they can. The sixties and early seventies may have witnessed some lunacies, but they were a time of hope. People felt they could do things: social evils could be challenged, social problems solved. Today, we have lost such hope.'[20]

Large numbers of people of every social class in Britain today are unemployed. School leavers cannot find work; middle-aged managers are 'retired early'; factory workers are laid off in their thousands. The problems of unemployment are well-documented: depression, anxiety, despair, aggression, ill-health. But the downward spiral suffered by individuals and therefore society as a result of mass unemployment is not helped by assumptions about the importance of work in people's lives, assumptions that urgently need questioning. Is work really the key to well-being? Or is it just that we regard it as such? Can it be right that one section of the population works itself into the ground, while another is destroyed by its lack of work? We would do well to recall the words of Hannah Arendt: 'Economic growth may one day turn out to be a curse rather than a good, and under no conditions can it either lead into freedom or constitute a proof of its existence.'[21]

Unemployment in the industrialised world reached 35 million in 1994. Politicians, increasingly driven by short-term necessities, have remained fixated on paid work of one form or another as the way forward for society, despite the fact that, in practice, their theories have seen only mass unemployment, an increasing health-and-wealth gap between rich and poor, and little evidence of improvement in the quality of life other than that measured by videos and TV sets. According to European figures, only Portugal has more people living in poverty than the UK. We need to ask ourselves what we mean by full employment, what we want from employment generally, and what is to happen to the millions of unemployed people in the meantime? It is curious that so little is done to introduce measures that might make unemployment less destructive, to make it easier for people to make something good of unemployment.

We know that the way in which unemployed people regard and use their time has a direct effect on how far they avoid the 'symptoms' of unemployment, with research showing that the ability to plan and fill time seems to reduce the distress of being out of work. The ability to play is also the ability to use time in a non-commercial, non-functional way, for one's own satisfaction. It helps us cope with the stresses of our lives, and it nourishes our sense of self-worth, so starved by the experience of unemployment in our culture. When you consider that the average working life is getting shorter and that substantial numbers of people are unlikely to get more than 35 years of work from 75 years of life, the need for skills that enable us to use non-paid time in creative, satisfying ways is unquestionable. I would go so far as to say that the phenomenon of mass unemployment is one of the single most persuasive reasons why play should be regarded as a crucial facet of adult life.

The ill-effects of unemployment are felt even by many of those who should theoretically be free of the pressure to work: people of retirement age and over. An increasing proportion of the population falls into that category, as a combination of increasing life expectancy and declining fertility and mortality rates results in an ageing population throughout Europe.[22] Compared with a few decades ago, fewer women are having children than before, and those who are have them later. There are more than 60 million people aged 60 and over in the European Community, and nearly one-third of the EC's population and one-fifth of the labour force are over the age of 50. By the year 2020, these figures will have increased considerably. Women in the EC can now expect to outlive men by an average of 6.6 years.[23] In France, women now live an average of 8.2 years longer than men. In the UK, the average life expectancy for a girl born in 1993 is 79 years. Three per cent of all women are now aged 85 and over, and this figure is expected to rise to 5 per cent by 2031. On demographic grounds alone, we can no longer afford to ignore the importance of play.

The cost to society of ill health in old age is considerable and increasing; it is seen in the financial costs of residential care, medical treatment and services, and it is seen, though not so easily measured, in the emotional costs of sheer human misery. As individuals and as a society, we need to invest in the later stages of life for, in the absence of paid work, the importance of rewarding activities increases. With an ageing population at hand, we need healthy, satisfied old people who can contribute to society with their experience, skills and time, and who can use those same attributes to fulfil their own potential.

More Than A Job's Worth

Work may be the devil we know best, but imagine a society where it was perfectly acceptable, even admirable, to work a two- or three-day week, and have the other four or five days for family, friends, other interests. In such a society, more of us would be in work, but at the same time work would take up less of our lives. In 1934, Bertrand Russell called for a four-hour working day: 'I want to say, in all seriousness that a great deal of harm is being done in the modern world by belief in the virtuousness of work, and the road to happiness and prosperity lies in an organised diminution of work.'[24] Instead of heeding Russell's warning, we have allowed our obsession with work to flourish unchecked, at the expense of our play. 'Modern methods of production', wrote Russell, 'have given us the possibility of ease and security for all; we have chosen instead, to have overwork for some and starvation for others . . . there is no reason to go on being foolish for ever.'[25]

A continuing belief in the virtuousness of work has squeezed the impulse to play into the narrowing margins of our lives. Today, those of us with employment devote a large proportion of our time to work, very often at the expense of play, while those without work feel profoundly unentitled to play, even though they may have the time for it. There is a kind of madness in it all that confounds reason and intuition alike.

It is time to cure ourselves of this collective insanity, not for selfish reasons but because our individual and communal well-being depends upon it. Instead of living to work, we should be finding ways of working to play.

Working To Play: An Opportunity For Change

As we near the end of the twentieth century, radical changes are taking place in the structure of employment throughout Europe and the United States. While these changes are being greeted with a mixture of dismay, anxiety, scepticism and, in some quarters, enthusiasm and delight, the extent of change and the significance of that change is not yet clear. However, in all the discussions about the future of employment, whether seen to be dire or rosy, what has been consistently overlooked so far is that women are now uniquely placed to shape that future. Women are both invaluable and undervalued members of the work force. As such they are in the best possible position to put an end to our culture's obsession with paid work as the panacea for all ills, to lead the way out of the workmire into a way of living that respects and values and cherishes the experience of play.

Women are an increasing presence in the work-place, and an increasingly necessary presence there. They are in a position where they could start to insist on changes that might improve the quality of life, not just for women, but for everyone. Arguably, their mere presence may achieve change: as more women are in paid employment and engaged in the frantic knife-edge juggling of domestic and professional commitments, more men will be affected too, as partners, colleagues, employees and employers. What to do with the children will increasingly become an issue that impinges on men's time and consciousness too. This could provide the necessary spur to action, even without more vocalised calls for change.

Neither kind of impetus to change will have any impact, however, unless women can resist the pressure to behave like men in the workplace, and refuse to polarise the two aspects of their lives. Hitherto, we have tended to suppress our experiences, to mould our ways of living and thinking and working to accord with the dominant male trends which characterise society, to accept that work – often of a grossly undervalued kind – is a women's lot. What we must do now is remind ourselves and others that we do not need to feel grateful for work – employers should feel grateful to *us*. We have to remind ourselves that work creates problems for women as well as solving them. We have to get into the habit of saying to ourselves and to others: 'I do want to work, but I'm not going to pretend that it has solved all my problems; nor am I going to cover up the fact that going out to work has brought a whole lot of *new* problems.' We have to start believing that our paid work has enormous financial value to society, whether it is full-time, part-time, flexi-time, term-time, or job-shared; more than that, we have to believe that our *unpaid* work is of enormous value to society too. And, above all, we have to believe that society should not make it any harder for us to contribute these forms of work by its refusal to acknowledge the pressures and strains and stresses under which this work puts us.

Women's conditions of work need to be improved, *not* so that women can work still harder, but so that they can be more often and more easily free of the tyranny of work, and free to realise their capacity for play. The issue of women's work cannot and should not be seen in isolation from the issue of women's play. As Charles Dickens pointed out, 'There can be no effective and satisfactory work without play.' Play is not an alternative to work, it is a prerequisite.

Changes in women's work obviously take place in the context of overall changes in the world of employment and, obviously, men's work too is in a state of enormous flux, characterised by increasing insecurity, increasing pressure to perform, increasing risks of redundancy. Less than half the working population in the UK has a full-time, long-term job; more than a million people now have more than one job; there are twice as many people in part-time employment and self-employment as there were fifteen years ago. Similar trends are taking place across Europe. In all probability unemployment is here to stay, so is shift work, fixed-term contracts, sub-contracting, franchising, temporary jobs, homeworking, teleworking and job-sharing. These are the key features of the new-look world of work. They could create pressure to work even longer hours than they do already; or they could make it easier for people to make time and space in their lives for things other than work. New technology will put some people out of work, and create jobs for others; new attitudes to employment will fulfil some workers, devastate others; as computers, faxes and modems release us from the office, this will create problems of isolation and lack of support. We may well be coming to the end of job security, or even, as American author William Bridges argues, witnessing the death throes of the job itself. According to Bridges 'Unless we can begin soon to re-educate our work forces in these new expectations and the economic realities that have shaped them, we are in for decades of economic chaos that will damage our organisations and devastate several generations of workers.'[26] I propose that we see these changes as an opportunity, not a catastrophe; that we take the chance presented by the changes in employment structure and practice to put work back in its place, to remember that there is much more to life than work.

Various commentators have drawn parallels between the changes now taking place in employment structures, and those which occurred at the end of the eighteenth century with the process of industrialisation. Then, a whole way of life was overturned. Industrialisation effected far-reaching change: as historian E.P. Thompson has explained, it 'entailed a severe restructuring of working habits – new disciplines, new incentives, and a new human nature upon which these incentives could bite effectively'. The enormous changes in employment patterns and structures that took place alongside industrialisation went hand in hand with the erosion of play as a central and valued aspect of daily life. Reflecting on the long-term implications of the Industrial Revolution, Thompson wondered if a time would come when people 'might have to re-learn some of the arts of living' that were then lost.[27] That time may now have arrived. Now, with a radical alteration again taking place in the organisation of working time, we have the opportunity to reinstate play, both as a cultural concept and a daily reality.

At the end of Eric Hobsbawm's *The Age of Extremes*, the historian argues that the future fails to compel us, for we have lost our faith in and hope for the future. He issues a dire warning: that unless society changes, it will face 'darkness', but he offers no solutions, no means to effect that change.[28] I am less despairing, for increasingly there *are* signs of change. People are increasingly unhappy with a life that leaves them so little time to talk to their partner, play with their children, see their friends. Instead, one can hear, faintly, but distinctly, a growing murmur of dissent. In 1993 a new magazine called the *Idler* appeared on the news-stands, its aim in the words of its founder, Tom Hodgkinson, 'to turn the dominant guiding ideas – work is good, sloth is bad – upside down, and encourage a culture where the opposite is true, where manic working is seen for what it often is: a sign of some unresolved inner conflict, a lack of creativity, of spirituality, of self-knowledge'.[29]

All around there are signs of a growing dissatisfaction with the culture of work, work and more work. People are calling for sabbaticals, for banking time, for four-day weeks, for paternity leave; they are opting for self-employment, or seeking refuge in full-time mothering. A small but significant number of people are questioning the value of paid work, turning instead to other ways of living, with the emphasis on personal fulfilment, communal values and quality of life. In the States, a growing band of disaffected workers are taking courses in Voluntary Simplicity (VS), with the aim of 'downshifting', getting out of the rat-race, lowering their financial requirements in order to raise their overall quality of life. According to the Trends Research Institute of Rhinebeck, New York, 15 per cent of people in their thirties and forties will be partially or wholly committed to a VS way of life by the year 2000.[30] This is not dropping out, according to Duane Elgin, author of *Voluntary Simplicity*, it is dropping in: 'You don't just go down to the coffee house and hang about with other prime-of-life slackers. Through simple living you're actually dropping in: to community, to family, to relationships.'[31] Whereas 25 years ago, only 1 person in 20 in Britain rejected conspicuous consumption, now 1 in 5 do.[32] A random sample of 800 Americans, commissioned by the Merck Family Foundation, found that 82 per cent agreed that 'we buy and consume far more than we need', and 28 per cent had taken practical steps to move away from a consumerist lifestyle. These 'post-materialists' reject the consumption-led economic recovery much touted by politicians; they prefer small scale, grass-roots organisations to large institutions, and, significantly, have no interest in the 'job for life', favouring flexible working and the idea of doing several jobs in a lifetime.

Can there be any doubt that we must now set about resurrecting the concept of play and reintroducing it into the fabric of our lives? Without play, we are little better than machines, merely carrying out an endless sequence of tasks of varying degrees of simplicity or complexity. Unlike the items paraded across television screens and billboards as elixirs of happiness, play costs absolutely nothing; it is, if you like, recession proof. It can take place anywhere, anytime, for free, a sound investment with guaranteed returns.

It is nearly two centuries since Jeremy Bentham wrote the words with which the first chapter of this book began and with which the last chapter is about to end: 'There are two ways of doing injury to mankind: one, the introduction of pains; the other, exclusion of pleasures. Both are acts of tyranny, for in what does tyranny consist, if not in this?'[33] Play, by contrast, is about freedom, the very opposite of tyranny. On an individual level, play is the experience of freedom of mind, body and soul; on the social level, play is the experience of interdependence, co-relation, co-existence. In play, we find a reality which is profoundly connecting – to ourselves, to the world we inhabit and have inhabited, to the world we aspire to inhabit, to the people with whom we inhabit it. Play is not something we can do without, without doing profound harm to ourselves, individually and collectively. As women, we understand about connection all too well; if we could fuse that understanding with the freedom to play, we could make lives for ourselves which would be happier, healthier, more fulfilled, more hopeful. For our own sake, for the sake of the people we love, for the sake of the society we live in, and the society our children will have to live in, it is time to relinquish the obsession with work. We must put work back in its place, and delay no longer in reclaiming our right to play, in asserting and celebrating our playful selves.

Bibliography

AAUW. *Shortchanging Girls, Shortchanging America* (Washington, DC, 1991) (Original data: AAUW/Greenberg-Lake Full Data Report, Greenberg-Lake, Washington, DC, 1990)

Abrams, R. 'Children on the Frontline', *She*, 1993

Abrams, R. *Woman in a Man's World* (Methuen, London, 1993)

Achterberg, J. *Woman as Healer* (Rider, London, 1990)

Amussen, S.D. 'The Gendering of Popular Culture in Early England', in T. Harris (ed). *Popular Culture in England, c. 1500-1850* (Macmillan, London, 1995)

Anderson, B.S. and Zinsser, J.P. *A History of Their Own: women in Europe from prehistory to the present*, Vol. 2 (Penguin, Harmondsworth, 1990)

Arber, S. and Ginn, J., eds. *Connecting Gender and Ageing* (Open University Press, Buckingham, 1995)

Arendt, H. *On Revolution* (Faber and Faber, London, 1963)

Argyle, M. *The Psychology of Happiness* (Routledge, London, 1989)

Argyle, M. and Lu, L. (1990) 'The Happiness of Extroverts', *Perons.individ.Diff.*, Vol. 11, no 10, pp. 1011-17

Aries, E. (1982) 'Verbal and Nonverbal Behaviour in Single-Sex and Mixed-Sex Groups: Are Traditional Sex Roles Changing', in *Psychological Reports* 51.127-134

Aries, P. and Bejin, A. *Western Sexuality – practice and precept in past and present times* trs Anthony Forster (Basil Blackwell, Oxford, 1985)

Austin Knight UK. *The Family Friendly Workplace* (Company report, London, 1995)

Beauvoir, S. de. *Memoirs of a Dutiful Daughter,* trs James Kirkup (Penguin, London, 1970)

Beauvoir, S. de. *The Ethics of Ambiguity,* trs Bernard Frechtman (Citadel, New York, 1964)

Bentham, J. *Theory of Legislation* First published 1802 (Kegan Paul, London, 1891)

Birch, H.G. (1945) 'The Relation of Previous Experience to Insightful Problem-solving', *Journal of Comp. Physiol. Psychol.,* No. 38, pp. 367–83

Blakney, R.B., trs. *Meister Eckhart: a modern translation* (Harper and Row, New York, 1941)

Blauner, R. *Alienation and Freedom: the factory worker and his industry* (University of Chicago Press, Chicago, 1964)

Block, J.H. (1983). 'Differential premises arising from differential socialization of the sexes: some conjectures', *Child Development*, Vol. 54, pp. 1335-54

Boynton and Ford (1933) 'The Relationship Between Play and Intelligence', *Journal of Applied Psychology*, 17

Bradley, I. *The Call To Seriousness* (Jonathan Cape, London, 1976)

Bridges, W. *Jobshift: how to prosper in a workplace without jobs* (Nicholas Bradley, London, 1995)

Brown, G.W. and Harris, T. *The Social Origins of Depression* (Tavistock, London, 1978)

Bruner, J.S., Jolly, A. and Sylva, K. *Play: its role in development and evolution* (Penguin, Harmondsworth, 1976)

Bruner, J.S. (1972) 'Nature and Uses of Immaturity', *American Psychologist*, Vol. 27, no 8

Buonaventura, W. *Serpent of the Nile: women and dance in the Arab world* (Saqi Books, London, 1989)

Burchell, B. 'The Effects of Labout Market Position, Job Insecurity, and Unemployment on Psychological Health', in *Social Change and the Experience of Unemployment,* eds. D. Gallie, C. Marsh and C. Vogler (Oxford University Press, Oxford, 1994)

Burchell, B. and Rubery, J. 'Divided Women: Labour Market Segmentation and Gender Segregation', in *Gender Segregation and Social Change: men and women in changing labour markets,* ed. A. MacEwen Scott, (Oxford University Press, Oxford, 1994)

Burke, P.J. (1989) 'Gender Identity, Sex and School Performance', *Social Psychology Quarterly,* Vol. 52, no 2, pp. 159-69

Cadogan, M. *Women With Wings: female flyers in fact and fiction* (Macmillan, London, 1992)

Campbell, A. *The Sense of Well-being in America* (McGraw-Hill, New York, 1981)

Chodorow, N. *The Reproduction of Mothering* (University of California Press, Berkeley, 1978)

Clarke, J. and Critcher, C. *The Devil Makes Work: leisure in capitalist Britain* (Macmillan, Basingstoke, 1983)

Clulow, C. and Mattinson, J. *Marriage Inside Out: understanding problems of intimacy* (Penguin, Harmondsworth, 1989)

Corsaro, W. and Rizzo, T. 'Disputes in the Peer Culture of American and Italian Nursery School Children', in *Conflict Talk,* ed. A. Grimshaw (Cambridge University Press, Cambridge, 1990)

Coward, R. *Our Treacherous Hearts: why women let men get their way* (Faber and Faber, London, 1992)

Csikszentmihalyi, M. *Beyond Boredom and Anxiety* (Jossey-Bass, San Francisco, 1975)

Csikszentmihalyi, M. (1982) 'Toward a psychology of optimal experience', *Review of Personality and Social Psychology*, 3, pp. 13–36

Csikszentmihalyi, M. and Kubey, R. (1981) 'Television and the rest of life: a systematic comparison of subjective experiences', *Public Opinion Quarterly*, 45, pp. 317–28

Csikszentmihalyi, M. and Larson, R. *Being Adolescent* (Basic Books, New York, 1984)

Curtis, J. (1993) 'Satisfying work if you can find it', *British Social Attitudes.*

Davies, B. and Ward, S. *Women and Personal Pensions* (HMSO, London, 1992)

Deem, R. *All Work and No Play: the sociology of women and leisure* (Open University Press, Milton Keynes, 1986)

Demos Quarterly, No. 5, 1995, 'The Time Squeeze' (Demos, London)

Dex, S., Clark, A. and Taylor, M. *Household Labour Supply,* British Household Panel Survey, Wave 1 Report (Department of Employment, London, 1995)

Dickinson, E. Selected Poems, ed. J. Reeves, (Heinemann, London, 1959)

Dixey, R. (1988) 'Eyes Down: A Study of Bingo' in E. Wimbush and M. Talbot (eds.), *Relative Freedoms: women and leisure* (Open University Press, Milton Keynes)

Donkin, H.B. 'Hysteria', in *Dictionary of Psychological Medicine,* ed. D.H. Tuke, pp. 619, 620 (Churchill, London, 1892)

Douglas, S.J. *Where the Girls Are: growing up female with the mass media* (Penguin, London, 1994)

Dumazedier, J. *Toward a Society of Leisure* (Collier: Macmillan, London, 1967)

Dunbar, R. 'Why gossip is good for you', *New Scientist,* 21 November 1992

Dunlop, H.L. 'Games, sports, dancing and other vigorous recreational activities and their function in Samoan culture', in *Sport, Culture and Society,* eds. Loy, Jr, J.W. and Kenyon, G.S. (Macmillan, London, 1969)

Elias, N. and Dunning, E. *The Quest for Excitement* (Basil Blackwell, Oxford, 1986)

Erikson, E. *Play and Development* (W.W. Norton, New York, 1972)

Erikson, E. *Childhood and Society.* First published 1950 (Vintage, London, 1995)

Erikson, E. *Insight and Responsibility* (W.W. Norton, New York, 1964)

Erikson, E. *Identity: Youth and Crisis* (Horton, New York, 1968)

Erikson, E. 'Womanhood and the inner space', in *Women and Analysis,* ed. J. Strouse (Grossman, New York, 1968/1974)

Ermisch, J. *The Economics of the Family: applications to divorce and remarriage* (Centre for Economic Policy Research, No. 140, 1986)

Etzion, D. (1984) 'Moderating effect of social support on the stress-burnout relationship', *Journal of Applied Psychology,* 69(4) pp. 615–22.

Evans, J.G. *Health: Abilities and Wellbeing in the Third Age* (Carnegie, United Kingdom Trust, 1992)

Fagot, B.I. (1978). 'The influence of sex of child on parent reactions to toddler children', *Child Development,* Vol. 49, pp. 459-65

Feynman, R.P. *'Surely You're Joking, Mr. Feynman!'* (Vintage, London, 1985)

Finch, J. and Groves, D. *A Labour of Love: women, work and caring* (Routledge and Kegan Paul, London, 1983)

Finnis, J. *Natural Law and Natural Rights* (Oxford University Press, Oxford, 1980)

Formanek, R. and Gurrian, A. *Women and Depression: a lifespan perspective* (Springer, New York, 1987)

French, M. *The War Against Women* (Hamish Hamilton, London, 1992)

Freud, S. *Wit and Its Relation to the Unconscious* ed. A.A. Brill, (Kegan Paul, London, 1922)

Freud, S. *Three Essays on the Theory of Sexuality,* ed. J. Strachey (Penguin Freud Library, Vol VII/Penguin, Harmondsworth, 1991)

Freud, S. *Beyond the Pleasure Principle.* First edition 1920, trs. James Strachey (Hogarth Press, London, 1950)

Gallie, D., Marsh, C. and Vogler, C., eds. *Social Change and the Experience of Unemployment* (Oxford University Press, Oxford, 1995)

Gambetta, D. (1994), 'Godfather's gossip', *Arch. europ. social.*, 35, pp. 199–223

Gaskell, J. *Gender Matters: from school to work* (Oxford University Press, Oxford, 1992)

Gavron, H. *The Captive Wife* (Penguin, Harmondsworth, 1966)

Gershuny, J. *Social Innovation and the Division of Labour* (Oxford University Press, Oxford, 1983)

Gewirtz, J.L. 'The Course of Infant Smiling in Four Child-rearing Environments in Israel', in *Determinants of Infant Behaviour,* Vol. III, ed. B.M. Foss (Wiley, New York, 1965)

Gibbon, E. *The History of the Decline and Fall of the Roman Empire,* Vol. II ed. D. Saunders (Penguin, Harmondsworth, 1991)

Giddens, A. (1964) 'Notes on the Concepts of Play and Leisure', *Sociological Review,* N.S. xii

Gilligan, C. *In A Different Voice: psychological theory and women's development* (Harvard University Press, Cambridge, Mass., 1982)

Gilligan C., Lyons, N.P., and Hammer, T.J., eds. *Making Connections: the relational worlds of adolescent girls at Emma Willard school* (Harvard University Press, Cambridge, Mass., 1990)

Gittins, D. *The Family In Question: changing households and familiar ideologies* (Macmillan, London, 1985)

Glasser, R. *Leisure – Penalty or Prize?* (Macmillan, London, 1970)

Glen, H. *Vision and Disenchantment: Blake's Songs and Wordworth's Lyrical Ballads* (Cambridge University Press, Cambridge, 1983)

Goldschmied, E. and Jackson, S. *People Under Three: children in their third year* (Routledge, London, 1994)

Golombok, S. and Fivush, R. *Gender Development* (Cambridge University Press, Cambridge, 1994)

Goodwin, M.H. 'Children's Arguing', in *Language, Gender and Sex in Comparative Perspective,* eds. S.V. Philips, S. Steele and C. Tang (Cambridge University Press, Cambridge, 1987)

Gordon, L. *Charlotte Bronte: a passionate life* (Chatto and Windus, London, 1994)

Gordon, R. 'The Creative Process: self-expression and self-transcendence', in S. Jennings, ed. *Creative Therapy,* (Kemble Press Limited, Banbury, 1983)

Gove, W.R. (1972) 'The relationship between sex roles, marital status, and mental illness,' *Social Forces,* 51, pp. 34–44

Gove, W.R. (1984) 'Gender differences in mental and physical illness: the effects of fixed roles and nurturant roles,' *Social Science and Medicine,* 19, pp. 77–91

Government Office for London. 'City Walks in London', consultation document, (1995)

Graef, R. *Living Dangerously: young offenders in their own words* (Harper-Collins, London, 1992)

Graham, H. *The Magic Shop* (Rider, London, 1992)

Green, E., Hebron, S. and Woodward, D. *Women's Leisure, What Leisure?* (Macmillan, London, 1990)

Gregson, N. and Lowe, M. 'Too much work? Class, gender and the reconstitution of middle-class domestic labour', in *Social Change and the Middle Classes,* eds. T. Butler and M. Savage (University College London Press, London, 1994)

Greif, Blank E. *Sex Role Playing in Pre-School Children,* in J.S. Bruner et al., *Play; its role in development and evolution* (Penguin, Harmondsworth, 1976)

Griffin, C. *Typical Girls? Young Women from School to the Job Market* (Routledge and Kegan Paul, London, 1985)

Griffiths, V. (1988) 'From "playing out" to "dossing out": young women and leisure', pp. 48–59, in E. Wimbush and M. Talbot (eds), *Relative Freedoms: women and leisure* (Open University Press, Milton Keynes)

Griffiths, V. (1988) 'Stepping out: the importance of dancing for young women', pp. 115–125, in E. Wimbush and M. Talbot (eds), *Relative Freedoms: women and leisure* (Open University Press, Milton Keynes)

Groos, K. *The Play of Animals* (London, 1898)

Groos, K. *The Play of Man* , trs. E.L. Baldwin, (Heinemann, London, 1901)

Hakim, C. (1995) 'Five myths of female employment', *British Journal of Sociology,* 46 (3), 429-55

Hall, G.S. *Adolescence, its Psychology* (London, 1905)

Hampton, J. (1989) 'Play and development in rural Zimbabwean children', *Early Child Development and Care,* Vol. 47, pp. 1-61

Hansard Official Report. 'Parents' responsibilities', Vol. 538, no 27 p.479 (24.6.92)

Hardyment, C. *Perfect Parents* (Oxford University Press, Oxford, 1995)

Hargreaves, J. 'Sex, gender and the body in sport and leisure: Has there been a civilizing process?', in E. Dunning and C. Rojek (eds), *Sport and Leisure in the Civilizing Process* (Macmillan, London, 1992)

Harvey, A. 'The Evolution of Modern British Sporting Culture 1793–1850'. Unpublished doctoral thesis. University of Oxford, 1995

Haskey, J. (1984) 'Social Class and Socio-Economic Differentials in Divorce in England and Wales', *Population Studies* no 38, pp. 419-38

Hawkins, R.C., Turrell, S. and Jackson, L.S. (1983) 'Desirable and undesirable masculine and feminine traits in relation to students' dietary tendencies and body image dissatisfaction', *Sex Roles*, 9, pp. 705–24

Hendry, L.B. *Growing Up and Going Out* (Aberdeen University Press, Aberdeen, 1983)

Hendry, L.B., Shucksmith, J. and Cross, J. 'Young people's mental well-being in relation to leisure', in *Fit For Life*. Proceedings of a Symposium on Fitness and Leisure (Health Promotion Research Trust, Cambridge, 1989)

Hendry, L.B., Shucksmith, J., Love, J.G. and Glendinning, A. *Young People's Leisure and Lifestyle* (Routledge, London and New York, 1993)

The Henley Centre for Forecasting (1992) *Frontiers: planning for consumer change in Europe*

Heyn, D. *The Erotic Silence of the Married Woman* (Bloomsbury, London, 1992)

Hobsbawm, E. *The Age of Extremes: the short history of the twentieth century 1914–1991* (Michael Joseph, London, 1995)

Hope, A. and Timmel, S. *Training for Transformation – A Handbook for Community Workers,* Vol. 1. First published 1984 (Mambo Press, Gweru, Zimbabwe, 1989)

Huizinga, J. *Homo Ludens: a study of the play element in culture* (The Beacon Press, Boston; Routledge and Kegan Paul, London, 1949)

Hutt, C. (1966) 'Exploration and play in children', *Symposia of the Zoological Society of London,* no 18: pp. 61-81

Johnson, F. and Aries, E. (1983) 'The talk of women friends', *Women's Studies International Forum,* Vol. 6, no 4

Joshi, H. (1990) 'The cash opportunity costs of childbearing: an approach to estimation using British data'. *Population Studies,* 44

Katz, E. and Gurevitch, M. *The Secularization of Leisure* (Faber and Faber, London, 1976)

Kessler, S. and McKenna, W. *Gender: an ethnomethodological approach* (University of Chicago Press, Chicago, 1978)

Knox, B. (1992) 'A dangerously modern poet' *New York Review of Books,* Vol. XXXIX no 20

Koestler, A. *The Art of Creation* (Hutchinson, London, 1964)

Koestler, A. *The Ghost in the Machine* (Hutchinson, London, 1967)

Kristeva, J. *Language the Unknown – an initiation into linguistics* (Harvester Wheatsheaf, Hemel Hempstead, 1989)

Laffey, A.L. *Wives, Harlots and Concubines: the Old Testament in feminist perspective* (SPCK, London, 1990)

Lange, D. (1988) 'Using like to introduce constructed dialogue: how like contributes to discourse coherence'. Master's thesis. Georgetown University

Langlois, J.H. and Downs, A.C. (1980) 'Mothers, fathers and peers as socialization agents of sex-typed play behaviours in young children', *Child Development,* Vol. 51, pp. 1237–47

Laurence, A. *Women in England, 1500–1760* (Weidenfeld, London, 1994)

Lawson, A. *Adultery: an analysis of love and betrayal* (Oxford University Press, Oxford, 1990)

Layte, R. (1996) 'The material and cultural determinants of the domestic division of labour'. Unpublished doctoral thesis. University of Oxford

Leaman, O. *Sit on the Sidelines and Watch the Boys Play: sex differentiation in physical education* (Longmans, London, 1984)

Lees, S. *Sugar and Spice: Sexuality and Adolescent Girls* (Penguin, London, 1993)

Leyser, H. *Medieval Women: a social history of women in England 450–1500* (Phoenix, London, 1995)

'Leisure Time' (Mintel International Group Ltd, London, 1995)

Leonard, D. *Sex and Generation: a study of courtship and weddings,* (Tavistock, London, 1980)

Lever, J. (1976) 'Sex differences in the games children play', *Social Problems* 23: 478–87

Liddington, J. and Norris, J. *One Hand Tied Behind Us* (Virago, London, 1978)

Lissarrague, F. 'Figures of Women', in G. Duby and M. Perot (gen. eds). *A History of Women: from ancient goddesses to Christian saints* (Harvard University Press, Cambridge, Mass, 1992)

Lochhead, Liz, 'Men Talk', in *True Confessions and New Clichés* (Edinburgh, 1985)

Lorenz, Konrad. *Studies in Animal and Human Behaviour* (Methuen, London, 1971)

Lytton, H. and Romney, D.M. (1991) 'Parents' differential socialization of boys and girls: A meta-analysis', *Psychological Bulletin*, Vol. 109, pp. 267–96

Maccoby, E.E. and Jacklin, C.N. 'Gender segregation in children', in H.W. Reese, ed., *Advances in Child Development and Behaviour* Vol. 20, pp. 239–87 (Academic Press, New York, 1987)

Maine, M. *Father Hunger: fathers, daughters and food* (Gurze Books, Carlsbad, Ca., 1991)

Malcolmson, R.W. *Popular Recreations in English Society 1700–1850* (Cambridge University Press, Cambridge, 1973)

Mansfield, P. and Collard, J. *The Beginning of the Rest of Your Life* (Macmillan, London, 1988)

McLoughlin, J. *Up and Running: women in business* (Virago, London, 1992)

McRobbie, A. 'Working class girls and the culture of femininity', in *Women Take Issue* (Hutchinson, London, 1978)

McRobbie, A. and Garber, J. 'Girls and subcultures: an exploration', in *Resistance Through Ritual,* eds. S. Hall and T. Jefferson (Hutchinson, London, 1976)

Mendelsohn, J. 'The View from Step Number 16', in *Making Connections: The relational worlds of adolescent girls at Emma Willard school,* eds. C. Gilligan et al. (Harvard University Press, Cambridge, Mass., 1990)

Millar, S. *The Psychology of Play* (Penguin, Harmondsworth, 1968)

Miller, P.M., Danahar, D.L. and Forbes, D. (1980). 'Sex-related strategies for coping with interpersonal conflicts in children aged five and seven', *Developmental Psychology,* Vol. 22, pp. 543–8

Milligan, S. and Clare, A. *Depression and How to Survive It* (Ebury Press, London, 1993)

Mitchell, Lucy Sprague, *Here and Now Story Book,* (E.P. Dutton, New York, 1948)

Moir, Jan, 'Girl talk', *Guardian* (26.8.94)

Moss, H.A. (1967) 'Sex, age and state as determinants of mother-infant interaction', *Merrill-Palmer Quarterly,* 13, pp. 19–36

Moyle, J. *Just Playing? The role and status of play in early childhood education* (Open University Press, Milton Keynes, 1989)

Naber, P. 'Youth culture and life world', paper given at Alice in Wonderland Conference (Amsterdam, 1992). Cited in S. Lees, *Sugar and Spice*, op. cit.

Newham, P. *The Singing Cure* (Rider, London, 1993)

Nietzsche, F. *Thus Spake Zarathustra* (Penguin, Harmondsworth, 1969)

Noor, N. (1995). 'Work and family roles in relation to women's well-being: a longitudinal study', *British Journal of Social Psychology,* Vol. 34 pp. 87–106

Norberg-Hodge, H. *Ancient Futures: Learning from Ladakh* (Rider, London, 1991)

Office of Population Censuses and Surveys, 1994, OPCS Monitor DH2 94/2

Ogden, J. *Fat Chance: the myth of dieting explained* (Routledge and Kegan Paul, London, 1992)

O'Neill, G. *A Night Out With the Girls: women having a good time* (The Women's Press, London, 1993)

Opie, I. and Opie, P. *Children's Games in Street and Playground* (Oxford University Press, Oxford, 1984)

Orbach, S. *Fat Is a Feminist Issue* (Arrow, London, 1988)

Ovid, 'The Art of Love', *The Erotic Poems* (Penguin, Harmondsworth, 1982)

Paglia, C. *Vamps and Tramps* (Viking, Harmondsworth, 1995)

Pahl, R. *Division of Labour* (Blackwell, Oxford, 1985)

Parke, R.D. and Sawin, D.B. 'The Family in Early Infancy: Social interactional and attitudinal analyses', in F. Pederson, ed. *The Father-Infant Relationship: Observational studies in a family context* (Praeger, New York, 1980)

Parker, S. *The Future of Work and Leisure* (Praeger, New York, 1971)

Piaget, J. *The Language and Thought of the Child* (Routledge and Kegan Paul, London, 1926)

Piaget, J. *Play, Dreams and Imitation in Childhood* (Heinemann, London, 1951)

Pinkola Estes, C. *Women Who Run with the Wolves: contacting the power of the wild woman* (Rider, London, 1992)

Pitcher, E.G. and Shultz, L.H. *Boys and Girls at Play: The development of sex roles* (Praeger, New York, 1983)

Plumb, J. H. *England in the Eighteenth Century* (Penguin, Harmondsworth, 1950)

Pomeroy, S.B. *Goddesses, Whores, Wives and Slaves: women in classical antiquity* (Random House, London, Sydney, 1975)

Porter, R. *English Society in the Eighteenth Century* (Penguin, Harmondsworth)

Power, T.G. and Parke, R.D. 'Play as a Context for Early Learning: Lab and home analyses', in E. Sigel and L.M. Laosa eds. *The Family as a Learning Environment* (Plenum, New York, 1982)

Privette, G. (1983). 'Peak experience, peak performance, and peak flow: a comparative analysis of positive human experiences', *Journal of Personality and Social Psychology,* Vol. 45, pp. 1361–8

Rapoport, R. and Rapoport, R., *Leisure and the Family Life Cycle* (Routledge and Kegan Paul, London, 1975)

Reay, D. (1990). 'Working with boys', *Gender and Education* Vol. 2, no 3

Redgrove, P. and Mortimer, P. *The Wise Wound* (Victor Gollancz, London, 1978)

Rheingold, H.L. 'The effect of environmental stimulation upon social and exploratory behaviour in the human infant', in *Determinants of Infant Behaviour,* ed. B.M. Foss (Methuen, London, 1961)

Richardson, D. *Women, Motherhood and Caring* (Macmillan, London, 1993)

Richman, N. *Communicating With Children: helping children in distress.* Development Manual 2 (Save The Children, London, 1993)

Roberts, K. *Leisure* (Longman, London, 1970)

Roberts, K. *Youth and Leisure* (Allen and Unwin, London, 1983)

Roberts, M. in M. Wandor *On Gender and Writing* (Pandora Press, London, 1983)

Robbins, R.H. *Encyclopedia of Witchcraft and Demonology.* First published 1959 (Bonanza Books, New York, 1981)

Robinson, J. *Unsuitable For Ladies: an anthology of women travellers* (Oxford University Press, Oxford, 1994)

Rowbotham, S. *Woman's Consciousness, Man's World* (Penguin, Harmondsworth, 1973)

Rowbotham, S. *Hidden From History* (Pluto Press, London, 1973)

Rubin, J.Z., Provenzano, F.J. and Luria, Z. (1974) 'The eye of the beholder: Parents' views on sex of newborns', *American Journal of Orthopsychiatry,* 44, pp. 512–19

Russell, B. *In Praise of Idleness and Other Essays* (George Allen and Unwin, London, 1935)

Save the Children, *Growing Up With Conflict: children and development in the occupied territories* (London, 1992)

Schiller, Friedrich, *On the Aesthetic Education of Man* (First published 1795)

Schwartz, Judith, *The Mother Puzzle* (Simon and Schuster, London, 1993)

Scott, A. and Burchell, B. '"And never the twain shall meet?" Gender Segregation and Work Histories', in *Gender Segregation and Social Change,* ed. A. MacEwen Scott (Oxford University Press, Oxford, 1994)

Seabrook, J. *The Leisure Society* (Basil Blackwell, Oxford, 1988)

Seavey, A.A., Katz, P.A., and Zalk, S.R. (1975) 'Baby X: The effect of gender labels on adult responses to infants', *Sex Roles,* 1, pp. 103–9

Sellers, S. *Language and Sexual Difference: feminist writing in France* (Macmillan, London, 1991)

Shakin, M., Shakin, D. and Sternglanz, S.H. (1985) 'Infant Clothing: Sex labelling for strangers', *Sex Roles,* 12, pp. 955–63

Sheldon, A. 1990 'Pickle fights: Gendered talk in preschool disputes', *Discourse Processes,* 13, pp. 5–31

Sherborne, V. *Development Movement for Children: mainstream, special needs and pre-school* (Cambridge University Press, Cambridge, 1990)

Showalter, E. *The Female Malady: woman, madness and English culture, 1830–1980* (Virago, London, 1987)

Slim, H. *A Feast of Festivals* (HarperCollins, London, 1996)

Smith, M.A., Parker, S. and Smith, C.S., eds. *Leisure and Society in Britain* (Allen Lane, London, 1973)

Solomon, M. *Mozart: a life* (Hutchinson, London, 1995)

Sommers, C. Hoff. *Who Stole Feminism: how women have betrayed women* (Simon and Schuster, New York, 1994)

Spender, D. *Man Made Language* (Routledge and Kegan Paul, London, 1980)

Suomi, S.J. and Harlow, H.F. 'Monkeys at Play', from 'Play', a *Natural History Magazine* special supplement, December 1971. Reprinted in J.S. Bruner, A. Jolly and K. Sylva. (eds), *Play: its role in development and evolution* (Penguin, Harmondsworth, 1976)

Superwoman Keeps Going: understanding the female web. The National Council of Women of Great Britain, 1992

Sylva, K., Bruner, J.S. and Genova, P. 'The Role of Play in the Problem-Solving of Children aged 3–5 years old', in J.S. Bruner, A. Jolly and K. Sylva (eds) *Play: its role in development and evolution,* (Penguin, Harmondsworth, 1976)

Talbot, M. *Women and Leisure: a state of the art review* (SSRC, Sports Council, London, 1979)

Talbot, M. (1988) 'Beating them at our own game? Women's sports involvement', pp. 102–114, in E. Wimbush and M. Talbot (eds.) *Relative Freedoms: women and leisure,* (Open University Press, Milton Keynes)

Tannen, D. *You Just Don't Understand – men and women in conversation* (Virago, London, 1992)

Taylor, G.R. *The Angel Makers* (Secker and Warburg, London, 1973)

Tebbutt, M. *Women's Talk? a social history of 'gossip' in working-class neighbourhoods, 1880–1960* (Scolar Press, Aldershot, 1995)

Thompson, E.P. *The Making of the English Working Class* (Penguin, Harmondsworth, 1963)

Thompson, E.P. (1967) 'Time, Work-discipline and Industrial Capitalism', *Past and Present,* Vol 38, pp. 56–97

Thompson, P. and Abrams, R. 'On the edge of later life'. Final report to the ESRC (1992)

Thompson, P., Itzin, C. and Abendstern, M. *I Don't Feel Old: the experiences of later life* (Oxford University Press, Oxford, 1990)

Tolfree, D. *Restoring Playfulness: different approaches to assisting children who are psychologically affected by war or displacement* (Raada Barnen, Stockholm, 1996)

Turnbull, C. *The Forest People* (Simon and Schuster, New York, 1961)

Tysoe, M. *Love Isn't Quite Enough: the psychology of male–female relationships* (HarperCollins, London, 1992)

Uttley, A. *Country Hoard* (Faber and Faber, London, 1943)

Vicinus, M. *Independent Women: work and community for single women 1850–1920* (Virago, London, 1985)

The Virago Book of Fairy Tales (Virago, London, 1990)

Wakefield, G.S. (ed.) *A Dictionary of Christian Spirituality* (SCM Press, London, 1983)

Walker, A. (1993) 'Age and Attitudes.' Commission of the European Communities

Walker, J.C. *Louts and Legends: male youth culture in an inner-city school* (Allen and Unwin, London, 1988)

Warner, M. *From the Beast to the Blonde: on fairytales and their tellers* (Chatto and Windus, London, 1994)

Warr, P.B. *Work, Unemployment and Mental Health.* (Clarendon Press, Oxford, 1987)

Washburn, R.W. (1929) 'A study of the smiling and laughing of infants in the first year of life', *Genetics and Psychological Monograph,* 6, pp. 397–535

Watson, H. *Women in the City of the Dead* (C. Hurst and Co., London, 1992)

Weber, M. *The Protestant Ethic and the Spirit of Capitalism.* First published 1904 (Routledge, London, 1992)

Weeks, D. and James, J. *Eccentrics* (Weidenfeld and Nicolson, London, 1995)

White, J., J. (1989) 'The power of politeness in the classroom', *Journal of Curriculum and Supervisionn* 4:4, pp. 298-321

Williams, H. *Whale Nation* (Jonathan Cape, London, 1988)

Willis, Peter. *Learning to Labour: How working-class kids get working-class jobs* (Saxon House, 1978)

Wimbush, E. *Women, Leisure and Well-being: final report* (Centre for Leisure, Edinburgh, 1986)

Wimbush, E. and Talbot, M. (eds.) *Relative Freedoms: women and leisure* (Open University Press, Milton Keynes, 1988)

Winnicott, D.W. *The Child and the Outside World: studies in developing relationships* (Tavistock, London, 1957)

Winnicott, D.W. *Playing and Reality* (Tavistock Publications, London, 1971)

Wolf, N. *The Beauty Myth* (Chatto and Windus, London, 1990)

Wolfenstein, M. (1951) 'The emergence of fun morality', *Journal of Social Issues* 7,4

Wollstonecraft, M. *A Vindication of the Rights of Woman.* First published 1792 (J.M. Dent, London, 1992)

Women 2000, Mintel International Group Ltd., London, 1993

Woodham, A. 'Laughter: The Health Tonic', *Independent on Sunday* (13.8.95)

Worpole, K. and Greenhalgh, L. *Park Life: urban parks and social renewal*

(Comedia, Stroud, 1995)

Young, G.M. *Victorian England: portrait of an age* (Oxford University Press, Oxford, 1960)

Zahan, D. *La Dialectique du verbe chez les Bambaras* (Paris, 1963)

Zaidman, L.B. 'Pandora's daughters and rituals in grecian cities', in G. Duby and M. Perot (gen. eds), *A History of Women: from ancient goddesses to Christian saints*, (Harvard University Press, Cambridge, Mass., 1992)

Zimmerman, D.H. and West, C. 'Sex roles, interruptions and silences in conversation', in *Language and Sex: Difference and Dominance*, eds. B. Thorne and N. Henley (Newbury House, Rowley, Mass., 1975)

Notes

Introduction

1. Camille Paglia, *Vamps and Tramps,* p. x.

2. Friedrich Schiller, *On the Aesthetic Education of Man.* p. xv

Chapter 1

1. Curtis, J., 1993. 'Satisfying work – if you can find it', British Social Attitudes.

2. Ibid.

3. Research by Haskey (1984) found that unemployment and insecure employment are both factors that increase the risk of marital breakdown. Brendan Burchell (1994) suggests that this may be due to the similar negative psychological consequences of both unemployment and insecure employment.

4. See Ermisch J. 1986 'The economics of the family: applications to divorce and remarriage', Centre for Economic Policy Research Discussion Paper, no. 140.

5. This possibility is supported by the findings of an Israeli study by Dalia Etzion on the moderating effects of social support on work stress and life stress. Etzion, Dalia, 1984, 'Moderating effect of social support on the stress-burnout relationship', *Journal of Applied Psychology*, Vol. 69, no. 4, pp. 615–22.

6. According to a report in the *Observer* newspaper in January 1995, a condition has been identified called TATT, or Tired All The Time. Sub-acute fatigue syndrome, as it is also known, is characterised by 'inexplicable, pervasive lethargy and listlessness, despite sound sleep, healthy diet and exercise'. Related to, but milder than, ME (myaglic encephalomyelistis), it is often linked to stress and depression. The report concludes: 'TATT is largely inexplicable, but it is probably another by-product of high-speed modern living.'

7. Labour Force Survey, 1983–91, Table 31.

8. 'The Time Squeeze', *Demos Quarterly*, 1995.

9. *The Family Friendly Workplace,* Austin Knight UK Limited, 1995. Austin Knight surveyed 22 well-known British organisations representing over 1 million white-collar workers.

10. General Household Survey, 1991. These figures compare with 95% and 86% of men, respectively.

11. Labour Force Survey 1983–91, Table 29 and Table 31.

12. Department of Employment 1994. A survey by the public service union, Unison, among part-time cleaning and catering workers employed by Newcastle-upon-Tyne council found that 38% of cleaning staff had two part-time jobs, while 4% had three. Many women employed by the council, although officially classed as part-time workers, were working more than 30 hours a week.

13. British Household Panel Survey, 1995, Wave 1 Report, 'Household Labour Supply,' Dex, S., Clark. A. and Taylor, M.

14. Employment in Europe Survey, January 1996.

15. See Juliet Schor, *The Overworked American.*

16. Sociologist Earnest Blauner observed that 'That problem with the leisure solution is that it underestimates the fact that work remains the single most important life activity for most people, in terms of time and energy, and ignores the subtle ways in which the quality of one's worklife affects the quality of one's leisure, family relations and basic self-feelings.' Blauner, E. *Freedom and Alienation,* p. 184.

17. See for example Peter Warr, *Work, Unemployment and Mental Health.*

18. Jeremy Seabrook, *The Leisure Society,* p. 1.

19. British Household Panel Survey, op.cit.

20. *Independent on Sunday,* Annabel Ferriman, 29.1.95.

21. *The Family Friendly Workplace,* op.cit.

22. Roger Graef, *Living Dangerously: Young Offenders in Their Own Words.*

23. Figures from the British Heart Foundation show that deaths from coronary heart disease increase with age, for both men and women, but the comparative rates and the patterns of increase are very different. Office of Population Censuses and Surveys (1994); OPCS Monitor DH2 94/2, 'Deaths in 1993 by cause: provisional numbers'.

24. *Women 2000,* Mintel International, 1993.

25. C. Hakim, 'Five Myths of Female employment', British Journal of Sociology, 46(3): 429–55. September, 1995.

26. Burchell and Rubery (1994) show time out of employment affects prospects and earnings; Arber and Ginn (1995) how interrupted employment drastically affects pension receipts.

27. Scott and Burchell, 1994.

28. Gregson and Lowe, 1994.

29. According to the Labour Force Survey, 69.2% of women aged 35–39 in the UK are in paid employment; 74.7% of women aged 40–44 in the UK are in paid employment, and 72.8% of women aged 45–49 in the UK are in paid employment. The majority of these women are also married. See Table 6, pp. 64–5, and Table 29, pp. 78–9.

30. British Household Panel Survey, op.cit.

31. 'The Time Squeeze', *Demos Quarterly*.

32. 'My Second Working Family', Ginny Dougary, *The Times*, 14.1.95.

33. The exception is the subject of children's play, which became a fashionable topic in the 1960s and has remained so. This apart, virtually nothing has been written in post-WW2 literature about play, either as a philosophical concept, or as a significant sociological phenomenon.

34. R.L. Stevenson, *An Apology for Idlers*.

35. Helena Norberg-Hodge, *Ancient Futures*, p. 35–6.

36. Ibid. p. 37.

37. These books are all published by Thorsens. Their authors are, respectively, Alex Kirsta, Jacqueline M. Atkinson, Robert Holden, Leon Chaitow and Dr Kenneth Hambly.

38. *Independent on Sunday*, 29.1.95; *Observer*, January 1993.

39. Camille Paglia, op.cit. p.ix.

Chapter 2

1. In the field of social science research, this linguistic shift is particularly noticeable from the 1970s on, when play is no longer the subject of study, replaced instead by a rash of books on leisure. Tellingly, the *Concise Oxford Dictionary of Sociology* offers lengthy entries under both 'work' and 'leisure' but does not list 'play'.

2. K. Groos, *Play of Man*.

3. S. Freud, *Beyond the Pleasure Principle*.

4. Ibid. Freud makes the point that 'The unpleasurable nature of an experience does not always unsuit it for play', p. 16. He describes how unpleasant experiences can be repeatedly played out in an unconscious way

as part of contemporary experience, rather than as a remembered event belonging in the past. In analysis, the events, past and present, are replayed in such a way that, ideally, the patient is able 'to recognise that what appears to be reality is in fact only a reflection of a forgotten past', p. 19.

5. Ibid.

6. Jean Piaget, *Play, Dreams and Imitation in Childhood,* p. 87.

7. Ibid. Piaget suggests that a key aspect of this state of mind is one of domination: 'While imitation is a continuation of accommodation for its own sake, it may be said conversely that play is essentially assimilation, or the primacy of assimilation over accommodation . . . [Play] proceeds by relaxation of the effort at adaptation and by maintenance or exercise of activities for the mere pleasure of mastering them and acquiring thereby a feeling of virtuosity or power.', pp. 87–9.

8. Ibid., pp. 87–9.

9. M. Csikszentmihalyi, 1975. *Beyond Boredom and Anxiety.*

10. G. Privette, 1983. 'Peak experience, peak performance, and peak flow: a comparative analysis of positive human experiences'.

11. J. Huizinga, *Homo Ludens,* p. 154.

12. M. Argyle, *The Psychology of Happiness,* p. 89.

13. R. Glasser, *Leisure – Penalty or Prize?* pp. 145–6.

14. Hendry, Shucksmith and Cross, 'Young people's mental well-being in relation to leisure'.

15. M. Csikszentmihalyi, op.cit.

16. M. Argyle and L. Lu, 'The Happiness of Extroverts'. Argyle and Lu studied the leisure activities of 114 adults, 69 of whom reported having a 'serious' leisure activity.

17. Stanley Parker points out that 'industry needs the consuming time of workers as much as it needs their producing time. *The Future of Work and Leisure,* p. 56.

18. E. Gibbon, *The History of the Decline and Fall of the Roman Empire,* Vol. 11, pp. 34–5.

Chapter 3

1. A. Koestler, *The Act of Creation.* In *The Ghost in the Machine* Koestler explores the connection between scientific discovery and humour, showing how both exploit and explore the coming together of seemingly incompatible elements: 'Comic discovery is paradox stated, scientific discovery is paradox resolved.' (p. 186.) The playfulness that underlies

scientific discovery is central to its success, and is characterised by the scientist's willingness to explore the absurd, ludicrous and implausible. 'The history of science abounds with examples of discoveries greeted with howls of laughter because they seemed to be a marriage of incompatibles,' Koestler writes, 'until the marriage bore fruit and the alleged incompatibility of the partners turned out to derive from prejudice.' Ibid., p. 186.

2. D.W. Winnicott, *Playing and Reality,* p. 54.

3. There is an embedded reference here to the importance of the playwright's endeavour, the value of the theatrical creation, which is both a mirror of life and a tutorial on life. The value of *the* play, as well as the value of play, is being demonstrated, showing us that the play is, indeed, the thing.

4. H.L. Rheingold. 'The effect of environmental stimulation upon social and exploratory behaviour in the human infant'. The study compared the care of three-month-old babies living with their own families and those living in institutions, and found that, in addition to the play differential, the former were also fed four times as often and talked to five times as often as those in institutions.

5. D.W. Winnicott, 'Why Children Play, 1942' in *The Child and the Outside World.*

6. See J. R. Moyle, *Just Playing? The role and status of play in early childhood education,* p. 73.

7. Intelligent children played for fifty minutes longer each day than retarded ones, according to one study by Boynton and Ford, 'The relationship between play and intelligence'.

8. Suomi and Harlow, in *Play, its role in development and evolution,* eds. Bruner, Jolly and Sylva, pp. 490–96.

9. Ibid.

10. Relationship Play is based on the theories of Rudolf Laban, and was developed by Veronica Sherborne. It is used in the training of social workers, nursery workers, as well as in day centres. It has even been used, with considerable success, for parents who have previously abused their children. See V. Sherborne, *Development Movement for Children: mainstream, special needs and pre-school.* Also, E. Goldschmied and S. Jackson, *People Under Three.*

11. Sylva, Bruner and Genova, 'The role of play in the problem-solving of children aged 3–5 years old', in *Play, Its Role in Development and Evolution,* eds. Bruner, Jolly, and Sylva. The same is true of monkeys: animals that have been allowed to play with an object for a while are more adept at using it later for its functional purpose, such as scratching out insects from the earth with a stick. See Birch (1945); Schiller (1952), in Bruner et al., op.cit., p. 48.

12. D.W. Winnicott, 'Why Children Play', from *The Child and the Outside World,* p. 152.

13. This information is based on material I collected during a two-day visit to the community in 1987. A video about the Cotswold Community, 'The Recovery of Childhood', is available to buy or hire. For further information contact: The Cotswold Community, Ashton Keynes, Swindon, Wiltshire SN6 6QU; Tel. 01285 861239.

14. Save The Children, *Growing Up With Conflict: children and development in the occupied territories.*

15. N. Richman, *Communicating with Children: working with children in distress.*

16. David Tolfree, *Restoring Playfulness: different approaches to assisting children who are psychologically affected by war or displacement.*

17. R. Abrams, 'Children on the Frontline', *She* magazine, 1993.

18. M. Argyle, *Psychology of Happiness,* p. 141.

19. In their study of the happiness of extroverts, Michael Argyle and Luo Lu found that, regardless of personality, engaging in social activities enhanced happiness, while withdrawing from social situations reduced happiness. Summarising their findings, they assert that 'about half of the greater happiness of extroverts can be explained by their greater participation in social activities . . . The most important factor is not to avoid social contacts with other people.' The authors hypothesise that encouraging introverts to engage in more social activities would be likely to improve their happiness ratings. This research does not, however, adequately account for the fact that introverts may positively enjoy solitary activities, nor that certain social activities might make an introvert miserable. M. Argyle and L. Lu, 'The Happiness of Extroverts'.

20. From various sources, summarised in Argyle, *The Psychology of Happiness,* pp. 112–25.

21. Psychologist Maryon Tysoe makes the point that the effect on your relationship is unlikely to be a positive one if all you ever do together is the washing up. *Love Isn't Quite Enough,* pp. 98–100.

22. C. Clulow and J. Mattinson, *Marriage Inside Out.* p. 36.

23. E. Erikson *Play and Development.*

24. Fifty men and women aged 55–60 were interviewed about their past experiences and their present attitudes towards ageing. P. Thompson and R. Abrams, 'On the edge of later life'.

25. Thompson, Itzin and Abenstern, *I Don't Feel Old,* p. 247.

26. Hendry et al. *Fit For Life,* p. 144.

27. Ibid.

28. David Weeks and Jamie James, *Eccentrics,* pp. 100–1.

29. Ibid., pp. 149–59.

30. Ibid., p. 180.

31. 'Laughter'. The Health Tonic', A. Woodham, *Independent on Sunday,* 13.8.95.

32. Ibid.

33. *Independent on Sunday,* Lesley Gerard, 4.6.95: 'More Play is What the Doctor Ordered'.

34. Howard Friedman, Univ. of California, cited in the *Guardian.*

35. Konrad Lorenz, *Studies in Animal and Human Behaviour.*

36. R.P. Feynman, *'Surely You're Joking, Mr. Feynman!',* pp. 172–4.

37. Helen Graham, *The Magic Shop,* pp. 72–4.

38. Ibid., p. 74.

39. Rosemary Gordon, 'The creative process: self-expression and self-transcendence', p. 23, in S. Jennings, *Creative Therapy.*

40. Anne Hope and Sally Timmel, *Training for Transformation – A Handbook for Community Workers,* Vol 1, p. 71.

41. Giddens goes on to say, 'The more limited importance of play in adulthood is not due to biological differences between the youthful and adult organism, but to factors external to the individual which limit the time available for play.' Giddens is, of course, quite right in saying that lack of time is a reason for the lack of play in adulthood, but this is not grounds for saying it is less important.' Anthony Giddens, 'Notes on the Concepts of Play and Leisure', p. 73.

42. S.J. Douglas, *Where the Girls Are: growing up female with the mass media,* pp. 127–34.

43. Bryan Williams, Cedar Falls, Aspect 6, *Programme for Wholeness*

44. Pers.comm: H.S.

45. Campbell (1981).

46. Barker, Dembo and Lewin, 'Frustration and Regression'.

47. A 1981 study of 800 people in Camberwell found that 14.9% of women compared with 6.1% of men showed prevalence of psychiatric disorder (P. Beddington et al., 1981.) Ten years later, in 1991, a round-up of the

evidence for women being more vulnerable to psychological symptoms concluded that women were twice as likely to be treated for depression as men. See Eugene Paykel, 1991.

48. Women aged 30–40 appear to suffer the poorest mental health. From research cited in Michael Argyle, *The Psychology of Happiness,* pp. 156–75.

49. This is in part explained by the fact that women pay more attention than men to their mental health, and are quicker to identify symptoms of ill-health and to act on them. It is also possible that doctors are more willing to classify women as suffering from mental health problems than they are men. See S. Milligan and A. Clare, *Depression and How to Survive It,* p. 143.

50. Helen Graham summarises research in this area by pointing out that, 'housework is directly opposed to self-actualisation and personal growth because it provides no feedback about the self, no possibility of advancement, no intellectual challenge and, invariably, no recognition by others of the labours involved. At most it provides only a fleeting sense of accomplishment. Furthermore, it is often associated with some degree of social isolation, and the demands of young children.' Helen Graham, *The Magic Shop,* p. 94.

51. *Superwomen Keeps Going: understanding the female web,* A Survey of Women's Lives and Expectations, p. 9.

52. Erik Erikson, 'Womanhood and the inner space', in *Identity: Youth and Crisis,* p. 278.

Chapter 4

1. Plato, *Laws,* Book VII. This translation is given in J. Finnis, *Natural Law and Natural Rights,* pp. 407–10.

2. Plato's words, while abidingly relevant, must also be seen in the light of the contemporary history of Ancient Greece. The Athenians had been defeated in the previous generation by the Spartans in the Peloponnesian Wars, and Athens was no longer the great military power it had been. Plato belonged to a generation of Athenians who were turning away from war and commerce, and instead looking to education and culture as the way forward. Play, in Plato's scheme of things, was a serious business. I am indebted to Dr Stephen Harrison of Corpus Christi College, Oxford, for sharing his thoughts on Platonic notions of play and their historical context, as well as the place of play in Ancient Greece and Rome generally.

3. Plato, *Laws.* Here Plato argues that certain kinds of play, such as song and dance, prepared men for success in the serious business of war and politics. War, in turn, paved the way to peace, and further opportunities for play.

4. Bernard Knox, reviewing Charles Martin's translation of Catullus in the

New York Review of Books. Martin's analysis of the poems themselves, and in particular poems 11 and 16, reveals the way in which Catullus carefully exploited the conventions of play in order to create the desired literary effect. C. Martin, *Catullus*; C. Martin, *The Poems of Catullus*, Bernard Knox, 'A Dangerously Modern Poet', *New York Review of Books*, 3.12.92.

5. S. Pomeroy, *Goddesses, Whores, Wives and Slaves: Women in Classical Antiquity*, p. 30.

6. Ibid, p. 39.

7. Ibid, p. 36.

8. Ibid, p. 79.

9. F. Lissarrague, 'Figures of Women', p. 190, in G. Duby and M. Perot (general editors), *A History of Women*, (Harvard University Press, Cambridge, Mass., 1992).

10. L.B. Zaidman, 'Pandora's Daughters and Rituals in Grecian Cities', pp. 338–76, in G. Duby and M. Perot, ibid.

11. S. Pomeroy. op.cit., pp. 170–89.

12. H. Leyser, *Medieval Women: a social history of women in England 450–1500*, pp. 242–48.

13. B.S. Anderson and J.P. Zinsser, *A History of Their Own*, pp. 21–5.

14. J. Huizinga, *Homo Ludens*, p. 180.

15. M. Tebbutt, *Women's Talk? A social history of 'gossip' in working-class neighbourhoods, 1880–1960*, pp. 19–27.

16. William Kethe, 'A Sermon Made At Blandford Forum in the countie of Dorset', London 1571, in Robert Malcolmson, *Popular Recreations in English Society 1700–1850*, p. 9.

17. The impact of puritanism on popular recreation was limited at this stage. According to Malcolmson, 'The outlook of puritanism was too urban in character, too orderly and austere, to be fully acceptable to a pre-industrial society.' R. Malcolmson, op.cit. pp. 13–14.

18. It is has been estimated that in the period 1574–1821 28.5% of households had servants. Richard Wall in Laslett and Wall (eds), *Household and Family in Past Time*, pp. 152–3.

19. Anne Laurence, *Women in England, 1500–1760*. p. 149.

20. From Thomas Tusser, *Five Hundred Points of Good Husbandry*, 1580, in A. Laurence, op.cit., p. 109.

21. A. Laurence, op.cit., p. 216.

22. Susan Dwyer Amussen in T. Harris (ed.), *Popular Culture in England, c. 1500–1850,* pp. 61–2.

23. Roy Porter, *English Society in the Eighteenth Century,* p. 169.

24. H. Slim, *A Feast of Festivals,* p. 37. Amongst some Protestants this attitude to the Christmas festivities persisted into the nineteenth century. Peter Carey's novel, *Oscar and Lucinda,* begins with a fictional account of a singularly unfestive Christmas Day in 1856 in the household of a Plymouth Brethren minister. Havoc is wreaked by the cook's decision that the minister's son, Oscar, should not be denied the delights of plum pudding any longer.

25. Cited in Roy Porter, *English Society in the Eighteenth Century,* p. 250.

26. Friederich Schiller, *On the Aesthetic Education of Man,* XV.9, p. 107.

27. Ibid.

28. From 'A Letter Describing the General Appearances and Effects of the Expedition with Lunardi's Balloon', in M. Cadogan, *Women With Wings: female flyers in fact and fiction,* p. 12.

29. Ibid. pp. 16–17.

30. Max Weber, *The Protestant Ethic and the Spirit of Capitalism,* p. 166. Weber argued that the Protestant ethic of calling and duty (in its attempt to reconcile religious asceticism with the secularising effects of wealth) fuelled and fused with a capitalistic spirit to create a work ethic, which has characterised all industrialised nations since. Weber inveighed against the deadening effect of the work ethic; he did not, however, make the connection between the work ethic and the devaluation of play, although his analysis of the effects on nineteenth-century culture of the combined forces of Protestantism and capitalism sits comfortably with such a connection, and in places points firmly in the direction of one, for example, when he compares the duty-driven 19th century with 'the rosy blush of its laughing heir, the Enlightenment'. Ibid., p. 182.

31. According to Malcolmson, 'Recreation was commonly seen as an impediment, a threat of substantial proportions, to steady and productive labour.' R. Malcolmson, op.cit., p. 94.

32. Clarke and Critcher, *The Devil Makes Work,* p. 56.

33. Parliamentary Papers, 1845, xviii, p. 618, in Malcolmson, op.cit., p. 110.

34. Josiah Tucker recommended this for the following: 'all Places of public Resort and Diversion, such as public Rooms, Music-Gardens, Play-Houses, etc. also on Booths and Stands for Country Wakes, Cricket Matches, and Horse Racing, Stages for Mountebanks, Cudgel Playing, etc. more over on Fives Places, and Ball Courts, Billiard Tables, Shuffle Boards, Skittle Alleys,

Bowling Greens, and Cock Pits: Also Capitulation Taxes should be levied on itinerant Players, Lottery-men, Shew-men, Jugglers, Ballad Singers, and indeed on all others of whatever Class or Denomination, whose very Trades and Profession have a natural Tendency, and whose Personal Interest it is to make other People profuse, extravagant, and idle.' *Josiah Tucker,* ed. Schuyler, p. 261, quoted in Malcolmson op.cit. p. 98.

35. E.P. Thompson, 'Time, Work-Discipline and Industrial Capitalism', *Past and Present,* 38, 1967, pp. 56–97.

36. In the *Public Advertiser,* 2.9.1757, quoted in Malcolmson, op.cit. p. 98.

37. Quoted in I. Bradley, *The Call to Seriousness,* p. 108, from G.R. Taylor, *The Angel Makers,* p. 22.

38. Quoted in Malcolmson, op.cit.

39. G.M. Young, *Victorian England: portrait of an age,* pp. 1–2.

40. In Malcolmson, op.cit., p. 102.

41. Charles Maudie, who ran the Select Circulating Library, was a strict Evangelical, and had no qualms about vetting the books available to the library's 25,000 subscribers. W.H. Smith, a Methodist, similarly censored the books on sale in his station shops. See Bradley, op.cit., p. 98.

42. From Chapter 3 of *Little Dorrit.*

43. I am indebted to Anna Gambles of Nuffield College, Oxford, for this observation.

44. H. More, *Works,* 1834, II, 319; III, 105.

45. There is evidence to suggest that some men were fiercely resistant to their wives' church-related leisure, and on occasion resorted to physical violence to stop them going, providing an intriguing parallel with the response of some husbands in the 1970s, who reacted with great hostility to their wives going out to consciousness-raising groups. I am grateful to John Walsh of Jesus College, Oxford for our discussions on the role of the church in shaping Victorian women's leisure.

46. H.L. Dunlop, 'Games, sports, dancing and other vigorous recreational activities and their function in Samoan culture'.

47. Ibid., p. 110.

48. I. Bradley, op.cit., p. 106.

49. *Homo Ludens,* p. 192. Huizinga sees this overriding of the play-element in culture as being symbolised in the changes in fashion, men's in particular, from the *outré* wigs and fantastic frills of eighteenth-century clothing to the austerity of Victorian dress.

50. Adrian Harvey, unpublished doctoral thesis, 'The Evolution of Modern British Sporting Culture 1793–1850', University of Oxford, 1995.

51. Ibid.

52. As social historians Clarke and Critcher make clear in their account of the history of leisure. 'For most of the nineteenth and twentieth-centuries . . . [women's] time has been predominantly structured around the family, and women's free time seems to have been woven into the private spheres of family, street and neighbourhood rather than the public worlds of institutionalised leisure.' Clarke and Critcher, op.cit., p. 56.

53. For a fuller analysis of the relationship between women and mental illness in Victorian society, see Elaine Showalter, *The Female Malady: women, madness and English culture, 1830–1980.*

54. Of 58,640 certified lunatics in 1872, 31,822 were women, according to figures given in J. Mortimer Granville, *The Care and Cure of the Insane,* p. 230. Cited in Elaine Showalter, ibid., p. 52.

55. H.B. Donkin, 'Hysteria' in D.H. Tuke, *Dictionary of Psychological Medicine,* pp. 619–20.

56. J. Seabrook, op.cit., p. 5. Seabrook offers a more detailed analysis of the paradoxical relationship between work and leisure in his book than I have space for here.

Chapter 5

1. Department for Employment, 1990, 'Women in the labour market: Results from the 1989 Labour Force Survey', *Employment Gazette,* HMSO, London, pp. 619–43.

2. General Household Survey, 1994.

3. *Employment Gazette,* 1990.

4. Department for Employment, 1994.

5. Income Data Services, May 1993.

6. National Council of Women, 1992.

7. The Henley Centre for Forecasting, *Frontiers: planning for consumer change in Europe.*

8. 'The National Child Development Study', Social Statistics Research Unit, City University, London, 1993.

9. D. Gittins, *The Family In Question,* Chapter 6, 'Why is a woman's work never done?'

10. J. Liddington and J. Norris, *One Hand Tied Behind Us,* p. 217.

11. Rebecca Abrams, *Woman in a Man's World*, pp. 175–6.

12. 'The Time Squeeze', *Demos Quarterly*. Different surveys yield different margins between men and women's leisure time. There are significant regional differences for example. According to a report by Mintel, 'Leisure Time', women in Yorkshire and the North East get 10.5 hours less leisure a week than men, compared with only 30 minutes difference in London. All the surveys agree that women on average get less leisure time than men. 'Leisure Time', Henley Centre for Forecasting.

13. OPCS, 'Social Trends', pl.147, 1985, table 10.1.

14. Ibid.

15. Analysis of time-use diaries by Layte revealed that where women are employed outside the home, they have less total leisure time than men. Those in full-time employment get 44.68 minutes less per day (308.76 minutes per week); those in part-time employment get 26.03 minutes less per day (162.21 minutes per week). When these figures were broken down for average leisure time for weekdays and weekends, Layte found that women have less leisure then men, *regardless of either's employment status*. Women in full-time paid employment get 120.98 minutes less leisure time at weekends; women in part-time paid employment get 204.88 minutes less; unemployed women get 142.40 minutes less; full-time housewives get 75.12 minutes less. (These figures are computed from data drawn from the Household and Community Study. The respondents represent a stratified sample from six travel-to-work areas across the UK, and the data is part of the ESRC-funded Social Change in Economic Life Initiative.) R. Layte, 'The material and cultural determinants of the domestic division of labour', unpublished doctoral thesis.

16. Layte found that when a woman is in full-time employment, 8.87% of her leisure time is also spent doing domestic chores compared with 3.34% of a man's leisure time. When a woman is in part-time employment, 8.99% of her leisure time is also time spent doing housework, compared with 2.82% of a man's. Unemployed women spend 11% of their leisure time also working, compared with 4.6% for men. R. Layte, ibid.

17. P. Mansfield and J. Collard, *The Beginning of the Rest of Your Life.*

18. Carolyn Vogler, 'Unemployment, the household and social networks', in D. Gallie, J. Gershuny and C. Vogler, *Social Change and the Experience of Unemployment*, p. 238.

19. Ibid.

20. J. Gershuny, *Social Innovation and the Division of Labour*, pp. 149–50.

21. Ibid. p. 153.

22. R. Layte, op.cit.

23. See J. Schor, op.cit.

24. OPCS Monitor, 1990.

25. A study carried out in 1986 by Erica Wimbush examined the role and meaning of leisure for a group of Scottish mothers with pre-school age children. Wimbush found that parenthood had dramatically affected these women's lives, while seeming to have made little or no impact on the social lives of their men: 'The occasional night out with girlfriends or work mates or a day off to go shopping in town with a friend were commonly cited examples of special occasions when women had space and time for themselves. But the frequency of these kinds of personal leisure were restricted by both finances . . . and the availability of others . . . to look after the children.' Even women who had managed to create an existence beyond the home for themselves, remained primarily committed to meeting the needs of their children, husbands and homes, 'their [own] activities had to fit in around this'. Only a few saw their own well-being as in itself a contribution to the well-being of their family. E. Wimbush 'Mothers meeting', in E. Wimbush and M. Talbot, (eds) *Relative Freedoms*, pp. 63–9.

26. The man did an average of 1 hour and 46 minutes unpaid work per day and 6 hours and 22 minutes of paid work, while the woman did an average of 2 hours and 27 minutes of unpaid work and 5 hours and 39 minutes of paid work. The total amount of time spent working was 8 hours and 8 minutes for the man, 8 hours and 6 minutes for the woman. J. Gershuny, op.cit., pp. 153–6.

27. 'Leisure time', Mintel. These figures do not reveal longitudinal changes in the division of labour after having children. R. Layte found that men were doing considerably more housework than before, and that the increase was more pronounced than for women. However, there were two interesting aspects to this finding: first, men would do more of tasks that they had been doing already, but were extremely reluctant to take on new tasks. In other words, they would do more shopping if they had done some shopping before, but they would not take on the laundry if they had never touched the washing machine up until that point. Secondly, Layte found that while there was an increase in men's domestic work immediately after the arrival of children within five years this had tailed off and the division of household chores was right back to where it had been before having children. Whether women reclaim the tasks or men shrug them off remains unclear. R. Layte, op.cit.

28. M. Argyle, *The Psychology of Happiness,* pp. 70–78; 'Leisure Time', 1995, Mintel. Watching television is a key leisure activity for women, and soap operas are especially popular. Argyle suggests that this is because soaps offer a fictional community with which female viewers, in particular, can identify. Another explanation, not considered by Argyle, is that the familiar characters and slowly progressing plots mean that soap operas can easily be

watched at the same time as doing household chores, such as ironing, sewing, cooking or feeding children.

29. Samuel Richardson, *Pamela* (Penguin edn, 1980) p. 150.

30. Eliza Lynn Linton, 'The girl of the period', *Saturday Review,* 14 March 1868. In M. Vicinus, *Independent Women,* p. 3.

31. In 1851, there were 204,640 unmarried women over the age of 45 in England; by 1891, this figure had risen to 342,072. When younger women and widows of all ages are accounted for, the true number of single women in England in the second half of the nineteenth century is much higher. There were almost one million unmarried women over the age of 20 in England in 1901. M. Vicinus, ibid., pp. 27–30. See also, notes 42–5 on p. 306.

32. M. Vicinus, ibid., p. 5. Vicinus points out that the 'passion for meaningful work' was an important goal for nineteenth-century women, an escape route from the stultifying confines of domesticity and dependency.

33. Pers.comm. Cortina Butler, 1990.

34. Anthea Gerrie, 'Me-Time', *She* magazine, March 1992.

35. Wolf argues that the ideal of feminine physical beauty is socially constructed and manipulated in such a way that women are prevented, or distracted, from taking up the advantages that feminism has won for them. 'The more legal and material hindrances women have broken through, the more strictly and heavily and cruelly images of female beauty have come to weigh upon us . . . We are in the midst of a violent backlash against feminism that uses images of female beauty as a political weapon against women's advancement.' N. Wolf, *The Beauty Myth,* p. 10.

36. St Thomas Aquinas, *Summa Theologica.*

37. Louise Jury, 'Teachers and students welcome review', *Guardian,* 13.11.93.

Chapter 6

1. S. Orbach, *Guardian,* 13.6.92.

2. Rousseau, *Emilius,* cited in M. Wollstonecraft, *A Vindication of the Rights of Woman,* p. 54.

3. M. Wollstonecraft, ibid.

4. J. White, 'The Power of Politeness in the Classroom: Cultural Codes that Create and Constrain Knowledge Construction', *Journal of Curriculum and Supervision,* 4:4, 298–321.

5. D. Lange, 'Using like to introduce constructed dialogue: how like contributes to discourse coherence', Master's thesis, in Deborah Tannen,

You Just Don't Understand, p. 237.

6. Deborah Tannen, ibid., pp. 236–7.

7. 'Lady in the Lords', *Corridor Magazine,* 1982 (author's collection).

8. Aries, E. 'Verbal and Nonverbal Behaviour in Single-Sex and Mixed-Sex Groups: Are Traditional Sex Roles Changing'.

9. Sue Lees, *Sugar and Spice.*

10. The *Guardian,* 'Blood and Guts on the Glass Ceiling', 21.5.92. J. McLoughlin.

11. Ibid. McLoughlin explores how this impacts on a woman's ability to pitch for success in the business context.

12. J. Gaskell, *Gender Matters: from school to work,* quoted in S. Lees, *Sugar and Spice,* p. 159.

13. A. McRobbie, 'Working class girls and the culture of femininity'.

14. D. Reay 'Working with boys'.

15. V. Griffiths, 'From "playing out" to "dossing out": young women and leisure', in E. Wimbush and M. Talbot (eds)., *Relative Freedoms,* p. 50.

16. Ibid., p. 50.

17. 'Carers in 1990'. *General Household Survey.*

18. M. Argyle, *The Psychology of Happiness,* p. 78.

19. Semonides, *Diehl,* fragment 7, trs. Marylin Arthur, quoted in Sarah B. Pomeroy, *Goddesses, Whores, Wives and Slaves: women in classical antiquity,* pp. 49–52.

20. W.R. Greg, 'Why are women redundant?' *National Review* 15(1862), p. 436, cited in Martha Vicinus, *Independent Women: work and community for single women 1850–1920,* p. 4.

21. Cited in S. Lees, op.cit. p. 154.

22. J. Achterberg, *Woman as Healer,* Chapter 13, 'Midwifery: the mysterious office', pp. 113–32.

23. R. Abrams, *Woman in a Man's World,* pp. 10–11.

24. Ibid. pp. 120–21.

25. Maccoby and Jacklin, 1987; Pitcher and Shultz, 1963; Golombok and Fivush, 1994: 121.

26. N. Chodorow, *The Reproduction of Mothering,* p. 187.

27. J. Mendelsohn, 'The view from step number 16'.

28. Ibid., p. 243.

29. S. Lees, op.cit., pp. 105–48.

30. D. Gittins, in her study of changing family ideologies, has pointed out that, 'However a society has been organised, there has always been the assumption that a certain core of domestic work is by definition woman's work. This regardless of whether she engages in paid work, whether she is totally or partly dependent on a husband or father, regardless of whether she is single, married, widowed or divorced, young or old.' As Gittins makes clear, there is no equivalent for men. 'A man may empty the rubbish, bath the baby, wash the dishes or sweep the floor, but if he elects not to do so – as many have and do – he is in no way socially or economically ostracised or penalised. His domestic participation is totally and always voluntary. If a woman choses not to keep the house clean, not to supervise the children adequately, she is in danger of being labelled as a 'bad' mother or a bad wife – she can be divorced, she can have her children taken away from her. Housework and child-care are not voluntary for married women in contemporary society, unless their class position is such that they have the financial resources to pay others to carry out their responsibilities.' D. Gittins, *The Family in Question,* p. 131.

31. Despite the fact that many women, both in the past and in contemporary society, have been and are paid to do tasks such as child-minding, cleaning and ironing, this work is nevertheless not perceived as a valuable and marketable skill. Where women do this kind of work for free, its market value is even more obscured. D. Gittins, ibid., p. 116.

32. Thompson and Abrams, *On the Edge of Later Life*, ESRC.

33. National Council of Women of Great Britain, *Superwoman Keeps Going: understanding the female web.* p. 9.

34. F. Johnson, and F. Aries, 'The talk of women friends', Women's Studies International Forum, Vol. 6, no 4, quoted in S. Lees, *Sugar and Spice,* p. 71.

35. P. Naber, 1992, 'Youth culture and life world', paper given at Alice in Wonderland Conference, Amsterdam, June 1992, cited in S. Lees, *Sugar and Spice,* p. 100.

36. S. Orbach, op.cit.

Chapter 7

1. Peter Redgrove and Penny Mortimer argue in their book, *The Wise Wound,* that in cultures where menstruation is recognised as a physical symbol of women's life-giving powers, pre-menstrual tension and menstrual cramps do not exist. The difficulties that many women in modern western societies experience around and during their periods express and reflect the hostility that female physicality incurs more generally in those societies. P.

Mortimer and P. Redgrove, *The Wise Wound.*

2. Pliny the Elder, *Natural History,* AD 77, quoted in *In Her Master's Voice,* compiled by Tama Starr.

3. Cited in Olwen Hufton, 1995, *The Prospect Before Her,* London, HarperCollins, p. 43.

4. Cited in J. Achterberg, *Woman as Healer.*

5. 'Desert Island Discs', BBC Radio 4, June 1990.

6. Analysis of videotapes of school children in conversation reveals that while boys align their bodies at angles to one another, girls tend to face each other and look directly at each other. Another study found that girls were criticised by their peer group for standing out from the crowd, whether that be for excelling academically or wearing newer and more expensive clothes than the others. See M.H. Goodwin, 'Children's Arguing'. Deborah Tannen concludes that, 'appearing better than others is a violation of the girls' egalitarian ethic: people are supposed to express their connections and similarities.' D. Tannen, *You Just Don't Understand,* p. 217.

7. The 'Oxfordshire Eating Survey' is a longitudinal study of women aged 16–35 living in Oxfordshire. Findings are based on 15,000 self-completed questionnaires, 800 one-off interviews, and annual interviews with 250 respondents conducted over four years. 30% of respondents are students, a small proportion are at home with children, the rest are employed. 65% are single with no children. I am grateful to Dr Fairburn at the University of Oxford for granting permission for me to quote these findings.

8. Shakin, Shakin and Sternglanz (1985) found that girls were more likely to be dressed in decorative clothes, while boys were more likely to be dressed in functional ones. Rubin et al. (1974) in a study of parents of newborn infants found that the delicacy and prettiness of daughters was mentioned, whereas parents tended to comment on the strength and alertness of sons.

9. R.C. Hawkins, S. Turell and L.S. Jackson, 1983, 'Desirable and undesirable masculine and feminine traits in relation to students' dietary tendencies and body image dissatisfaction', *Sex Roles,* 9,705–24.

10. The tale of Cinderella has been in circulation for over a thousand years. In her extensive tour of the fairy story in *From the Beast to the Blonde,* Marina Warner points out that a Chinese version survives in written form dating from AD 850–60. This follows the familiar plot of the bereft daughter ill-treated by her step-mother and step-sister, who keep her sequestered at home. Magic intervenes, in the shape of a golden fish, and salvation comes through the device of a tiny gold shoe. 'There was not one that it fitted. It was as light as down and made no noise even when treading on stone.' M. Warner, *From the Beast to the Blonde,* pp. 202–3.

11. Figures from the Sir Norman Chester Centre for Football Research, 1995.

12. From a report in the Swansea *Evening Post,* July 1996.

13. '[In] the female narrative [of schizophrenics] the hectoring spirit . . . who jeers, judges, commands and controls . . . is almost invariably male. He delivers the running critique of appearance and performance that the woman has grown up with as part of her stream of consciousness.' Showalter's point is that in female schizophrenics, the hectoring spirit we are all familiar with is made manifest. E. Showalter, *The Female Malady,* p. 213.

14. Comedia/Demos conducted a survey of 12,000 people and 12 parks around Britain. See K. Worpole and L. Greenhalgh, 1995, *Park Life: Urban Parks and Social Renewal.*

15. City Walks in London (consultation document), 13.6.1995, The Government Office for London.

16. Hough and Mayhew, 'The Second British Crime Survey', 'The Greater London Women's Committee Study of Women and Transport', 1985; 'The British Crime Survey', 1993. The latest British crime survey showed that the average risk of becoming a victim is 1 in 150. Most at risk of attack are young men between 16 and 19. Women are less likely to be injured than men, while women over the age of 60 have only a 1 in 400 chance of an attack in the street.

17. Sue Lees, op.cit., p. 273.

18. V. Griffiths, in E. Wimbush and M. Talbot, op.cit., p. 51.

19. Ibid.

20. R. Dixey, 'Eyes down': A Study of Bingo', in E. Wimbush and M. Talbot, op.cit., pp. 91–101.

21. Golombok and Fivush, 1994.

22. Maccoby and Jacklin, 1987; Pitcher and Shultz, 1983.

23. Miller, Danahar and Forbes, 1986; Sheldon, 1990.

24. Opie and Opie 1984.

25. Moss, 1967; Parke and Sawin, 1980, Power and Parke, 1982.

26. Seavey, Katz and Zalk, 1975.

27. Further evidence for the rapidity and rigidity with which gender comes to identify us comes from studies of boy babies whose sex is wrongly designated at birth as a consequence of their genitals not being fully developed. When these children then have to be redesignated male at the age of eighteen months or two years, they experience considerable trauma as a result.

S. Kessler and W. McKenna, *Gender: An Ethnomethodological Approach.*

28. L.B. Hendry, *Growing Up and Going Out,* p. 45.

29. Research itself is often bounded by stereotypical notions of gender. A recent American study of 1,688 teenagers found that 'the degree of masculinity or femininity of their gender identities [accounted] for a significant portion of their school grades'; the more feminine the gender identity, the better the grades, not only in verbal-skills related subjects, but across the board. However, this particular research was entirely uncritical of conventional definitions of gender, and had assessed 'femininity' and 'masculinity' accordingly. Thus, 'sitting still' was deemed a feminine activity, while 'being disruptive' was deemed a masculine one! It is not particularly surprising that the disruptive children should do less well academically than those who sat still and concentrated, but what this says about gender identity remains unclear. P.J. Burke, 'Gender Identity, Sex and School Performance'.

30. 'Girls and boys are treated differently both by fathers and mothers from the moment of birth. By the time they reach their third year their gender identity is usually well-established and their play preferences are clearly influenced by perceptions of what is appropriate for boys or girls.' E. Goldschmied and S. Jackson, *People Under Three: children in their third year,* p. 146.

31. As American clinical psychologist Margo Maine has pointed out, 'Boys are encouraged to be independent and to take risks; girls are encouraged to be nurturant and to seek approval.' Margo Maine, *Father Hunger,* p. 66.

32. This finding is borne out by numerous studies in the UK and America. See Esther Blank Greif, *Sex Role Playing in Pre-School Children* for a study of American nursery school children from white middle-class professional families. Similar restraints on 'cross-playing' have been recorded in other parts of the world.

33. J. Hampton, 'Play and Development in Rural Zimbabwean Children', *Early Child Development and Care,* Vol. 47, pp. 1–6.

34. There are cultural factors at work here, too. A study of pre-school Italian children, aged 2–4, found that both sexes enjoyed heated discussion more than the activity set by the teacher (quietly drawing a picture). The children regarded arguing as an alternative activity and a more rewarding one, an opinion endorsed by Italian culture generally. See. W. Corsaro and T. Rizzo, 'Disputes in the peer culture of American and Italian nursery school children'.

35. Corinne Hutt, 1966.

36. Carol Gilligan et al., *Making Connections.*

37. According to Carol Gilligan, the adolescent girl is both an emergent woman, concerned with conventional notions of femaleness, such as nurturing and feeling, but she is also an emergent adult, concerned with a different set of attributes, such as self-sufficiency and independence. C. Gilligan et al. Ibid.

38. AAUW summary: *Shortchanging Girls, Shortchanging America* (Original data: AAUW/Greenberg-Lake Full Data Report, Greenberg-Lake, 1990, Washington, D.C.).

39. M. Maine, *Father Hunger*, p. 60.

40. C. Hoff Sommers, *Who Stole Feminism: how women have betrayed women*, pp. 137–51. Sommers argues that 'self-esteem' is inadequately defined in the survey, and inadequately tested for; she points out, for example, that controls were not made for gender differences in styles of self-reporting, nor for 'a gap in expressiveness' that exists between adolescent females and males, nor for the fact that high school drop-out rate is greater in males than females. On the basis of the original survey data, Sommers argues that the study actually suggests an inverse relation between self-esteem reports and success in school.

41. 'Ann' is a pseudonym for one of the women I interviewed for the research I carried out with Paul Thompson into ageing, entitled 'On the edge of later life', (ESRC, 1993). Nearly all the women I interviewed for this research described a similar suspension or diminution of play in adolescence, not matched in the interviews with men of the same age and class.

42. Hendry et al. *Young People's Leisure and Lifestyle*, p. 173.

43. Hendry et al., ibid. p. 40.

44. S. Rowbotham, *Woman's Consciousness, Man's World*, p. 20.

45. Hendry, et al: op.cit., pp. 126–7.

46. See P. Willis, *Learning to Labour*; J.C. Walker, *Louts and Legends: male youth culture in an inner-city school.* S. Lees, *Sugar and Spice.*

47. S. Lees, op.cit.

48. Social historians Clarke and Critcher point out that, 'The leisure of adolescent girls is more controlled from within and without than that of boys. The premium placed upon sexual attractiveness and its implied subordination and vulnerability to boys makes leisure a tentative enterprise for girls.' *The Devil Makes Work*, p. 157.

49. S. Lees, op.cit., p. 17.

50. S. Lees, ibid, p. 15.

51. McRobbie and Garber, 1976.

Chapter 8

1. J. Huizinga explains that the English word 'play' derives from Anglo-Saxon, 'plega', which has connotations of rapid movement, clapping and playing an instrument, as well as playing games. It survives in the modern German, *pflegen*, and Dutch, *plegen*, for play. Both derive from older words which do not mean to play, but to take a risk, to vouch, to expose oneself to danger for someone or something. J. Huizinga, *Homo Ludens,* p. 39.

2. An example of play used in this sense of 'delight' is given with these lines from a fifteenth-century poem:

> Alas! and walo-way! my child that was me lefe!
> My luf, my blood, my play, that never dyd man grefe!

3. There are 43,000 clubs affiliated to the Football Association in Britain, nearly all of these will have at least one football pitch, some will have several. The standard pitch size is between 4,050 square metres (45m × 90m) and 11,400 square metres (95m × 120m). Assuming an average of one pitch per club, that is in the region of 332 million square metres of official football pitch, and does not take into account the many hundreds of impromptu pitches set up by boys and men in streets, parks and recreation grounds all over the country.

4. Association football accounted for 49.48% of playing pitches in England in 1994. When all forms of football are taken into account, that figures rises to 49.77% (cricket accounts for 15.05%; Rugby Union and League account for 10.17%). Regional comparisons show that the amount of space devoted to football is remarkably uniform across the country, with football pitches accounting for around 45–50% of playing pitches in each region. The region with the most playing pitches, the north west, also devotes a higher than average proportion of those pitches to football (3,873 pitches; 53.60% of them for football); interestingly, Greater London has the lowest number of playing pitches, but the highest proportion of football pitches (1,618 pitches; 54.62% of them for football). The Sports Council, *Register of Recreational Land,* table 6.1.3, chart 6.1.1.

5. The high valuation of soccer and other all-male sports is clearly reflected in the number of column inches and the minutes of air space devoted to newspaper, radio and television coverage of these events. Magazines and books on predominantly female activities, such as knitting and cross-stitching, are also available, but they appear in places and spaces specifically designated for women, not in the apparently gender-neutral spaces of daily national news reports.

6. 'Fair deal overdue for fairer sex', Christine Spreiter, *The Times,* 1994. The problem of sponsorship exists across the board in women's sport, from athletics to judo. Tracey Edwards approached over 300 companies and had to sell her house to raise the £3 million capital needed for *Maiden*, her

female-crewed yacht. Women's Rugby Football Union receives no sponsorship, relying on membership subscriptions and gate money. Lack of publicity makes funding bodies and private investors less inclined to back women's sports, and the lack of money in turn makes it less 'sexy' to news editors and reporters: the circle of marginalisation is soon completed.

7. J. Hargreaves, 'Sex, gender and the body in sport and leisure: Has there been a civilizing process?' in E. Dunning and C. Rojek (eds), *Sport and Leisure in the Civilizing Process*, p. 179.

8. Spender makes the point that 'women occupy the zone of negative semantic space, they are unable to decree their own reality, thus they are 'wrong'. D. Spender, *Man Made Language.*

9. As Dale Spender explains, 'Language is not an insignificant dimension. To be inferior when it comes to language is frequently to be discounted.' Ibid. Spender was not the first person to point up the connection between language and sexism in society. She herself acknowledges the work of Elizabeth Cady Stanton in the mid-nineteenth century, as well as other feminist writers since, but Spender has been one of the most influential writers on the subject in recent years, going further and deeper than those before her into the connection between semantics and sexual inequality, and the implications for women and for society.

10. Nietzsche makes this point explicitly in *Thus Spake Zarathustra:* 'There are two things a true man desires: danger and play. Therefore desires he woman as the most dangerous of playthings . . . Let woman be a plaything pure and delicate as a jewel, illuminated with the virtues of a world that is yet to come . . . Man's happiness is, I will. Woman's happiness is, He will . . .' F. Nietzsche, *Thus Spake Zarathustra,* pp. 91–2.

11. A celebratory lunch for three hundred successful businesswomen, held in London in October 1993, was written up disparagingly in *The Times.*

12. Robert Philip, 'English rose blossoms in the mid-winter mud', *Daily Telegraph* 17.1.94.

13. Brian Oliver, 'Let out for being "straight"', *Daily Telegraph,* 17.1.94.

14. Barry Pickthall, 'Frank ousted from Whitbread', *The Times,* 10.11.93.

15. P. Davies, *I Lost My Heart to the Belles,* p. 15.

16. Gilda O'Neill, *A Night Out With the Girls,* pp. 13–20.

17. The word 'gossip' has an interesting etymology. M. Tebbutt writes, 'The earliest definitions of "gossip" were of a noun concerning the role taken by god-parents at a Christian baptism. The late Old English word *godsibb* was literally a 'relative in God', which emphasised spiritual closeness and care for the child's well-being. It could also apply to an intimate friend invited to a baptism, and over time the spiritual overtones became diluted to a more

secular form of caring as expressed in neighbourliness . . . By the fourteenth century the word's more spiritual overtones had broadened and acquired a meaning which characterised gossip as a particularly close friend and especially as someone who was neighbourly and took an interest in their friends' behaviour . . . [T]he sixteenth- and seventeenth-century definition of the noun [denoted] close female friends whom a woman invited to attend her at childbirth . . . [G]ossip gradually acquired a gender-specific meaning as idle, inconsequential female talk which in the eighteenth century received dictionary recognition from Dr Johnson who supplied a definition which 'for the first time' connected gossip unambiguously and officially with women as 'One who runs about tattling like women at a laying-in'. By the nineteenth century the gossip was well established as 'a person, mostly a woman, of light and trifling character, especially one who delights in idle talk'. M. Tebbutt, *Women's Talk? A social history of 'gossip' in working-class neighbourhoods, 1880–1960*, pp. 19–27. D. Gambetta points out that in Italian the word for god-father, *compadre*, has retained its original meaning, while *comare* or *commare*, originally the word for godmother, has come to mean a gossip. D. Gambetta, 'Godfather's Gossip', 1994, *Arch. Europ. sociol.* 35, pp. 199–223. M. Warner shows how a similar shift has taken place in French and English: 'In French, *commère* . . . originally a godmother . . . came to mean a gossip-monger, a telltale; the English "Cummer", now obsolete, also meant godmother, intimate friend and gossip, as well as midwife and wise woman until the last century.' M. Warner, *From the Beast to the Blonde*, p. 33.

18. Dale Spender makes the point that 'there are no terms for man talk that are equivalent to chatter, natter, prattle, nag, bitch, whine and, of course, gossip'. D. Spender, *Man Made Language*, p. 107. It should also be said however that women have a paradoxical weapon in their hands here, because if they choose to apply these words to men, they acquire an additional force. To call a woman a nag is to confirm her negative femaleness, but to call a man a nag is to criticise and to emasculate.

19. M. Roberts, *On Gender and Writing*, p. 65.

20. M. Tebbutt draws attention to the stereotyping that informed the British government's Home Front propaganda during the Second World War. The 1939 campaign against 'Careless Talk', targeted 'gossiping housewives'. The 'anti-gossip' campaign of 1940 was aimed at both men and women, but while gossiping men were embodied in the figure of Mr Pride in Prophecy, gossiping women were represented by Miss Leaky Mouth and Miss Teacup Whisper, 'encapsulating', as Tebbutt says, 'the altogether greater weight of male opinion'. M. Tebbutt, op.cit.

21. The Holy Inquisition was formed as early as 1022, and men and women were executed for devil worship from that point on. However, the witch hunts gathered pace from the fifteenth century, and by the end of the sixteenth century women were being tortured and killed on a horrifying

scale. Witch hunts gradually ceased towards the end of the seventeenth century, although the last official execution took place in Germany as late as 1775. Men were accused of witchcraft too, but never in anywhere near equal numbers. The ratio in some parts of Europe at the height of the witch mania was 10 women to 1 man. It has also been pointed out that while men were often singled out because they were politically inconvenient, women were targeted simply for being women. While there are no definitive figures for the number of women burnt as witches, estimates range from 200,000 to 9 million. According to R.H. Robbins, there are recorded burnings of 100,000 witches in Germany alone. (*Encyclopedia of Witchcraft and Demonology*) At the turn of the sixteenth century, Germany was described by a contemporary observer as 'almost entirely occupied with building fires for witches. Switzerland has been compelled to wipe out many of her villages on their account.' Cited in J. Achterberg, *Woman as Healer,* p. 85.

22. Cited in L. Gordon, *Charlotte Brontë: A Passionate Life,* pp. 64–5.

23. 'Girl Talk', J. Moir, *Guardian,* 26.8.94.

24. Dale Spender makes the point that 'Women have not been judged on the grounds of whether they talk more than men, but of whether they talk more than silent women.' Spender also argues that the idea that women's voices are high-pitched and therefore less pleasant than men's depends upon taking male voice-pitch as the norm. Spender cites research findings that indicate that sex differences in vocal pitch have a great deal to do with social convention. D. Spender, *Man Made Language,* p. 42.

25. A study by Zimmerman and West (1975) found that 98% of interruptions in mixed-sex conversation were by males. Deborah Tannen points out that all men do not interrupt more than all women, drawing attention to the importance of different conversational styles. High-involvement speakers of either sex are more likely to interrupt other people's speech than high-considerateness speakers of either sex. Jewish women, for example, are more likely to interrupt other speakers than women from other cultural groups because of the emphasis in Jewish culture on debate and discussion. Interruption is part of the Jewish linguistic style! Tannen also points out that when women are gathered together without men, they do interrupt each other. Tannen calls this 'co-operative overlapping', and argues that it creates rapport rather than signalling dominance. D. Tannen, *You Just Don't Understand,* pp. 201–7.

26. Robin Dunbar, 'Why gossip is good for you', *New Scientist,* 21.11.1992.

27. Ibid.

28. In *The Golden Bough,* Frazer mentions tribes where magic could be worked on a person 'just as easily through his name as through his hair, or any other material part of his person'. D. Zahan relates the case of the Bambaras of Sudan who regard speech as a total physical act, involving the

entire body. To speak is to utilise one's physical self to the highest degree, to speak is to give birth to words. See D. Zahan, *La Dialectique du verbe chez les Bambaras,* 1963. Julia Kristeva also points out the intrinsic connection between creation and speech in the Bible, where God's words in Genesis are synonymous with what he creates: 'God said, Let there be light, and there was light.' J. Kristeva, *Language the Unknown – an initiation into linguistics,* pp. 98–9.

29. Kristeva, following Hegel, argues that language is 'a signifying system in which the speaking subject makes and unmakes himself [sic]'. J. Kristeva, op.cit., p. 265.

30. L. Irigaray, in S. Sellers, *Language and Sexual Difference*, pp. 12–13.

31. 'Reality is constructed and sustained primarily through talk . . . Those who control the talk are also able to control reality.' D. Spender, op.cit., p. 119.

32. Lady Richmond Brown, *Unknown Tribes and Uncharted Seas,* Duckworth, 1924, in J. Robinson, *Unsuitable For Ladies: an anthology of women travellers,* p. 17.

33. See R. Parker, *The Subversive Stitch.*

34. The powerful sensuality of Arab dancing captured the imagination of westerners travelling in the east during the nineteenth century, who overlooked its role and significance as a form of private entertainment for and by women, and instead emphasised the sexual element of the dance, the element of women performing for men's pleasure, rather than women performing for their own pleasure. In *Serpent of the Nile: women and dance in the Arab world,* Wendy Buonaventura shows how in the course of the twentieth century, Arabic dance has been taken over by the west, who have glamorised it, simplified it, and in the process, lost most of its subtlety and potency. Nevertheless, 'as a social activity in the Arab world, the dance has retained its intimate nature and many of the customs surrounding it. It is still handed down from mother to daughter and performed by women for their own entertainment . . . And it remains an essential ingredient of any occasion when communities gather to enjoy themselves.' op.cit., p. 21.

35. L.S. Mitchell, *Here and Now Story Book,* in J. Bruner et al., *Play, its role in development and evolution*, and taken from a paper presented at the Second Lucy Sprague Mitchell Memorial Conference, 'Dimensions of Language Experience' by Courtney B. Cazden.

36. M. Warner, op.cit., p. 17.

37. The origin of Old Mother Goose is not known for certain, but the goose has numerous associations with women and with talking. In French, for example, the word *caquet* for the honk of a goose is used also to mean chatter. According to Marina Warner, 'The goose serves as the emblematic beast *par excellence* of folly and, more particularly, of female noise, of

women's chatter.' Ibid., pp. 51–66. For a more detailed analysis of the relationship between male authors, female sources and female narrators of fairytales, see ibid., pp. 12–25.

38. Ibid., p. xxi. See also chapter 23, 'The Silence of the Daughters: The Little Mermaid', in which Warner goes into the theme and meaning of female silence in some detail.

39. Feminist readings and rewritings of traditional fairy tales have cast doubt on the happiness of these happy endings, asking for instance if it is really so good that the spirited girl ends the story as a passive bride, and showing how the plots and themes of the stories uphold patriarchal values and stereotyped gender roles. In Angela Carter's collection, *The Bloody Chamber and Other Stories*, traditional stories are given a new and sometimes disturbing twist.

40. Most countries have developed formulaic openings and endings to their folk stories. Armenian fairy tales often start with the formula, 'There was and there was not, there was a boy . . .'; an Egyptian story begins, 'Neither here nor elsewhere lived a king'. All perform this same function of highlighting the fictionality of the narrative. As Angela Carter points out, 'Although the content of the fairy tale may record the lives of the anonymous poor with sometimes uncomfortable fidelity . . . the form of the fairy tale is not usually constructed so as to invite the audience to share a sense of lived experience. The "old wives' tale" positively parades its lack of verisimilitude.' *The Virago Book of Fairy Tales,* p. xi.

41. H. Watson, *Women in the City of the Dead,* pp. 12–16.

42. At the end of Helen Watson's stay in the City of the Dead, the women gather to hear 'a tale about trial and error and about knowing when enough is enough'. It is a story about a honey bee, who lands one day in a strange garden. 'There was nothing about the bee which made much sense at all. It was a mystery, a puzzle, a curiosity! Some said that the bee was simply deranged and this explained its curious ways. Others said that although it looked a lot like a bee, it wasn't a bee at all and this explained why it behaved in a most un-beelike manner . . . Certainly it was a very peculiar kind of bee with all kinds of peculiar habits and interests . . . Honey bees are busy by nature and this one was no exception. What was peculiar was how it kept busy. Honey bees collect honey and that's that, just honey, no more and no less! But this honey bee was not that kind of bee! This peculiar honey bee was happy to collect anything at all. Sometimes it found honey and sometimes it found worms. Both times it was equally happy . . . The honey bee also looked a little strange, not at all as you'd expect . . . it had astonishing spiky hair instead of the usual soft fluffy look of a honey bee. People tried to help because the bee had many well-meaning friends. But, sad to say, it went through numerous beautifying processes without any successful results.' Significantly, one of the most peculiar things about this

bee is its attitude to work. 'The honey bee worked very hard and was totally mad about work . . . [It] delighted in its work, which was another strange thing people noticed about it. It worked from dawn to dusk and moved at such a speed that it left a dust trail behind it.' Ibid., pp. 204–11.

43. Ibid.

44. 'There is romance and revelation in the telling of tales,' Watson writes. 'The romance is for everyone, the revelation is for those willing or able to perceive it. What is essential to all storytelling is that the ordinary and the extraordinary are interwoven into a rich tapestry which represents an alternative view of everyday life . . . Tales divert, warm, redeem, entertain and justify.' Ibid.

45. In *Language and Sexual Difference,* Susan Sellers the intellectual processes behind the narrative styles of these French feminists 'Cixous sees the type of textual composition woven from the multiple and heterogeneous possibilities generated by the writing process as challenging the rules of (linear) logic, objective meaning, and the single, self-referential viewpoint decreed by masculine law. She believes (feminine) writing has the potential to undermine and present another alternative to this law, and the hierarchy of linguistic, social and political relations the law creates.' op.cit., pp. 143–4. Monique Wittig puts the theory into practice in her work. 'The insistence on the feminine, on women and on circles as the (positive) symbol of woman's sex, is expressed both in the continual reference to these . . . , in the lists of women's names that appear at various points in the text . . . and in the series of circles repeated at intervals on otherwise blank pages.' ibid., p. 154. Another exercise in *écriture féminine* is to be found in the writing of Michèle Ramond, as Sellers describes: 'The text [of *Vous*] opens with a double blank page, beginning a narrative on page three in mid-sentence. The double blank pages are repeated at irregular intervals through the text, and the narrative is resumed in each case in mid-sentence and sometimes mid-word, and always at a different point from where it was broken off . . . Ramond's sentences also break with all the conventional rules of sentence construction, placing different propositions alongside each other, incorporating half-lines of blank space, and experimenting with the textual lay-out.' Ibid., p. 159.

Chapter 9

1. Adapted from J.R. Moyle, *Just Playing? The role and status of play in early childhood education*, pp. 136–7.

2. According to American sociologist Martha Wolfenstein, 'Playing with children was regarded as dangerous; it produced unwholesome pleasure and ruined the baby's nerves. Any playful handling of the baby was titillating, excessively exciting, deleterious. Play carried the overtones of feared erotic excitement.' M. Wolfenstein, 'The emergence of fun morality'.

3. John Watson (1928). *Psychological Care of the Infant and Child,* cited in C. Hardyment, *Perfect Parents,* p. 175.

4. 'Play, having ceased to be wicked, having become harmless and good, now becomes a new duty,' writes Martha Wolfenstein of the child-care ethos of the fifties. M. Wolfenstein, op.cit.

5. Cited in J. Schwartz, *The Mother Puzzle,* p. 242.

6. Piaget's theories of child cognitive development were reinterpreted by child-care experts as a series of rungs on an intellectual ladder. The parents' job was to help their child climb to the top as fast as possible. As Hardyment puts it, 'The concept of an elastic mental age was taken as a challenge.' C. Hardyment, *Perfect Parents,* p. 246.

7. J. Schwartz, op.cit., p. 243.

8. Ibid., p. 231.

9. Ibid.

10. Clare Garner, 'The loss of innocence', *Independent,* 15.8.1991.

11. Ibid.

12. A. Uttley, *Country Hoard.*

13. Goldschmied and Jackson, *People Under Three,* Chapter 1.

14. From *The Hurried Child* by David Elkind, quoted in J. Schwartz op.cit., p. 231.

15. Goldschmied and Jackson point out that the process of exploration in the play of small children is 'very like the activity of scientists who develop their knowledge by carrying out the same experiment over and over again with tiny variations . . . one thing leads to another in a pleasurable process of discovery, which in turn leads to practice and the growth of skill.' *People Under Three,* p. 123.

16. Goldschmied and Jackson, ibid., p. 138.

17. Corinne Hutt in 'Exploration and play in children', from *Symposia of the Zoological Society of London,* no 18, pp. 61–81. Hutt's study involved 30 nursery school children aged between three and five. She observed a wide range of exploratory activities embedded in the act of playing.

18. According to Leo Hendry, 'This type of play has a valuable function . . . whether the child is reducing his fears, exploring his feelings, trying to understand a puzzling event or altering it to make it pleasant to himself, he is reducing the world to manageable proportions.' L.B. Hendry *Growing Up and Going Out,* Chapter 3, 'Play and pre-adolescent leisure', p. 36.

19. It has also been suggested that 'Middle childhood is a period when the

sexes draw apart to rehearse sex roles in their play'. Children may prefer same-sex rather than mixed groups at this age because they provide 'safe havens' in which to explore these fledgling aspects of their social selves. See L.B. Hendry, op.cit., p. 41.

20. Hendry, op.cit.

21. Sheila Rowbotham recalls her fascination with the Beat movement when she was a young woman, reading *On The Road*, listening to Howl, identifying with the men 'because they were exciting and adventurous', trying not to notice the absence of enticing female role models. 'The fact that the girls invariably got a rough ride in the Beat movement never really dawned on me until later. I just thought it was somehow inevitable that girls were meant to be heroically tough and miraculously soft at the same time. Exhaustingly I tried to live the contradiction.' *Woman's Consciousness, Man's World*, p. 15.

22. Arthur Koestler, *The Act of Creation*, p. 96.

Chapter 10

1. S. de Beauvoir, *The Ethics of Ambiguity*, Chapter 3. These words appear in the context of an argument about the fallacy of attempting to save time as a route to happiness.

2. Luke, 10:38–42, Holy Bible, New Revised Standard Version, Oxford, OUP.

3. C. Turnbull, *The Forest People*. Cited in Bruner et al. op.cit.

4. S. de Beauvoir, *Memoirs of a Dutiful Daughter*.

5. M. Solomon, *Mozart: a life*, p. 165. These letters are 'famous for their exuberant comic language, which is rich in obscenities and obscurities'. Solomon spends some time on the subject of Mozart's 'addiction to the play-impulse', p. 280, arguing that it served a crucial psychological function by allowing Mozart to reinvent himself and limit his father's influence over him; its role was not just an outlet for excessive creative energy, but an essential instrument of subversion. See pp. 277–83.

6. Richard P. Feynman, *'Surely You're Joking, Mr. Feynman!'*, p. 173.

7. Ibid, p. 174.

8. Robert F. Hobson, *Forms of Feeling*, p. 243.

Chapter 11

1. P. Newham, *The Singing Cure*, pp. 236–9.

2. C. Pinkola Estes, *Women Who Run with the Wolves: contacting the power of the wild woman*, pp. 28–33.

3. J. Ogden, *Fat Chance*, p. 87.

4. Ibid., pp. 20–21. Sociologist Ralph Glasser points out that the diet industry works conveniently closely with the food industry, in particular the confectionery industry: 'Both are indulgence activities. Both give satisfaction in their respective negative ways, the one by cosseting in its infantile pursuit of the sensual, the other by buying punishment, an equally infantile indulgence, by pursuing a guilt-ridden discipline. *Both serve to blot out a deeper hunger for a sustaining emotional purpose.*' [my itals], R. Glasser, *Leisure – Penalty or Prize?* p. 153.

5. William Perkins (1558–1602), cited in R. Malcolmson (1973), p. 9. John Northbroke complained of the 'monstrous thumping of the feete, to pleasant soundes, to wanton songues, to dishonest verses'. J. Northbroke, 'Spiritus est vicarius Christi in terra. A Treatise wherein Dicing, Dauncing, Vaine plaies or Enterludes with other idle pastimes, etc. commonly used on the Sabbath day, are reprooved.' Ibid.

6. W. Buonaventura, *Serpent of the Nile*, p. 25.

7. See G.S. Wakefield (ed.), *A Dictionary of Christian Spirituality*, pp. 102–3. God the Player is a recurring theme in philosophy and theology. The fourteenth-century mystic and scholastic Meister Eckhart emphasised God's playful aspect: in one of the Legends, he meets a beautiful boy who riddles with him for a while before disappearing. Eckhart explains, 'For it was God himself – who was having a bit of fun.' In a Sermon on the playfulness of God, he explains that a playful divinity is potentially present in human action: 'For truly, God plays and laughs in good deeds, whereas all other deeds, which do not make for the glory of God, are like ashes before him.' Raymond B. Blakney, *Meister Eckhart*, p. 143. Other scholars, before and since, have explored the connection between human and divine play. John Finnis ends his work on law and ethics, by arguing for play as *the* divinely-given aspect of human life. '[I]f we ask why God creates, no answer is available other than the one implicitly given by Plato: play – a free but patterned expression of life and activity, meaningful but with no further point . . . Practical reasonableness, therefore, need not be regarded as ultimately a form of self-perfection. That is not its final significance. Nor, on the other hand, are its requirements sheer categorical imperatives; they gain practical force from the most basic explanation that can be provided for them – that they are what is needed to participate in the game of God. Play, too, can now be more adequately understood. It is to be contrasted with business, with responsibilities, with the serious things of life. But, in the last analysis, there is a play that is the *only* really serious matter. In such a "final analysis", in which we seek an understanding going beyond our feelings, the "serious things of life", even atrocious miseries, are really serious only to the extent that they contribute to or are caught up into a good play of the game of the God who creates and favours human good.' J. Finnis, *Natural Law*

and Natural Rights, pp. 409–10.

8. W. Buonaventura, op.cit., p. 25.

9. A swan is born', Sue Gaisford, *Independent on Sunday,* 8.11.92.

10. W. Buonaventura, op.cit, pp. 199–201.

11. Vivienne Griffiths studied the experience of dancing for 12–16-year-old girls in West Yorkshire over the course of a year, and found that disco-dancing was enjoyable partly because of the element of 'active yet acceptable sexual suggestiveness', but also for a chance to get together with friends and have a laugh. The girls in Griffiths's sample saw the dances predominantly as an all-female activity, involving dressing up, sensual pleasure and self-expression. They were self-aware and self-absorbed in their dancing. V. Griffiths, 'Stepping out: the importance of dancing for young women, in E. Wimbush and M. Talbot, op.cit., p. 118.

12. L.B. Hendry, J. Shucksmith, J.G. Love and A. Glendinning, op.cit., pp. 58–74.

13. Thompson and Abrams, 'On the edge of later life'.

14. G. O'Neill, *A Night Out With the Girls: women having a good time,* Chapter 6, 'Jumping for Joy: Women's Sport and Exercise', pp. 98–119.

15. 'Health Survey for England'. The survey was conducted in 90 areas of England and involved 3,300 adults.

16. From research by Dr Neil Armstrong, University of Exeter, cited in the *Guardian,* 24.11.92.

17. J. Grimley Evans, *Health: abilities and wellbeing in the third age.*

18. Figures from the Sports Council and the Women's Sports Foundation.

19. N. Elias and E. Dunning, 'The Quest for Excitement in Leisure', *The Quest For Excitement,* pp. 63–91.

20. M. Talbot, 'Beating them at our own game? Women's sports involvement', p. 105, in E. Wimbush and M. Talbot, op.cit.

21. Ibid., pp. 102–114.

22. Ovid, *Art of Love,* 3, 11.352–369. Ovid also exhorts women to master the faked orgasm, and encourages in general a degree of self-objectification that one translator, Peter Green, says bears comparison with Henry Miller. Ovid advises would-be temptresses on their clothes, hair, make-up, and warns against 'rank goatish armpits and bristling hairs on your legs'; he urges regular tooth-brushing, dainty table-manners, and, above all, guile: 'Shut your door,/Don't reveal the half-finished process. Most of your actions/Would offend if you didn't conceal them: there's a lot/Men are better not knowing.' 11.228–230. Never mind Henry Miller, much of Ovid's

advice could be straight out of *Cosmopolitan* in the 1990s.

23. N. Wolf, *The Beauty Myth,* p. 139.

24. J. Milton, *Paradise Lost,* Book IX, 11.1027–32.

25. A 1980 survey by American *Cosmopolitan* of 106,000 women found that 41% had had extramarital affairs; a 1986 survey of college-educated working women by Thor Data of New York City found that 41% of the married respondents were having or had had affairs. Cited in Dalma Heyn, *The Erotic Silence of the Married Woman,* p. 26.

26. Figures from the *Elle*/Durex Sex Survey, 1992, based on 1,000 questionnaires randomly selected from 3,500 responses. No breakdown of age or class of respondents was given. A more statistically rigorous survey of 1,000 British men was conducted at around the same time by MORI for the men's magazine, *Esquire.* Its findings on infidelity make interesting comparison: 7% of the 473 married men were unfaithful on a regular or irregular basis. This tallies with the findings of the 1992 National Survey of Sexual Attitudes and Lifestyles which found that most married people are monogamous, but that twice as many women as men are monogamous. The National Survey also found a clear correlation between social class and sexual activity, with people in social class one and two (professional and managerial) twice as likely to have had two or more partners in the past year as people in social classes four or five.

27. Stringent rules governing female sexuality are found in most societies. Marilyn French points out in *The War Against Women,* p. 140, that 'all past societies constricted women's sexuality: it was a criminal act for women, but not for men, to commit adultery, which different societies punished with varying degrees of severity, including death. Punishments from beatings to imprisonment in convents to death were inflicted on girls who lost their virginity before marriage – even if they were raped, and even if by a family member.' Female circumcision is still practised in many African and Asian communities, not only in Africa and Asia, but throughout Europe and America; an estimated 10,000 girls in Britain are at risk of circumcision, according to the Foundation for Women's Health Research and Development in London. The practice of female circumcision is carried out explicitly in order to curb sexual desire and sexual activity in women.

28. D. Heyn, *The Erotic Silence of the Married Woman,* p. 286.

29. J. Huizinga, op.cit., p. 192.

Chapter 12

1. Aine McCarthy, *Guardian,* October 1993.

2. Goldschmied and Jackson, *People Under Three,* p. 233.

3. 1991 figures, General Household Survey.

4. Ibid.

5. R. Abrams, 'The father of all battles', *Guardian,* 25.10.95.

6. Study of household surveys in US, Brazil and Ghana, by Duncan Thomas, University of California in L.A., cited in E. Balls, 'Working women hold the key to children's future', *Guardian,* 5.9.94.

7. *Superwoman Keeps Going,* 1992, National Council of Women.

8. These figures are from a survey of 580 women and 420 men carried out in 1992 by the Centre for Criminology at Middlesex University, and commissioned by the London Borough of Islington. The survey found that 28% of women have suffered physical injury from a partner and 19% of men have struck their partners, 5% of the women had suffered broken bones because of attacks, 40% had difficulty sleeping as a result of a partner's violence, 46% felt depressed because of it.

9. *Hansard Official Report,* 'Parents' Responsibilities', Vol. 538, no 27, p. 479, 24.6.92.

10. I am grateful to Ellen Jackson for referring me to Zamyatin's work.

11. Many of the older meanings of 'play' given in the dictionary relate to its characteristic of movement, and more specifically, *freedom of movement.* Amongst the various definitions of play given in the OED, we find 'free or unimpeded movement; free action; freedom; opportunity, or room for action; scope for activity'.

12. Louis MacNeice, 'Autumn Journal, 1938' in *Collected Poems, 1925–48.*

13. R. Glasser, op.cit., p. 213. Glasser likens the destructiveness of the enraged frustrated child to the destructiveness of the profoundly frustrated adult. He calls for a 'spiritually committed society' to fill the void of consumerism and empty 'leisure'. Glasser argues that the spiritual dimension of human experience must be recalled to counter the excessive emphasis on functionalism and commercialism. Interestingly, there has been an increasing interest in spirituality since the early 1980s, but worryingly a major aspect of this has been the rise of religious extremism. Fanatical, intolerant, rigid and restrictive, it has hardly brought about the benefits Glasser envisaged.

14. 'The Protestant ethic made very early a sharp separation between what one does when young and what one does later, with the transition very sharply defined. In the western tradition, there grew a puritan separation of the "works of the adult" and "the play of babes".' J.S. Bruner 'Nature and uses of Immaturity', *American Psychologist,* vol. 27, No. 8, 1972. Republished in Bruner et al., op.cit., pp. 28–64.

15. Stephen Tunnicliffe, letter to the *Guardian,* December 1993.

16. 'Play is represented not as a specialised and threatened area of experience . . . but as a mode of interaction which informs and is essential to the creative continuance of a whole community.' H. Glen, *Vision and Disenchantment,* p. 138.

17. Ibid., p. 137.

18. Ibid., p. 133.

19. Ibid., p. 144.

20. D. Donnison, 'We All Pay the Price for Unemployment', *Guardian,* 1.9.93.

21. Hannah Arendt, *On Revolution,* Chapter 6.

22. A report by the Commission of the European Communities, 'Age and Attitudes', states that 'a child born in 1990 may expect to live almost 10 years longer than one born in 1950', Alan Walker, 'Age and Attitudes', p. 4.

23. Ibid.

24. Bertrand Russell, *In Praise of Idleness and Other Essays.*

25. Ibid.

26. W. Bridges, *Jobshift: How to Prosper in a Workplace without Jobs.* Extracted in 'The death of the job', *Independent on Sunday,* 5.2.95.

27. E.P. Thompson, 'Time, Work-Discipline and Industrial Capitalism', op.cit.

28. E. Hobsbawm, *The Age of Extremes: the short history of the twentieth century 1914–1991.*

29. T. Hodgkinson, 'Positively idle', *Guardian,* 9.11.94. The *Idler* magazine takes its name from Dr Johnson's series of bi-weekly essays, 'The Idler', published in the eighteenth century at about the same time as the *Observer,* the *Rambler,* the *Bystander* and the *Spectator* were launched, their titles reflecting the value, since lost, attached to the intellectual play of contemplation and reflection.

30. Cited in Walter Schwarz, 'Volunteers for a new America', *Guardian,* 25.10.95.

31. Ibid.

32. Survey by MORI. These findings are part of the World Values survey.

33. J. Bentham, *Theory of Legislation,* 'Principles of the Penal Code', p. 380.

Index